"What the *Mayflower* was to Massachusetts in 1620 the *Hector* was to Pictou County in 1773. The first Scottish emigrant ship to Nova Scotia, a trickle of less than 200 men, women and children, ultimately became the torrent that made Nova Scotia truly and forever New Scotland."

ATLANTIC INSIGHT

BOOKS BY DONALD MACKAY

The Lumberjacks (1978)

Anticosti: The Untamed Island (1979)

Scotland Farewell: The People of the Hector (1980)

Empire of Wood: The MacMillan Bloedel Story
(1982)

Heritage Lost: The Crisis in Canada's Forests
(1985)

*The Asian Dream: The Pacific Rim and Canada's
National Railway* (1986)

The Square Mile: Merchant Princes of Montreal
(1987)

*Flight from Famine: The Coming of the Irish
to Canada* (1990)

*The People's Railway: A History of Canadian
National* (1992)

*Train Country: An Illustrated History of Canadian
National Railways* (1994) (with Lorne Perry)

Donald MacKay

SCOTLAND FAREWELL

THE PEOPLE OF THE HECTOR

NATURAL HERITAGE / NATURAL HISTORY INC.

For my mother, and the MacRaes
who in olden times at Castle Eilean Donan
wore "The Mackenzie's Shirt of Mail."

ACKNOWLEDGEMENTS

The Publisher acknowledges with gratitude the cooperation, information and illustrations provided by The Ship Hector Foundation, Pictou County Chamber of Commerce, Pictou County Tourist Association, Pictou Waterfront Development Corporation, The Hector Centre Trust, the deCoste Entertainment Centre, and the Office of the Town Clerk and Treasurer, Pictou, Nova Scotia, for the 2001 edition of this book.

Published by Natural Heritage/Natural History Inc.
P.O. Box 95, Station O, Toronto, Ontario M4A 2M8

Cover design by Blanche Hamill, Norton Hamill Design

Printed and bound in Canada by Hignell Printing Limited

Fourth Printing May 2001

Canadian Cataloguing in Publication Data

MacKay, Donald, 1925-
        Scotland farewell : the people of the Hector

Includes bibliographical references and index.
ISBN 1-896219-12-8

1. Scots – Nova Scotia – History. 2. Hector (Ship). 3. Scots – Nova Scotia – Pictou (County) – History. 4. Nova Scotia – Emigration and immigration. 5. Scotland – Emigration and immigration. I. Title.

Canada

THE CANADA COUNCIL | LE CONSEIL DES ARTS
FOR THE ARTS | DU CANADA
SINCE 1957 | DEPUIS 1957

We acknowledge the financial support of the Government of Canada through the Book Publishing Industry Development Program (BPIDP) for our publishing activities, the support received for our publishing program from the Canada Council Block Grant Program and the assistance of the Association for the Export of Canadian Books, Ottawa.

Contents

Preface

In the history of Scottish emigration no name is more cherished than that of a leaky old brig named the *Hector*. Celebrations honouring her voyage to Pictou, Nova Scotia, in 1773 have drawn pilgrims in their thousands from Scotland, the United States and wherever Scots have settled.

There were almost 200 people aboard the *Hector*. Their descendants number more than 40,000 and are spread throughout Canada and the United States. Some call her the "Scottish *Mayflower*," although in truth her voyage bore little semblance to that of the Plymouth pilgrims 150 years earlier. Others more accurately identify the *Hector's* fearful voyage as the genesis of that great flood of emigration which was to make Nova Scotia's eastern mainland, and Cape Breton, truly Scottish. In the Nova Scotia forests they sang homesick songs of "Lochaber No More," dreamed of lone shielings and the misty isles of home, but few ever went back to Scotland.

For all the pageantry and pomp which has celebrated the *Hector* at Pictou, the story of her people has come down to us in a series of tableaux rather than in any cohesive account of how they lived and why they emigrated. This book is an effort to explore their lives, in Scotland as well as in Nova Scotia, the hardships which drove them and the promises which lured them to the New World, long before the Highland Clearances forced crofters off their rented land in favour of the "four-footed clansmen," the black-faced sheep from Scotland's southern borders.

The *Hector* passengers, or most of them, were obscure, illiterate crofters and artisans from the northern reaches of the Highlands who spoke only Gaelic when they came and left little written record of their lives. For many, their only memorials are their descendants and some tombstones at Iron Bridge cemetery by the railway tracks at New Glasgow, Nova Scotia, or at the graveyard amid the elms and honeysuckle near Durham, on Pictou's West River.

Our main sources of information about how they lived and prospered in the backwoods of Nova Scotia are two books written more than a century ago by the Rev. Dr. George Patterson of Pictou County, grandson of the *Hector* passenger, John Patterson, and also, on his maternal side, grandson of the settlers' first permanent minister, whose life he recorded in *Memoire of the Rev. James Mac-Gregor, D.D.* Patterson also had access to the journals of William Mackenzie of Loch Broom, one of the few educated men aboard the *Hector*, but those journals have long disappeared, apparently lost by the printer who published Patterson's *History of the County of Pictou* in 1877. Writing three generations after the *Hector*'s arrival, Patterson bemoaned the difficulties of obtaining accurate information.

"With the exception of copies of grants and similar papers, preserved in public records, there is scarcely a document of that period in existence, and these serve very imperfectly to give us an insight into the life of the early settlers. We are thus indebted for all our knowledge of that era, almost entirely to unwritten sources, and the difficulty of obtaining exact information in this way can only be understood by those who have made an attempt of the same kind."

However, during Dr. Patterson's lifetime there were people still living who had sailed as young children on the *Hector,* and these he "expiscapated," to use his old Scottish term, anxious that with their passing the history of the patriarchs would be lost forever. At a time when historians dealt mainly with the famous, his was a pioneer work in the oral history of ordinary men and women.

Apart from Patterson's books, sources are fragmentary and largely contained in the Public Archives of Nova Scotia in Halifax, although there are some at the Hector Centre in Pictou. To read accounts of how the *Hector* people lived in Scotland and why they emigrated, one must travel to Edinburgh and the Scottish Records Office. There, in what Hugh A. Taylor of the Public Archives of Nova Scotia describes as "paper archeology", letters, journals, newspapers and, above all, the records of the Forfeited Estates give us a great deal of information about the social and economic conditions of the Highland glens from whence the *Hector* people came two centuries ago. It was from the estates of Lord Lovat and the Earl of Cromarty, annexed by the government, and neighbouring parishes to the north which were closely linked with the Lovat and Cromarty estates, that most of the people of the *Hector* came in the break-up of the clan system which continued long after the cataclysm of the battle of Culloden.

In dealing with these records I encountered the usual difficulties with Highland names, and particularly with the spelling of patronymics. The same name might appear in three or four different ways—Mc, Mac, or even simply M', followed sometimes by a capital, as in MacDonald, or more often by a lower case letter, as in Macdonald. The spelling seemed to change with whim or fashion, but since most of the renderings of the time gave the lower case I have tried to standardize in that way. Since all references to the Rev. Thomas McCulloch and the Rev. James MacGregor render their names with upper case, I have followed suit. I found the *New Century*

Cyclopedia of Names (New York, 1954) full of sensible advice.

With regard to another controversial area I had less difficulty, for although it used to be thought that the name of the ship which carried Pictou's Yankee settlers from Philadelphia was named the *Hope*, the shipping records prove conclusively, I think, that she was the *Betsey*.

One of the pleasures in researching a book is the infinite number and variety of kind and helpful people that one meets along the way. On the other hand, one of the frustrations is trying to do justice to that kindness. In an effort to record my gratitude I would like to mention the following people:

Clyde Sanger of Ottawa for suggesting this book; Penny Sanger for accompanying us on a Highland research expedition which ended in a rented crofter's hut on Coigach Peninsula, Loch Broom; and Richard Sanger for his photo research in Edinburgh.

John Imre and his staff at the Scottish Records Office; the staff of the National Library of Scotland; Donald Whyte of the Scottish Genealogy Society, Edinburgh; I. R. Mackay, Inverness; William Muir, the salmon fisherman of Achiltibuie, Loch Broom, for a copy of a rare manuscript on early life in Coigach Barony.

In particular I thank George Dixon of Edinburgh and Glasgow whose scholarly guidance led me to new information on circumstances surrounding the *Hector* voyage, and to John Prebble for his early advice and inspiration. My search for information about the brig *Hector*, one of half a dozen ships of that name listed in Lloyd's Register in the 1770s, was abetted by Kay Chapman of the National Maritime Museum, London, and the Registrar of British Ships, HM Customs and Excise, Greenock.

Mrs. Kay MacIntosh of Halifax and Henry R. Beer of Montreal, both natives of Pictou County, generously loaned me their own excellent research and to them I owe special thanks. I received much help from such descendants of the *Hector* people as Donald F. Maclean, Halifax; Jean and David Maclellan, Ottawa; Colin B. Mackay, Rothsay, N.B.; Weldon Fraser, Pictou; Helen Carson, Pictou; and Page Harshman, Toronto. Roger Nason of Fredericton shared with me the scholarship he has lavished on the Pagan commercial enterprise which organized the *Hector* expedition.

At the Hector Centre in Pictou, Mrs. Juanita Brittain provided much enthusiastic assistance and advice, as did the former archivist at the Centre, Mrs. Ruth Spicer. I am most grateful to the staff of the Public Archives of Nova Scotia, and in particular Allan C. Dunlop, Senior Research Assistant, who gave generously of his time and scholarship.

I wish to acknowledge, also, a research grant from the Explorations Program of the Canada Council, as well as travel assistance from Air Canada.

Many thanks also to Robin Brass and Elaine Aboud of McGraw-Hill Ryerson.

To all those who offered help and encouragement, including my friends Robert McCleave of Halifax and George Whalen of Sudbury, and those in Pictou County, where my own paternal ancestors once settled, my sincere thanks.

Donald MacKay
Montreal, Quebec
March 1980

Introduction

For a nation whose chief export has been her men, women and children, Scotland has had little success in founding colonies of her own, under the Scottish flag. In colonizing, as in fighting foreign wars, the Scots had to exercise their considerable talents under banners other than their own white cross of St. Andrew.

At first the Scots were in the habit of going abroad to take service in the armies of the Continent, such as when the Earl of Douglas took 7,000 men to France in the 15th century to support Charles VII against the invading English. By the 17th century, Scottish mercenaries had become a tradition on the Continent, exported from Scotland under licences, some fighting for Protestant kings, some for Catholic. The clan Mackay, for example, supported the Protestant Reformation; in 1626 Donald Mackay raised

3,000 men and 36 pipers to serve the Protestant cause in the Thirty Years War, first under Christian IV, King of Denmark, and then, in the Scots Brigade, under Gustavus Adolphus, King of Sweden, and "Lion of the North," against "the Roman Emperor and the Catholicke League in Germanie." There were 10,000 Scots in the Swedish army and as many again in the French, and somewhat fewer in the armies of the Netherlands, Russia and other countries. There was an understanding that should Scot meet Scot on opposing sides, they would not fight each other.

Nor were the Scots in Europe only soldiers; in 1598 the much-travelled Scottish writer Fynes Moryson reported artisans and traders "flocking in great numbers into Poland." There were so many—one report said 30,000—that King Stephen Batory granted them land at Cracow, "and in these kingdoms they lived at this time in great multitudes, rather for the poverty in their kingdom than for any great traffic they exercised here." The tradition of self-exile had begun.

Early in the 1600s, King James VI began to settle 50,000 Protestant, mostly Lowland, Scots in northern Ireland as a counterweight to the Irish Catholics. Later these Scotch Irish, as they came to be called, flocked to the North American colonies in their tens of thousands. The results of King James' resettlement policy haunt us to this day on the streets of Belfast, but the royal efforts to establish Scotland in the New World at the same time have almost been forgotten.

In the 1620s, a few years after the English *Mayflower* had landed her pilgrims at Plymouth, Sir William Alexander took possession, under royal charter, of the land between the St. Croix River and the Gulf of St. Lawrence on the questionable basis that it had once been claimed for the Crown by John Cabot. Sir William, an officer of the Royal Court, a poet and enthusiastic Latinist, called the colony "Nova Scotia," thinking it fitting there should be a New

Scotland as well as a New England. The Knights Baronets of Nova Scotia were created from among those merchants in Scotland willing to contribute six men and 1,000 merks in cash, a "merk" being 13 shillings. Each baronet was to receive 10,000 acres. In 1629, the baronets, "that they may be the better knowne and distinguished from other persouns," were given the right to wear around their necks an orange ribbon with the arms of Nova Scotia. That was one of the few tangible returns they ever got for their money. Few, if any, of the baronets ever went to Nova Scotia to see their land. However, the law demanded that the granting of their patents include a formal presentation of symbolic earth and stone and this ceremony was always carried out at Edinburgh Castle, as a matter of convenience. From this tradition sprang up the erroneous belief that a piece of ground at Edinburgh Castle had been legally declared a part of Nova Scotia, which, in fact, was not so. A bronze plaque commemorating the symbolic transfer of earth and stone was unveiled near the castle's main gate in 1953.

A settlement was founded by Sir William at Baleine Bay on Cape Breton Island in 1629, but it lasted only a few weeks before being destroyed by marauding soldiers from a French ship. Sir William's second effort at Fort Charles (named for Charles I) on the Bay of Fundy, where the French had established their own short-lived Port Royal in 1605, lasted a few years, until King Charles ceded Nova Scotia back to the French in 1631 and the colony ceased to be Scottish territory. It became Acadia again under the Treaty of St. Germain-en-Laye, and the Scots returned home, although King Charles promised to maintain the rights of the baronets in Nova Scotia and continued to grant rather meaningless charters for Nova Scotia baronies right up to 1637. But it would be nearly 150 years before another shipload of Scottish settlers came to Nova Scotia—the people of the *Hector*.

Far to the south, Scottish colonies were founded in New

Jersey and South Carolina in the 1680s, but Scotland's greatest effort, while still more or less an independent nation with its own parliament (although sharing a king with England), came late in the 1690s. The Scots set out to compete with England and Spain for a share of New World wealth by establishing a trading colony on the Isthmus of Panama. The colony of New Edinburgh was doomed from the start, as much for its location as for opposition from the English and military attacks from the Spanish, who claimed the neck of land joining North and South America as their own. Before the disaster ended, Scotland had lost 2,000 settlers—some drowned at sea, some died of yellow fever in the malarial swamps, others perished in battle with the Spaniards. Scotland also lost hundreds of thousands of pounds, perhaps half of its available national wealth, in the effort, and within a few years of this national tragedy, under the Act of Union of 1707, it also lost the right to colonize abroad. Under the British flag, however, Scottish emigration was to swell, particularly during the Highland Clearances, and peak in the 19th century.

As early as the 1650s, we find Scots in the American colonies, some having migrated willingly and others banished there as criminals or political prisoners. When Cromwell defeated the Scots and imposed military government, 1,000 political prisoners were shipped out to New England and Virginia. The tradition grew of sending common criminals, murderers, robbers, beggars and whores to the colonies, for terms of seven years to life. The records of the Royal Burgh of Stirling for the late 1600s contain a bill for two fathoms of rope "to tye Laurance M'Lairen quehen sent to America," and although we do not know his crime, it may not have been serious. In September 1763, Elizabeth Campbell, wife of a soldier of the Argyllshire regiment, arrested for picking pockets at a fair, "was found guilty, art and part, and was banished to the plantations not to return for seven years." Another method of getting cheap labour for the plantations was established in the 1740s in the brisk, ill-concealed trade of enticing—even kidnapping—young Scots boys. One victim, Peter Williamson, wrote that he had been shanghaied in Aberdeen at the age of 11 and sold for £16 in the colonies. During the Highland famine of 1740 there are accounts of parents selling their sons for one shilling. Although jails were used as way stations in this traffic, the authorities turned a blind eye so that it was impossible to discover just how many boys were whisked off to the New World. Certainly there had been more outcry in the 1730s when Sir Alexander Macdonald of Sleat and his brother-in-law, the Macleod laird of Dunvegan, arranged to ship off 100 of their own clansmen to Pennsylvania. Serfdom was not uncommon and was to flourish in the coal mines in Scotland until almost 1800.

By the 1730s there were Scots in most of the 13 colonies, as far south as Georgia where 100 mercenaries came from Sutherlandshire to guard the southern frontiers against the Spanish in Florida. The Highlanders' favourite colony was North Carolina where, encouraged by the Scots-born Governor Gabriel Johnson, they settled for 100 miles up the Cape Fear River Valley. They were to come in their greatest numbers only after the collapse in 1746 of the remnants of the clan system, with the defeat of Prince Charles Stuart's Jacobite rebellion at the battle of Culloden.

Prince Charles had tried to achieve what his father, James Francis Edward, the Old Pretender, had failed to do in 1715—put a victorious end to the series of dynastic battles between the House of Stuart and the Protestant kings in London which had begun in 1688, when William of Orange had become King of Great Britain by deposing the Catholic James II. Henceforth those clans—whether Catholics, Episcopalian or Presbyterian—who supported the Stuarts were Jacobites, from the Latin *Jacobus* or James. Those loyal to Orange and Hanover, and there were many among the Protestant clans, were Whigs, a name taken from a once-derisive term used in the western Lowlands. Both factions were to suffer at Culloden, the last battle fought on British soil, but the Jacobites suffered more.

For hundreds of years Highland life had been based upon the *clan*, whose mystic, bonding power was vested in its chief, the father who governed and protected his children in time of peace and called them out in time of war with the Fiery Cross which was carried by runners from glen to glen. Any weakening of the chief's powers was bound to weaken the whole clan. Erosion of clanship was apparent at least as early as Cromwell's military occupation of Scotland in the mid-1600s. But for another century the government in London more or less tolerated the chiefs and the clan system—until Prince Charles rose in rebellion in 1745, frightening the English so much they resolved to break the chiefs and end their power. The harassment and disruption of tribal life carried out by the English after the Jacobite defeat at Culloden led, inevitably, to emigration, despite, and sometimes because of, efforts by the English to replace the old ways with the modern methods of the south.

Emigration took some 20 years to grow after the shock of Culloden Moor, and when it came it was in waves rather than a steady stream. By the late 1760s gentry who had once derived power from the now-weakened chiefs were migrating to the colonies, taking dependent clansmen with them. Between 1768 and 1771, 1,600 settled in North Carolina, and in 1772 the governor reported that "near a thousand people have arrived at Cape Fear River from the Scottish Islands since the month of November with a view to settling in the province." "Tacksmen," the middlemen who had rented land from the chiefs and leased it at a profit to lesser tenants, obtained vast tracts of land in the colonies and brought out so many people that by 1775 there were 15,000 Highlanders in North Carolina alone. Highlanders settled in Virginia, Maryland and as far north as the Mohawk Valley in New York. After the outbreak of revolution in 1775, the second anti-Hanoverian revolution they had witnessed in their lifetimes, they moved on to found Glengarry County in eastern Ontario.

Those who were not sponsored by tacksmen and lairds often pawned their freedom in order to emigrate. "If they could not pay their passage," wrote Thomas Pennant in the 1770s, "they sold themselves to the captains of vessels, who at the port resold them to Plantations." As late as 1805, New York newspapers ran advertisements like this one: "A wench: Eight and a half years of the time of a healthy wench for sale; she is honest and sober, and understands the work of a family generally. Enquire etc." This young Scots woman, observed the *Greenock Advertiser* in Scotland on February 26, 1805, "sailed with many others from the Clyde to improve her fortune, and who, as is most common, had lost her liberty to defray her expenses." Nor was it uncommon to find notices in colonial newspapers seeking information about runaway Scottish servants as well as runaway black slaves.

After the Jacobite defeat at Culloden, more than 600 Highlanders were deported to the colonies from among the 3,500 prisoners taken during the 1745-46 rising. The Crown Solicitor in London, Philip Carteret Webb, suggested that they be branded so they could be detected and arrested if they tried to return to Scotland. Fortunately nothing came of this atrocious suggestion, and the idea was as unnecessary as it was cruel because few ever did return. Most of them—farmers, herdsmen, ploughmen, shoemakers, smiths, tailors, carpenters, weavers—hardly any of them professional soldiers, were still in the colonies 30 years later when the American Revolution began. Surprisingly, given their treatment by the English, they not only declined to join the American rebels but also signed up by the thousands in the King's Royal Highland Emigrant's Regiment to fight the men who had, perhaps, less cause than they to hate the House of Hanover. Some 3,000

Highland soldiers were raised for the King in North Carolina, including middle-aged men who had fought the English as lads at Culloden. They were by instinct royalists, and the practice of levying Highlanders to fight England's wars was nothing new.

Fifty years earlier the Black Watch, clad in dark tartan and assigned at first to police the Highlands, had been raised by the British and eventually sent to fight on the Continent in 1745, the year Prince Charles' rebellion began. When the Seven Years War (in the colonies the French and Indian War) began in 1757, Sir William Pitt again sent to the Highlands for men. In a clever move which both drained the glens of troublesome young fighters and brigaded them against their old allies, the French, Sir William raised 10,000 Highland men before the war ended in 1763. One of these regiments was the famous 78th, or Fraser Highlanders, 1,800 strong. It was raised in one month by Simon Fraser of Beauly, the repentant Jacobite son of one of the most powerful of the old-time chiefs, Lord Lovat, who lost his head on Tower Hill, London, for supporting the wrong cause once too often in the rising of 1745. Frasers, Macleods, Chisholms, Camerons, Mackays and other clansmen, in kilted dark "government plaids" and bonnets trimmed with black feathers, fought as keenly *for* the English cause as they, or their kinsmen, had fought *against* it a few years earlier at Culloden. They fought at Louisbourg and again at the Heights of Abraham, losing 200 men. Nor did they bear ill will toward their commander, the Englishman James Wolfe, for all his draconian measures as an area commander during the military occupation of the Highlands after the Culloden battle, and it is said that Wolfe died in the arms of a Fraser Highlander. For his part, Wolfe found the Highlanders "hardy, intrepid, accustom'd to a rough country, and no great mischief if they fall. How can you better employ a secret enemy than by making his end conducive to the common good?" As a reward for their loyalty and courage, or perhaps merely to preserve a British presence in a defeated land, King George III, after the Treaty of Paris gave the New World to the English in 1763, granted lands to those Highlanders who wished to remain. Nearly 200 men applied, settling on grants—ranging from 3,000 acres for a captain to 50 for a private,—at Murray Bay, named for Wolfe's successor, General James Murray, or in remote places where one can still find Frasers or Macdonalds who speak only French. Some settled on Isle St. Jean, which had been seized from the Acadians and became known as St. John Island before being renamed Prince Edward Island in 1795. They described their lives as landowners in letters to kinsmen in Scotland living in the land-hungry glens where uncertain rental of one or two poor acres was all that could ever be hoped for. Some of the Fraser Highlanders who went home to pay off at Inverness resolved to return and two of them sailed in the *Hector* to Pictou, Nova Scotia, just across the strait from P.E.I., in the summer of 1773.

Thus it was not Nova Scotia but the Island of St. John which received the first permanent Highland settlers in Maritime Canada. In 1767 the rich red soil of the island was divided into 67 townships, each one 20,000 acres, at a time when the Nova Scotia peninsula was filling with New Englanders. The island was portioned out by lottery in London to army officers, supporters of the British government and influential merchants for peppercorn rents, on condition they settle one Protestant family for every 200 acres, within ten years. Most never even attempted to fulfil this condition, but sold parcels of land to jobbers who rented them to working tenants, hampering proper colonization for decades to come. When Governor Walter Patterson, who had served in the army in the southern colonies and owned an island grant, arrived to take up his duties in 1770, he complained there were only 150 families there.

The Fraser Highlanders on the island had come from the

shires of Ross, Inverness, Sutherland and Argyll; the first contingent direct from the old country arrived in the spring of 1770 on the ship *Falmouth* from Greenock on the Clyde. Sir James Montgomery, Lord Advocate of Scotland, having obtained one of the original grants of land in 1767 and having increased it to 80,000 acres, brought out 60, mainly Protestant, settlers from Perthshire—Mcewans, Macgregors, Maclaughlans, Shaws, Aulds, Taylors, Browns. They paid a shilling an acre for land around Covehead and although they would have considered this cheap enough in Scotland, when they found the land uncleared they felt cheated. They were, however, fortunate in arriving early in the summer with time to establish themselves, as less fortunate by far were the 200 Highlanders aboard the *Annabella* who sailed from Campbeltown in Argyll to settle Colonel Robert Stewart's grant on Richmond Bay near Malpeque. On board were 60 Mackenzies, Mackays, Ramsays, Macdougalls, Macarthurs, and Macintoshes. The *Annabella* was wrecked off the northeast shore in a snowstorm, the emigrants lost their clothes and food and survived only with the help of kindly Acadian settlers.

It was not, presumably, a passenger from the *Annabella* or even from the *Falmouth* who wrote to the *Scots Magazine* in Edinburgh in July of the next year painting a picture of Eden in the St. Lawrence Gulf. It sounded more as if it had been written by a land agent. Perhaps it was, for it harped on the need for men. "Ours in general is very fertile, good for pasture as well as culture, a deal of it well adapted for hemp and flax; excellent greens and roots of all kinds; we want nothing here but hands . . . the winter is long but pleasant and healthy for the most part clear weather and sunshine; plenty of game of all sorts. The settlers sent over by an Hon. Gentleman are doing very well. When these people write to their friends I dare say we shall have more sent over, as we are told they are oppressed by their lairds; and here they will be lairds themselves. We are a distinct government, tax ourselves and make our own laws." This was written at the time when the Rev. William Drummond, who had accompanied the *Falmouth* settlers, was recording in his journal for July 20, 1771: "Found the people all in health but some of them mutinous," or again on August 25, "the people still discontented and mutinous."

It was to the Island of St. John that Captain John Macdonald, Laird of Glenaladale in the green saucer of land above Loch Shiel in western Inverness, led his Roman Catholic clansmen to escape religious persecution in 1772. Although John Macdonald had been only five years old at the time of Culloden, his father, Alexander, had been among the first to welcome Prince Charles from France and stood with him in the rain at nearby Glenfinnan on August 19, 1745, when the Prince raised the red and white silk standard of rebellion "to redress the wrongs which Scotland suffered since the Union with England in 1707." One hundred and fifty Glenaladale men fought at Culloden and John had grown up amid tales of the persecution of the Catholics who had numbered about one-half of Prince Charles' troop strength on Culloden Moor. He was 29 when he learned that his kinsman, Colin Macdonald, Laird of Boisdale on the island of South Uist, had taken it into his head to force his Catholic tenants to embrace the Protestant faith. One of Boisdale's bullying methods was to stand in the road and try to herd Catholics into the Protestant church with his yellow cane. The islanders had taken to calling his faith *Credimh a bhata bhui*, "the religion of the yellow stick." Having tried unsuccessfully to indoctrinate children in the schools, Boisdale threatened that if his tenants refused to renounce Catholicism, they would be driven from their homes. Glenaladale resolved to help them, mortgaged his estate and used the money to buy land on St. John Island. Chartering the ship *Alexander* at Greenock, he transported there more than 200 tenants in the spring of 1772—Campbells, Mackinnons, Mackenzies,

Maceacherns. Although Glenaladale offered them long leases on what he considered generous terms (he was not a rich man), many were unhappy to find themselves still tenants, with no land of their own. Some drifted off to other parts of the island or across the strait to Cape Breton Island.

The Highlanders had come with the prompting or aid of lairds and tacksmen who brought the ravelled remnants of the clan caste system with them. But by the early 1770s, a new breed of emigrant appeared—disbanded soldiers, artisans, independent farmers—freed from the clan system, but impoverished, all responding to the advertisements of emigration agents and the new land companies. Such were the people of the *Hector*, which sailed from Loch Broom and arrived, much the worse for wear, at Pictou Harbour, Nova Scotia, on September 15, 1773.

They came for many reasons: the famine of the previous spring, the pressures of recent population increases due to a higher birth rate, intolerable rent increases, trouble with the law, the hunger of landless men to own land of their own. Most had a little money, at least enough to pay their passage and a bit to spare. Most, as it happened, came from the Forfeited Estates, ancestral lands of the Mackenzies, Macleods, or the Lovat Frasers, which the Crown had seized from the chiefs who had risen with Prince Charles in the 1745 rebellion. One thing the *Hector* people held in common—they were of the generation which had grown up after Culloden, the battle which, like a thick black ledger line drawn through Highland history, had put an end to feudal tribalism. What they had experienced on the long road from Culloden Moor had instilled in them the need to emigrate.

The arrival of the *Hector* in Nova Scotia, although it was an expedition which disappointed both the organizers and, initially, the emigrants themselves, started a new pattern of Highland emigration. "That stream of Scottish emigration," wrote Dr. George Patterson, grandson of one of the *Hector* passengers, "which in after years flowed, not only over the county of Pictou, but over much of the eastern part of the Province, Cape Breton, Prince Edward Island, portions of New Brunswick, and even the Upper Provinces, began with this voyage, and even, in a large measure, originated with it, for it was the representations of those on board to their friends, that others followed, so the stream deepened and widened in succeeding years." In the next half century many thousands of Scots, mostly Highlanders, poured through Pictou Harbour making northeastern Nova Scotia a true New Scotland.

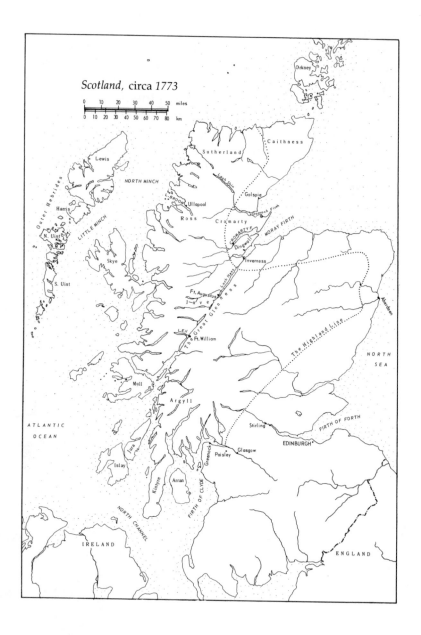

Scotland, circa 1773

Orkney

Lewis

NORTH MINCH

Outer Hebrides

Harris

LITTLE MINCH

N. Uist

S. Uist

Skye

Sutherland

Caithness

Loch Shin

Loch Broom
Ullapool

Golspie

Dornoch Firth

Ross

Cromarty F.

CROMARTY F.

MORAY FIRTH

Dingwall

Inverness

Ft. Augustus

Loch Ness

I~n~v~e~r

Loch Oich

The Great Glen

Loch Lochy

L.Eil
Ft. William

The Highland Line

Aberdeen

NORTH
SEA

ATLANTIC
OCEAN

Mull

Argyll

Jura

Islay

Kintyre

Arran

Greenock
Paisley

Glasgow

FIRTH OF CLYDE

Stirling

FIRTH OF FORTH

EDINBURGH

NORTH CHANNEL

IRELAND

ENGLAND

0 10 20 30 40 50 miles
0 10 20 30 40 50 60 70 80 km

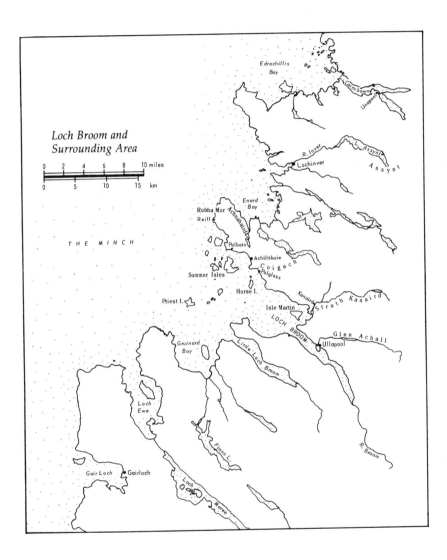

Loch Broom and
Surrounding Area

0   2   4   6   8   10 miles
0   5   10   15   km

Edrachillis Bay

Càrnbawn

Unapool

R. Inver

Lochinver

Assynt

A s s y n t

Enard Bay

Rubha Mor   Achnahaird

Reiff

T H E   M I N C H

Polbain

Achiltibuie

C o i g a c h

Polglass

Summer Isles

Horse I.

Priest I.

Isle Martin

Kanaird   S t r a t h   K a n a i r d

L O C H   B R O O M

G l e n   A c h a l l

Ullapool

Gruinard Bay

Little Loch Broom

Loch Ewe

Fionn L.

R. Broom

Gair Loch   Gairloch

Loch Maree

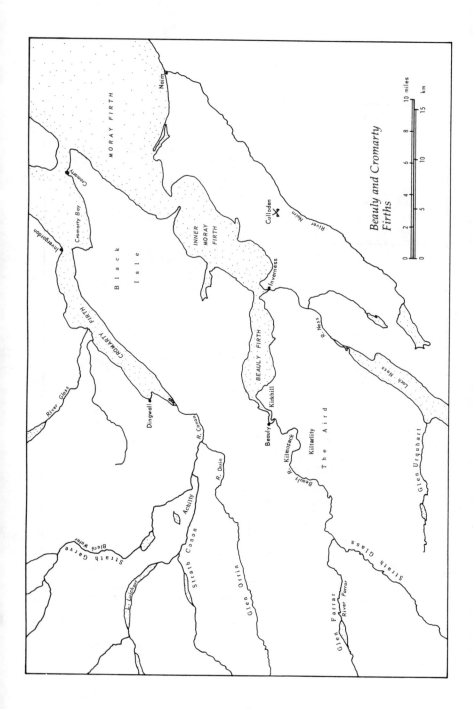

Beauly and Cromarty Firths

PART ONE

After Culloden

*Nothing but fire and sword can cure their
cursed, vicious ways of thinking.*

THE EARL OF ALBEMARLE,
COMMANDER OF KING GEORGE'S ARMY
IN SCOTLAND IN THE SUMMER OF 1746.

CHAPTER ONE

Loch Broom

It was not yet noon when Alexander Cameron heard the drums. Wrapped in his plaid, he had been standing since dawn in the rain-soaked heather on the northern slopes of Culloden Moor watching the rebel army of Prince Charles forming into line-of-battle. Beyond the straggled tartan rows of Macdonalds, Frasers, Mackintoshes, Macgillivrays, Appin Stewarts and the rest, stood the Camerons, perhaps 600 strong, led by Donald, "the Gentle Lochiel," with whom Alexander claimed kinship.

Alexander Cameron, who was nearly 18 and whose home lay in the far west country over by Loch Broom, had risen in the dark that morning, April 16, 1746, to do his chores on the farm where he was apprenticed. Few chores were completed, for streaming down the road from Inverness were throngs of people—men, women and boys of

2

his own age and younger—off to see "the battle." Without a word to his master, Alexander had joined them. There were boys from the Grammar School of Inverness, five miles away, and there was a boy about his own age, Alexander Fraser, who had walked more than 15 miles from Beauly to watch his three older brothers fight for Prince Charles. With the rain now turned to sleet, the boys stood in a knot behind the left flank of the Jacobite army and strained to see what might happen next as the drums drew closer through the mist.

They had not long now to wait. First they saw the Cameron scouts, who had been dogging the movements of the English army since dawn, falling back warily through the mid-day gloom. Then other figures could be seen, alone or in small groups—scouts for the English. And then, in a watery glint of sunshine, appeared the awesome might of *An-t-Arm Dearg*, the Red army, 9,000 men in white and scarlet, silken standards snapping in the wind. There were 800 mounted dragoons, a train of artillery, English regiments and Scots—Lowland units such as the Royal Scots Fusiliers and, among the Highlanders, the Campbells of the Argyll Militia or the men in Lord Laudon's companies. Among them somewhere was their leader, the King's son, the 25-year-old Duke of Cumberland. Marching to the measure of their drums (although the normal beat of two and a half miles an hour was slowed by the mud and soggy heath), the English army advanced across the brown moor toward the waiting rebels.

The Jacobites were little more than half the strength of the English army, but now, outnumbered, the sleet in their faces, hungry and weary, they raised a cheer that soared above the quickening bagpipes.

The Highlanders, standing in mud and rain since seven o'clock that morning, had slept less than three hours the previous night and the lucky ones had eaten a chunk of bread and nothing else. On orders from Prince Charles they wore blue bonnets with the cockade of the Stuarts—five white bows with a laurel wreath—and the plaid and kilt of their clan. In earlier battles, at Prestonpans and Falkirk, they had bested the English, but now they were weak and fighting a rearguard action. That morning some had been singing the Twentieth Psalm: "Jehova hear thee in the day, when trouble he doth send."

By one o'clock, after a crab-like manoeuver for position, the English army faced the rebels across 500 or 600 yards of sloping moorland. What followed was more a massacre than a battle. Within ten minutes Cumberland's three-pounders had silenced the makeshift rebel artillery with roundshot and, changing to grapeshot, savaged the helpless rows of clansmen. A third of the rebels closest to the English ranks were killed or wounded before Prince Charles thought to order the one manoeuver that had won him victory in the past—the Highland charge with sword, axe, war cry and ranting bagpipe. At last the shout for "claymores!" went up and down the Highland line but by then it was too late. The redcoats waited for the rebels with their bayonets, but few of the charging Highlanders got that far.

Alexander Cameron saw his clansmen running toward the English "in the smoke, the Lowland wind and rain." They had thrown away their muskets for the charge, and were running uphill, their targets or shields held above their heads, their claymores in their hands. A few of the Camerons broke through the line of English bayonets; Major James Wolfe, who was to lead the sons of some of these Highlanders on the Heights of Abraham in Quebec, was there that day and observed that his English soldiers "were attacked by the Camerons (the bravest clan amongst them) and t'war for some time a dispute between the swords and bayonets; but the latter was found by far the most destructible weapon."

Within 40 minutes the battle was over and the rebels were in retreat. The Chevalier de Johnstone, a Franco-Scot

4

who fought with the Jacobite army and also fought on the French side against Wolfe at Quebec, had stood among the Macdonalds not far from where Alexander Cameron watched. "What a spectacle of horror," wrote Johnstone. "The same Highlanders who had advanced to the charge like lions, with bold and determined countenance, were in an instant seen flying . . . " On the field among the dead and dying, Alexander Cameron saw his kinsman, the chieftain Donald of Lochiel, both legs broken by shot. Four men rescued him, and although they were almost captured by dragoons when they hid him in a shed, they got him safely away.

Alexander Fraser, the lad from Beauly who claimed kinship with the lordly Lovats, saw two of his three brothers shot down and his namesake, Ensign Alexander Fraser, who was also known as Maciver, wounded in the thigh by a musket ball and taken prisoner. In the press of bodies he may not have seen a redcoat shoot the wounded Charles Fraser of Inverallochie. Charles, only 20 years old, was leading the Frasers that day in the absence of old Lord Lovat's son Simon, who was to serve Wolfe on the Heights of Abraham 13 years later.

By now the Highland army was melting away, some in orderly retreat, some fleeing in panic before the flashing sabres of the English dragoons. Donald Campbell of Airds, who was with the Argyll Highlanders on the English side and who kept a battle diary, reported, "There never was a more compleat victory obtain'd. We got all the enemies cannon, ammunition and a great part of their baggage." His Colonel, Archibald Campbell, claimed the rebel dead numbered 1,000 and the prisoners 500. Considering those wounded who later died on the moor, the number was probably much higher. The English put their own casualties at 50 killed and 259 wounded.

With the dragoons harrying the countryside looking for rebel survivors, the two young Alexanders managed to slip away in the mist. Fraser set out for Beauly, but even there he would not be safe from 400 of Cumberland's red-coats looting and burning the Fraser country north of Inverness. Those who could fled into the western hills. One incident which Alexander Fraser never forgot—and he lived to be a very old man at Middle River in Pictou County, Nova Scotia—involved his kinsman, Ensign Alexander Fraser of Wellhouse in Kilmorack Parish near Beauly. After his capture at Culloden, the Ensign was taken along with 18 other prisoners to a dyke and ordered to prepare for death. After firing at point-blank range, the English soldiers methodically clubbed to death those who were still alive. Observing signs of life in the Ensign, one of the soldiers struck him in the face with the butt of his gun, gouged out one of his eyes, broke his nose and shattered his cheek and left him for dead. With the help of a sympathic Highland officer, young Lord Boyd who served with the English troops at Culloden, Ensign Fraser found sanctuary in a mill where he was cared for. In time he recovered from his wounds and returned to his home near Beauly.

As for Alexander Cameron, he fled from the moor until he reached his master's farm. The farmer, busy with his own work and knowing nothing about the battle, scolded the boy for going off without permission. Angered further by Cameron's improbable tale, the farmer ran after the boy and slipped and cut himself with the dirk he wore at his knee. By then the neighbours had got word of the battle at the moor and persuaded the farmer to hide himself in the hills lest the marauding English should find him wounded and kill him as a refugee from the battle.

Cameron set out, like many of the survivors, for the western mountains and came at last to Loch Broom where years later, as a middle-aged man, he was to again meet Alexander Fraser when the two boarded the emigrant ship *Hector* on their voyage to Pictou, Nova Scotia. What they had seen that day would change their lives.

Of all the parishes that sent men over the mountains to

follow Prince Charles, Loch Broom and the neighbouring parish of Assynt to the north were the most remote. But even Loch Broom was not safe from the King's men, who came that summer not by land but by ship. From the cliffs at Reiff and the high fields of Polbain the people of the crofts saw the white sails beating up from the southwest; by evening the squadron had anchored beside the herring boats in Kanaird Bay, under the lee of Isle Martin. Among them was the sloop-of-war *Furnace*, commanded by Captain John Fergusson who had already cast a long shadow.

In the weeks since the battle his marines had raided the western isles and sea lochs; failure to catch the fugitive Prince Charles Edward Stuart had not improved the captain's temper. Although Fergusson was considered an efficient officer by his superiors and was given command of a 50-gun ship in later years, according to Bishop Robert Forbes who knew him, Fergusson had always been bloody-minded, "a fellow of very low extract, born in the country of Aberdeen, who, being naturally of a furious, savage disposition thought he could never enough harass, misrepresent and maltreat everyone whom he knew, or supposed to be, an enemy of the good cause he himself was embarked on."

Like many a Scot in the English army, Fergusson stamped out the dying embers of rebellion with great ferocity. Whether for personal reasons, or because the English distrusted all Scots and he wanted to prove his loyalty, he carried his own hangman and his ship was a floating prison. Those suspected of knowing the Prince's whereabouts were flogged until, as one recalled, "blood gushed out both my sides." Fergusson burned crofts and crops. He arrested the gentle Flora Macdonald on the isle of Skye and sent her to face trial in London for aiding the Prince, whom she had found "maigre, ill-coloured, and overrun with scab . . . having had no meat or sleep for two days and two nights, sitting on a rock, beat upon by rains, and when that cleared ate up by flies." Dressing the Prince in her maid's frock and kerchief, and calling him

Betty Burke, she helped him escape. Fergusson had been outwitted, but his men boasted of having captured the wily old Lord Lovat as the chief of the Frasers hid in a hollow tree, many miles from his home at Beauly on the east coast, in the Moidart country in the west near Fort William. And now Fergusson had arrived in Loch Broom.

Loch Broom had known many raids in its history that dates back to 1227, when a holy man named Mathew built a chapel on the apron of alluvial soil at the lochhead, 20 miles from the open sea. Its name, long anglicized, derives from a fresh water lake, Loch à Bhraoin (Loch of the Showers), high among the mountains. From this lake flows the River Broom, down past the parish church which now stands where Mathew built his chapel. Above the loch the mountains, with names such as Mantle of White Stone, are silent, sometimes bright, other times somber, in the shifting Highland light.

The raids always came from the sea. A document dated 1596 tells how Torquil the Usurper, Torquil Dow Macleod, came from the Hebrides with 700 men, "who committitt [sic] barbarous and monstrous crewalities as the lyk of haid nocht bene herid of, spairing nayther man vyfe nor bearne." In 1655 Cromwell's men came sacking and burning "as a lesson" to the nation he had defeated.

Discounting the 32-mile cattle track from Dingwall on the east coast across the glens and passes, there were no roads to Loch Broom in 1746, so the redcoats came by sea. In the early light of the northern summer morning, herdsmen on the shirts of Ben More Coigach saw them row ashore, 80 soldiers including a detachment of Royal Scots Fusiliers who had fought in the government front line at Culloden a few weeks earlier. With a drummer rattling the pace, they marched off up the green easy strath of Kanaird and came to a halt six miles away, in front of the fine stone farmhouse of Mackenzie of Langwell. The Laird was not there but his wife, nursing her children through smallpox, watched them pillage her home and burn a trunk containing family papers, including the wadset, or deed, to the land. Not only had her husband supported the rebellion, but she herself was a close relative of the Earl of Cromarty, George Mackenzie of Tarbat, who had led Jacobite troops, and owned the northwest reaches of Loch Broom parish, a wild tract of land known as the Barony of Coigach.

Perhaps because of the smallpox, the soldiers did not tarry. Driving off 50 head of Mackenzie's shaggy black cattle, they marched down the valley, pausing to burn a tenant's croft and steal his scrawny sheep. For eight days Fergusson's men harried Loch Broom, the black smoke from roof-trees and sodden heather thatch drifting down the loch. Then they were gone. But the people of Loch Broom might count themselves lucky, for across the mountains to the south and east the retribution of *An-t-Arm Dearg*—the Red Army—had been at once more terrible and more prolonged.

In the dying days of May, the Duke of Cumberland marched eight battalions of his victorious army from Inverness, where they had settled in after the Culloden battle, down the Great Glen through the now-silent Lovat Fraser country of Strath Errick and on to Fort Augustus. Theft and pillage and rape and murder were rampant. "Parties were sent out from Fort Augustus all around the Highlands," reported the *Scots Magazine* of Edinburgh in June 1746. "Wherever these came they left nothing that belonged to the rebels. They burned all the houses and carried off the cattle." Eight thousand of the soft-eyed, long-haired beasts, which were the Highlander's cash crop, were stolen by the soldiers and slaughtered for food or sold to drovers who had heard of the ravaging and had come up from England. Clansmen who had been encouraged to surrender their arms in return for pardon were jailed and sometimes shot. An officer writing to *London Magazine* boasted that his men "carried fire and destruction as they passed, shooting vagrant Highlanders they met in the mountains, and driving off the cattle."

In July the *Scots Magazine* reported: "The troops continue their diligence in searching for rebels through the hills and isles and distressing their estates," "distressing" being a quaint euphemism for pyromania. From Lovat's Castle Dounie on the gentle slope above Beauly Firth in the east, to the home of the Camerons at Achnacarry on Loch Eil in the west, and then north into Loch Broom, the soldiers burned and looted. "Jacobite rebellious spirit is so rooted in the nation's mind that this generation must be pretty well wore out before this country will be quiet," said the 25-year-old Prince whom the English called "Sweet William." The Jacobites called him "Butcher Cumberland" and named one of their worst weeds "Stinking Willie," so called to this day.

With rebel hunting waning for want of fuel, Cumberland relinquished his command to the Earl of Albemarle and returned to an admiring London, where he suggested that whole clans of unruly Highlanders be shipped to the colonies. English newspapers, not to be outdone, urged that the people of that "cursed country" be denied seed grain for their crops and that other steps be taken to get rid of them so their lands could be resettled with "decent God-fearing people from the south." The Londoners were still reacting to the fright they had suffered a few months earlier when Prince Charles' makeshift Highland army had marched within 127 miles of the capital before turning back north.

As a result, two laws were passed by Parliament which proved to be draconian enough. First came the "Act for the more effectual disarming the Highlands; and for restraining the use of Highland dress." It became a serious offence for a Highlander to possess arms or even to own a set of bagpipes which the English feared, not without reason, as "a weapon of war." Unless a clansman belonged to one of His Majesty's Highland regiments, he was barred from wearing tartan, kilt or plaid, and had to wear the clothing of the Sassenach. Highlanders were given a year to buy trousers or sew and dye their plaids and kilts into parodies of Lowland clothing. They faced six months in jail for a first offence of wearing Highland garb and seven years transportation to the colonies for a second. Englishmen such as Edward Burt, stationed in the Highlands with the army, might scarce appreciate, however, why this was such a blow to Highland pride since Englishmen thought little of Highland dress until the romantics of the Sir Walter Scott school taught them better in the 19th century. "The common habit of the Highlander," wrote Burt, "is far from being acceptable to the eye. A small part of the plaid . . . is set in folds and girt round the waist to make it a short petticoat that reaches halfway to the thigh, the rest is brought over the shoulders and fastened before, below the neck . . . so that they make pretty nearly the appearance of the poor women in London when they bring their gowns over their heads to shelter themselves from the rain. The dress is the *quelt*, and for the most part they wear the petticoat so very short that in a windy day, going up a hill, or stooping, the indecency of it is plainly discovered."

Whatever indignities were occasioned by the Disarming Act, or Dress Act, it was another Act, the next year, for the Abolition of Heritable Jurisdictions, which was the more destructive. This Act removed the feudal hereditary power of the chiefs, which was more than 700 years old. Although this power had been waning for generations it had once been almost absolute. The estates seized belonged to rebel chiefs, but even those who were neutral or loyal to the Crown could not longer dispense justice or order their people to fight clan battles. The military organization of the clan was broken and the value of a chief's estate began, more than in the past, to be reckoned in money rather than men. All this absolved the chiefs, so they thought, of the traditional fatherly responsibility for their clansmen, which led to dislocation and suffering particularly among those clans whose chiefs had used their powers well. Although the Prince Charles rebellion in

1745-46 had been actively supported by only a fraction of the Highland population—some say one-third were Jacobite, one-third Whig and one-third neutral—the new laws affected all Highlanders—Jacobite, neutral or Whig.

Late in the summer of 1746, the Highland people turned to the Presbyterian ministers, whose beliefs had always been rejected by the Roman Catholic Stuarts and the Jacobite cause. By now, however, Catholic priests were so hounded they could give little help to their parishioners. "As most of the parish is burnt to ashes and all the cattle belonging to the Rebels carried off by his Majesty's forces," wrote a minister in the *Caledonia Mercury* of Edinburgh, "there is no such thing as money or a pennyworth to be got in this desolate place . . . My family is now much increased, by the wives and infants of those in rebellion in my parish crowding for a mouthful of bread to keep them from starving." To this the government had no better advice than to urge this Presbyterian clergyman, and all his brethren, to turn informer. "The clergy," said the *Scots Magazine*, "have been directed to give a list of all those in their respective parishes that have or who have not been, concerned in the recent rebellion. Tis said that a few have complied, but others have declined."

Among those who made no secret of their support for the Protestant King in London was the minister of the parish of Loch Broom. The Reverend James Robertson had been appointed a year earlier, before the Jacobite rebellion had begun, and neither his place of origin nor the manner of his coming had endeared him to his parishioners. In a world where people from an adjoining parish might be called strangers, he had come from the distant Atholl country of the south central Highlands. He had been recommended by the Duke of Atholl, but since the patron of Loch Broom parish, the Earl of Cromarty, had been busy plotting rebellion and had forgotten to register the appointment with the Moderator within six months, the Presbytery had bestowed the appointment on a local man, the Reverend Robert Mackenzie. When the Duke of Atholl persisted, the Presbytery reversed its decision.

Robertson's influence in Loch Broom in the generation following the uprising was considerable, for James Robertson was no ordinary man. He was large, muscular, militant and evangelical when he came to Loch Broom at the age of 45 to labour "with much earnestness and zeal." He was not shy about using the weight of his tremendous arm when faced with what was termed "the grosser indelicacies" of the mountain men in his parish, which at 400 square miles was one of the biggest in the Highlands. There was the case of Donald Mackenzie. Having found the 44-year-old crofter from the remote fringes of the Coigach peninsula "grossly ignorant" of religion, Robertson refused to baptise the child whom Mackenzie had carried 20 miles. Being bold as well as powerful, Donald Mackenzie next waylaid the minister on a footpath far from the manse and tried again. After a quick examination, Robertson found the man as ignorant as before and again refused; whereupon Mackenzie laid violent hands on the minister and swore he would not release him until he had baptised the child. In the struggle Mackenzie, finding the minister too strong to hold, drew his dirk and stabbed Robertson in the arm. Despite his wound Robertson continued the struggle and wrestled free, but took no further action at the time.

An incident which gained Robertson respect and fame occurred while he was visiting the Reverend Donald Ross, former Loch Broom minister, at Ross' new parish at Fearn across the mountains on the east coast. During divine service the roof of the old kirk, built of flagstones rather than the usual tile or thatch, collapsed. Amid dust and falling masonry, Robertson ran to the door as the lintel threatened to give way. Holding it like a Samson, he gave the congregation time to escape into the churchyard and then he rescued his friend, Ross, who lay half-suffocated in the dust and rubble of the altar canopy. Forever after, and to this day, James Robertson has been known as *Am Ministeir Laidir*, "The Mighty Minister."

During the Jacobite rebellion, with its elements of civil war, Robertson, to his dismay, discovered that the parish patron, the Earl of Cromarty, was a rebel leader who expected his Coigach tenants at Loch Broom to be rebels, too. But when the awesome *Am Ministeir Laidir* preached at them to stay home in their glens, they heeded him, even when the braggart Coll Macdonald of Barisdale rode from the south in search of men for the Glengarry regiment. He got a cold welcome and men took to the hills to keep out of his way. Young William Mackenzie, who was one of the *Hector* immigrants to Pictou, Nova Scotia, many years later used to regale his friends with tales of how his Uncle Colin, then 20 years old and the brother of William's father, Sir William Mackenzie, Laird of Ballone, Loch Broom, took up his sword and demanded that Barisdale leave him in peace. But as 1745, the Year of the Prince, drew to a close, Cromarty raised his own regiment and sent his son John (known as Lord Macleod because of his mother's people) to Loch Broom. The men felt obliged, because of tradition or fear of losing their rented land, to follow Cromarty into battle at Falkirk in January 1746. By February even the Reverend Robertson had been drawn into the struggle, although on the government's side.

The rebels had taken the town of Inverness, forcing the civil administrator of Scotland, Lord President Duncan Forbes, and one of the King's generals, Lord Laudon, to flee northwest through the snowy passes to Assynt, north of Loch Broom. Wishing to gain refuge in the loyal Macleod country of Skye, but trusting no one in the intervening country, they sent a messenger to Robertson to ask for help in their passage through his parish. Robertson agreed, but the cloaked and booted messenger had been seen by the commander of Jacobite troops encamped in the glen above the manse, and the minister was arrested. Whatever Robertson told the commander—and the only hint we have is that "he acquitted himself with his usual coolness and presence of mind"—he was freed the next morning. Presumably he had deceived the Jacobites so that they moved away, and not only did the government men pass safely through the parish but also stayed the night in Robertson's house.

His efforts to keep his own parishioners out of the war were less successful. On March 17, a month before the battle of Culloden, the Earl of Cromarty's son again came recruiting for his father's regiment. "He unexpectedly surprised the poor people," Robertson recounted later in pleading for their lives, "snatching some out of their beds. Others, who thought their old age would excuse them, were dragged from their ploughs, while some were taken off the highways. One I did myself see overtaken by speed of foot, and when he declared he would rather die than be carried to the rebellion, was knocked to the ground by the butt of a musket and carried away all bleed."

Within the month, one day before the battle of Culloden, these untrained, reluctant men saw action in a skirmish fought at Golspie in Sutherlandshire north of Inverness. Cromarty was no general and the affair was soon over. According to the *Scots Magazine*, "The party commanded by the Earl of Cromarty was attacked on the 15th at Golspie by Lord Sutherland's people and routed, only 30 having escaped. About 40 of them were killed or drowned, and some were wounded." One hundred and sixty prisoners were taken to Inverness aboard the sloop H.M.S. *Hound*, among them the Earl of Cromarty, his son and many of Robertson's parishioners: Lieutenant Alexander Mackenzie of Corrie, Ensign Hector Mackenzie, the Earl's Coigach forester, Captain Colin Mackenzie— brother of Sir William Mackenzie of Ballone—and Robertson's farm servant, Roderick Mackenzie.

With so many gone from Loch Broom, there was little planting that spring. The glens were full of rumour about the Prince hiding in the islands to the south, with a price on his head. The Jacobites, it was said, were trying to rally at Lochaber for one more battle. A French fleet with 3,000 soldiers commanded by the Duc d'Anville lay at Brest awaiting invasion orders to come to the support of their Jacobite allies; however the orders were never given and instead the French sailed to Nova Scotia to try to recapture Louisbourg in the ill-fated campaign in which many of the French were drowned.

To south and east the Red soldiers were on the rampage, but once the brief naval raid on Loch Broom was over it was considered a safe hiding place for many strangers. Survivors of the battles at Culloden and Golspie straggled home in little groups, scurrying down in darkness from the hills behind the manse so as not to be seen, although the Rev. Robertson knew who they were as well as their reasons for going to battle.

That summer there was only one more alarm at Loch Broom. Long after the *Furnace* had gone, Lord Albemarle, by then commanding the King's army in Scotland, heard rumours that Prince Charles had been seen at Loch Broom, and despatched the warship *Serpent* to hunt him down. But soon after, the elusive Prince was "seen" in Glendessary and the *Serpent* was recalled. Such hide-and-seek went on until French ships arrived in late September to carry the Prince, the wounded Lochiel and others from Lochaber to France.

Throughout the summer small groups of rebels straggled to their homes in the west. Times were desperate with the redcoats on the loose, and for young John Macdonnell, a Jacobite courier arriving at Loch Broom, his first impression was of the lawlessness which is certain to follow civil war. Sailing from France on April 16, the very day of the Culloden battle, and taking the northern route around the top of Scotland to avoid English ships, Macdonnell knew nothing of the battle until he reached Loch Broom during the first week of May. Carrying £1,500 in French gold for Prince Charles, he rode south from Loch

Broom, still in Mackenzie country, "thinking ourselves as safe as in the heart of France," and stopped to sample the hospitality of Laggy, on Little Loch Broom, with Colin Dearg Mackenzie and his men. During toasts to Prince Charles, Macdonnell noticed that the heavy canvas bag containing his clothes and the gold had disappeared from his side, but he was reassured by Colin Dearg that, since Macdonnell would soon be on his way again, a servant had put the bag on Macdonnell's horse to save him the effort. Macdonnell discovered this to be true, but when he came to open the bag that night upon reaching his destination, he found two-thirds of the gold missing. He returned to Laggy and accused Colin Dearg of stealing it, but Dearg denied any wrongdoing. Since Dearg was attended by armed followers, Macdonnell was obliged to continue his journey with what money he had left. Two years later he returned to Laggy with armed companions and although he wrung an admission out of Colin Dearg, the money had already been distributed among the Mackenzie clan or spent. Macdonnell, who was only 18 when he was robbed, moved to the colonies in 1773 like so many others, fought for the British in the American Revolution and died of old age at his farm at Cornwall, Ontario.

About the time Macdonnell was smuggling gold, the Rev. James Robertson had gone to Inverness. He was certain that many of his parishioners held prisoner there had been impressed into the Jacobite army against their will. He had heard that the English now intended to send them to London for trial. Cumberland had made it plain he had no faith in Scottish justice and grumbled that "one half of the magistracy had been either aiders or abettors to the Rebellion, and the others dare not act through fear of offending the Chiefs or hanging their own cousins." To plead their cause, one day early in May Robertson walked up Strath More behind his manse to Corrieshalloch Gorge and continued on for 37 miles to Dingwall, from where he travelled south to Beauly, then 12 miles further to Inver-

17

ness—called the Highland capital although it actually lies in eastern lowlands. A town of 500 sandstone houses, a castle, a Tolbooth jail, two churches and normally a population of 3,000, Inverness was bursting with redcoat soldiers. Robertson was received not only by the patrician Duncan Forbes of Culloden, but also by the Duke of Cumberland himself. What the pudgy 25-year-old son of King George II and the raw-boned, middle-aged parish cleric had to say to each other was not recorded. It is known that the Duke asked the minister to write to him and this Robertson did for as long as Cumberland remained in the Highlands that summer. The Duke also presented the minister with a "stand of arms" to carry home as protection against roving bands of "broken men." But none of this brought the release of even one of Robertson's imprisoned parishioners who, early in June, were taken from the prison camps of Inverness and despatched to London on cargo ships: *Jane of Leith, Alexander and James, Thane of Fife* and, ironically, *Property and Liberty*. The prisoners, even the sick ones, lay on ballast without bedding; after a three-week voyage through a North Sea storm, 300 of the Loch Broom men were taken to Tilbury Fort, a star-shaped redoubt on the lower Thames. There they lay under the brick arches of the abandoned powder magazines. Some were transferred to prison hulks such as the *Pamela*, where a surgeon from the Commission for the Wounded, no friend of the Jacobites, was moved to observe: "On looking down into the hold where the prisoners were, was saluted with such an intolerable smell that it was like to overcome me, tho' I was provided with proper herbs and my nostrils stuffed therewith." Perhaps one-fifth of the prisoners died on the voyage from Inverness or during the weeks they awaited trial for treason. Few spoke English. They were homesick and half-starved. Their crime, for most of them, was that they had obeyed their chiefs and, however reluctantly, gone to war.

In the autumn Robertson followed them south 700

miles, the length of Britain, and most of it afoot. In London he found the citizens still celebrating the great victory, and arrived in time to attend the trial of Ensign Hector Mackenzie, one of those he had listed as being impressed into Jacobite service involuntarily. The Ensign was held in the former debtors' prison at Southwark, just across London Bridge. Robertson went to the trial each day, spoke on Mackenzie's behalf and was horrified when the 45-year-old game keeper was sentenced to death for treason. Only then did Robertson turn to the Duke of Cumberland, who sent him to the King's minister, the Duke of Newcastle. After hearing Robertson out, Newcastle promised that Hector Mackenzie would be pardoned but as time wore on and no pardon was forthcoming, Robertson once more presented himself at Newcastle's door. To get rid of him, the busy Duke repeated his promise and this time offered his hand upon it, whereupon Robertson grasped Newcastle's fingers in such a grip that it seemed as if he would not let go until the man was pardoned. The Duke gasped, "Yes, yes, Mr. Robertson, you shall have him. You shall have him." The court records bear witness that Ensign Hector Mackenzie, "by intercession of the Reverend James Robertson, was released on condition of leaving the country permanently and transporting himself to America."

In the case of the 20-year-old Captain Colin Mackenzie, Robertson told the court that the young man had been so loyal he had threatened to take up arms against Barisdale in order to stay out of the war, that he was well disposed to the government and that he had joined the rebellion in the end only because Cromarty's men had threatened his property if he refused. Colin Mackenzie was acquitted along with nine others, but that was the extent of Robertson's success.

It has been recounted that he saved another of his parishioners. One day as he was walking along the Thames, he heard a voice hail him in Gaelic from a prison hulk moored near Gravesend. "Oh Mr. James," said the voice, "are you going to leave me here?" Robertson recognized the man as Donald Mackenzie, the crofter who had tried by force to have his child baptised when Robertson was new to Loch Broom.

"Ah Donald," replied the minister, "do you remember the day of the dirk?"

"Oh, Mr. James," said the crofter, "a bad place for remembrance is this."

And the story goes on that an all-forgiving Robertson won Donald Mackenzie, the crofter who had hurt him with a dirk, a pardon. But in cold fact Donald Mackenzie's name appears on the list of those transported in March of 1747 to the colonies. Of the 218 prisoners from Cromarty's regiment, the majority from Loch Broom parish, 152 were transported and only six ever saw Scotland again. They were simple men: John Macleod, 57, a farmer who lived a few miles down the Loch at Ullapool; a second John Macleod, 21, who worked for Mackenzie of Langwell; and Kenneth Mackenzie, 25, whose description on the prison rolls was simply that "he lived with his father at Loch Broom." There was Alexander Macleod, 40, a ploughman; Alexander Maclennan, 28, a blacksmith at Achnahaird far out on Coigach peninsula; George Mackenzie, 32, a Coigach farmer; and Robertson's farm servant Roderick Mackenzie, whom the minister had been unable to save any more than he could William Maclean, who was only 14 when he was transported with the rest. Six Loch Broom men are known to have perished in prison and another 48 were listed as "fate unknown" and are presumed to have died.

The man who had led them, George Mackenzie of Tarbat, the Earl of Cromarty, like the other captured leaders of the '45 rebellion—the Lords Lovat, Kilmarnock and Balmerino—was locked in the Tower of London, tried for treason and sentenced to death by beheading. He had pleaded guilty and his appeal against the death sentence was that of a broken man. "Nothing remains, my lords," he said, "but to throw myself, my life and fortune, upon your lordships' compassion. I have involved an affectionate wife, with an unborn infant, as parties to my guilt, to share its penalties; I have involved my eldest son, whose infancy and regard for his parents hurried him down the stream of rebellion. I have involved also eight innocent children, who feel their parent's punishment before they know his guilt. . . . But if after all, my lords, my safety shall be found inconsistent with that of the public, and nothing but my blood can atone for my unhappy crime, if the sacrifice of my life, my fortune and family is judged indispensibly necessary for stopping the loud demands of public justice; and if the bitter cup is not to pass from me, not mine, but Thy will, O God, be done."

It was not his rhetoric but his wife who won the hapless Earl a conditional pardon. Having entrance to the court she pleaded, in her pregnant condition, with the royal family and swooned at their feet. Cromarty's pardon was conditional on his living out his days under government supervision in the south of England where his last years were spent in poverty. A letter he wrote from Layhill in Devon on September 5, 1748, begged pardon of the government if he was "any way troublesome" and asked for permission to seek better housing because his "house is in a manner ruinous, not even necessary furniture in it, hardly a Chair to sitt on." He died of natural causes in London in 1760, long after his co-defendants had died under the axe, Lovat having been the last to lose his head in April 1747. The government eventually began the slow process of taking over and running their estates, forming the Forfeited Estates Commission.

In time, it would also provide assistance and improvements, although nearly 30 years after Culloden Dr. Samuel Johnson, no particular friend of the Highlanders, was to write of English policy: "They have created a desert and called it peace." And in the desperate winter of 1746-

47, with snow on the hills and ice in the lochs, his words rang true. A government spy, Patrick Campbell, travelling the northwest Highlands late in 1746, reported, "The inhabitants of the rebellious countries begin to be in misery for want of provisions; steal they must, or leave their country, which is as bad as death." They would leave in their thousands in the years to come.

CHAPTER TWO

Land of the Mountain and the Flood

"The Highlanders are a savage and untamed nation, rude and independent, given to rapine, easy-living, of a docile warm disposition, comely in person but unsightly in dress, hostile to the English . . ."

JOHN OF FORDUN, ABERDEEN, 1380

Before Culloden, the picture that emerged was bleak and feudal. This was not surprising since the writers were usually southern travellers, Lowlanders and English, who found the prospect starkly different from their own lands. They told of peasants, superstitious and illiterate, speaking an outlandish language described as "Irish," sharing hovels of earth and stone with farm animals, tending hopeless strips of oats on slopes eroded by

23

mountain floods, stealing cattle as a way of life, in bondage to their chiefs, reliving ancient feuds. They were "utterly barbarous" wrote their King, James VI, in the 1590s; nor had the gloomy picture brightened much by the 18th century. "Upon the whole the Highlands, some few estates excepted, are the seat of oppression, poverty, famine and wild despair," wrote John Knox, a London bookseller and traveller. "Neglected by government, forsaken or oppressed by the gentry, cut off during most of the year by impassable mountains and impracticable navigation from the seats of commerce, industry and plenty, living at considerable distance from human aid, without the necessaries of life . . ." Knox's views, although they did not encompass those Highland virtues romanticized later by Sir Walter Scott, were more sympathetic than those of most 18th-century Englishmen whose fashion, until well into the 19th century, was to speak ill of "the wild Highlanders." There was ample precedent for their disparaging comments.

"Highlanders are great thieves," wrote Dio Cassius in A.D. 200. Some 800 years later Gildas called the Picts "a set of bloody free-booters, with more hair on their thieves' faces than clothes to cover their nakedness." Medieval writers spoke of the *Bestiales Picti* and a 14th-century writer called them "wyld wykked he-lend men." In 1597 James VI proposed to "reform and civilize the best inclined among them, rooting out or transporting the barbarous and stubborne sort and planting civilitie in their roomes." Nor were the fears and prejudices of the Lowlanders abated when, in 1678, an army of Highlanders—"The Highland Host"—was quartered on the western Lowlands by the government in Edinburgh to frighten militant Covenanters into accepting the Episcopacy of the Church of Scotland. This army was accused of looting £200,000 worth of household goods in Ayrshire.

Early in the 1700s Martin Martin, a Highlander, appealed for greater understanding and less scorn in his *Description of the Western Islands*. But any Englishman desiring unbiased information about the Highlands on the eve of the union between England and Scotland in 1707 was woefully provided for. Daniel Defoe, while calling Highlanders "formidable fellows" and wishing the English army had 25,000 of them, could not resist a fashionable sneer. "Certainly the absurdity is ridiculous to see a man in his mountain habit, armed with a broadsword, target, pistol, at his girdle a dagger, and staff, walking down the High Street so upright and haughty as if he were a lord and withal driving a cow!"

The historian Thomas Morer, a clergyman, contented himself with such generalities as "once or twice a year great numbers of them get together and make a descent into the Low-lands where they plunder the inhabitants and so return back and disperse themselves. And this they are apt to do in the profoundest peace, it being natural to them to delight in rapine." Nor did they raid only the Lowlands; clan raided clan. Mad Colin Campbell, Laird of Glenlyon, told of how the Macdonalds "masterfully reft, spulzied and took away from the said complainer and his servants, four score head of kye, eleven horses and mares, together with the whole insight and plenishings of their homes." Mad Colin would be indirectly avenged when the Campbells massacred 38 Macdonalds on a snowy night in Glencoe, a century later.

General George Wade, Commander-in-Chief of "North Britain," or Scotland, from 1725 to 1740 and builder of 243 miles of civilizing roads—none of them north of the Great Glen which slants from Inverness west to Fort William—wrote that periodic raids were still reported in his time but he blamed specific clans rather than the whole Highland community. "The clans in the Highlands most addicted to rapine and plunder are the Camerons in the West of the shire of Inverness, the Mackenzies and the others in the shire of Ross who were

25

vassals of the late Earl of Seaforth, the Macdonalds of Keppoch, the Broadalbin men [the Breadalbane Campbells, presumably] and the Macgregors on the borders of Argyllshire. They go out in parties of from ten to thirty men, traverse large tracts of mountains until they arrive at the Lowlands . . . drive the stolen cattle in the night time and in the day remain in the tops of the mountains or in the woods . . ." In 1545 the Macdonalds and Camerons had stolen 2,100 cattle and 5,200 sheep and goats from Glen Urquhart in the Highland's biggest raid. By the 18th century such predatory habits were on the wane.

General Wade, in his report, was struck by "the Servile and Abject Obedience" the clansmen paid to their chiefs. But even some of those chiefs looked upon the "children" of their clans with impatience. Simon Fraser, eleventh Lord Lovat and a chief who did more than most to prolong the dying days of ancient clanship, told his King in the 1720s that the Highlands "do remain to this day much less civilized than other parts of Scotland." Lord President Duncan Forbes, who had done his best to prevent his fellow Highlanders from rebelling in 1745, wrote in his sadness and despair after Culloden: "The inhabitants stick close to their ancient land and idle way of life; retain their barbarous customs and maxims, depend generally on their chiefs as their Sovereign Lords and Masters; and being accustomed to the use of Arms, and inured to hard living, are dangerous to the public peace." Even as he wrote the government in London was taking steps to change all that—more than Forbes could ever wish.

Few Englishmen understood the Highland way of life, although Captain Edward Burt, in his *Letters from Scotland* written before the 1745 rebellion, certainly made an effort. But it is an appendix to Burt's book, a document written one year after the battle of Culloden by a Lowland Whig, Graham of Gartmore, and entitled "Causes of the Present Disorderly State of the Highlands of Scotland," which brings to light the conditions of that era.

"The poverty of the people is occasioned and continued," said he, "by a custom that is presently in use, and hath long obtained in that country, viz., the practice of letting many farms to one man, who, again, subsetts them to a much greater number than those can maintain, and at a much higher rent than they can afford to pay. There are many instances of 16 families living upon one *plough* of land (a plough being as much arable as will feed four horses and as much pasture land as will feed 40 or 50 cows)."

Their houses, huddled in a *baile*, or hamlet, by stream or loch, were of fieldstone piled in dry-wall fashion without cement, or of wattle-work, like monster baskets, or again of mud and turf so that "at a distance they look like so many heaps of dirt." They were roofed with sods and thatches of heather held down against the wind by plaited straw ropes weighted with stones. "The poor, mean smoaky cold hutts, without any door or window-shutter, and without any furniture or utenseills, and which a man may build in three or four days, accustom the people to bear any accommodation that are sufficient for cows or hoggs," said Gartmore. Windows, if any, were slits that could be plugged with heather against the gales of winter. A peasant's bed was a pile of heather in the corner, his chair, a rough wooden stool or perhaps a rock, his light, a peat fire augmented on occasion by candles made of fir roots gathered from the peat bog. In winter cattle, goats, sheep and hens were known to share the same accommodation.

The inquisitive Captain Burt found such homes occupied even by the gentry, such as the tacksman who offered him hospitality one rainy day: "He afterwards invited me to his hut, which was built like the others, only very long but without any partition; where the family was at one end and some cattle at the other. He was without shoes, stockings, or breeches, in a short coat with a shirt not much longer, which hung down between his thighs and just hid his nakedness from his two daughters, almost seventeen or eighteen who sat over-against him." There were no chimneys save a hole in the roof through which the peat smoke from the fire in the middle of the room found its way out. The people called their sooty dwellings "black houses" and in such a cold, dank climate, where their ragged woollen clothes were wet as often as they were dry and rheumatism and ague were common companions, no one cared about dirt so long as there was warmth. Burt told how the few dishes he saw were hardly ever washed and milk soon turned sour in them, and there was a belief that "if the butter has no hair in it the cow will not thrive." Dung heaps sat outside the door and served as privies. Disease or illness was an "act of God," accepted with fatalism. In some years 15 per cent of children under ten died of smallpox. "The young children of the ordinary Highlanders," he wrote, "are miserable objects indeed and are mostly overrun with the distemper which some of the old men are hardly ever freed of in their infancy."

On the other hand, one of Burt's contemporaries was surprised at how children flourished in spite of these adversities. The author of the book *A journey through part of England and Scotland, along with the Army*, signed only "a Volunteer" and published in 1747, wrote: "I have seen in their Huts when I have been walking, and forced to retreat thither for Shelter from the Rain, their Children, sometimes many in a Hut, full of the Small Pox at their Heighth, they having been lying and walking about in the Wet and Dirt, the Rain at the same time beating through the Thatch with Violence; so that I used to get from one End of the house to the other to keep dry; but it was all in vain; the Rain soon following me. These children at the same time seemed hearty, drinking Whey and Butter-milk, Wet and Cold, with the Inclemency of the weather, and yet so well!"

Their work shirts, laundered only by the rain from heaven, came from the hairy brown wool of the original Highland sheep, which were hardly bigger than collie dogs. They were the predecessors to the Cheviot sheep, which were brought in late in the century at the beginning of the Highland Clearances. The wool was spun, just as it came from the sheep's back, into a sort of sacking. Over this they wore a plaid, seven or eight yards long and usually grey and black, which served as a cloak by day and a blanket by night. Writing early in the 1700s, Morer described how "they cover the whole body with 'em from the neck to the knees excepting the right arm which they mostly keep at liberty. Many of 'em have nothing under these garments besides waistcoats and shirts which descend to lower than the knees, and they so gird 'em about the middle as to give 'em the same length as the linen under 'em and thereby supply the defect of drawers and breeches." They were partial to blue bonnets but not to shoes, which they wore to the kirk or during frost and snow—clumsy home-made brogues slit across the toes to let the water run out. The women wore shifts of sack-like material, dressing up for church or other occasions in a bit of coarse linen and the tartan plaid. The *philabeg*, or little kilt, came into fashion in the 18th century, only to be banned after Culloden by the Dress Act. By 1755 the plaid and kilt were worn infrequently. An agent for the Forfeited Estates Committee recalled that his crofters dressed "in short blue Cloath Coats or other short Coats of one colour in place of Tartan, and Trousers of one colour resembling the little Kilts, with this difference, that they were sewed up the middle."

They had few possessions: some spoons of melted horn, some wooden plates and bowls, a few pots, an iron dirk, a primitive flail for threshing the grain from its husk and a quern, or stone handmill, for grinding it.

Oatmeal was their staple food, until the potato was introduced in the 1750s from Ireland. Oats appeared as porridge with thin milk, as boase when mixed with pea-meal and strained water from boiled greens and as soup with kale or occasionally with barley. They had sowans, the starchy husk of oats boiled into jelly, and bread and bannocks of oats or barley which they ate with cheese and sometimes an egg, but rarely with a bit of meat, which was reserved for the gentry. Their oats was largely the inferior grey, hairy type and their barley the variety known as Scotch bear, which can thrive in the wet ground and a short season while better barley cannot. So scarce was grain in the bad years, and so hungry the people, that it was harvested before it was ripe. "I saw a woman cutting green barley in a little plot outside her hut," wrote Burt. "This induced me to turn aside and ask her what she intended it for, and she told me it was to make bread for her family. The grain was so green and soft that . . . when she had prepared it, certainly it must have been more like a poultice than what she called it, bread."

The anonymous author of *The Highlands in 1750* reported that the cottars, while "generally the soberest and honestest of the whole," inhabited the meanest part of a tacksman's land. "Their food all summer is milk and whey mixed together without any bread, the little butter or cheese they are able to make is reserved for winter .provision. They sleep away the greatest part of the summer, and when the little Barley they sow becomes ripe, the women pull it as they do flax, and dry it on a large wicker machine over the fire, then burn the straw and grind the corn upon Quearns or hand mills. In the End of Harvest, and During the winter, they have some Flesh, Butter and cheese with great scarcity of Bread. All their business is to take care of the few Cattle they have. In spring, which is their only season in which they work, their whole food is bread and gruel without so much as salt to season it." One crop failure meant the difference between a living of sorts and famine.

Nor did the chiefs escape lean times for, as Burt reported, "Although they have been attended at dinner by five or six servants, yet with all that state, they have often dined upon oat meal varied several ways, pickled herrings, or other cheap and indifferent diet." There were also times, at the height of their barbaric splendour, when chiefs such as the eleventh Lord Lovat's father and his household ate 140 pounds of meal a day, as well as beef, mutton, poultry and game, entertained the while by bards and pipers. Imported wine and spices were also plentiful.

When Daniel Defoe described the Highlanders he encountered, it was obviously not of peasants but of gentry that he spoke: "They are large bodies, and prodigiously strong; and two qualitities they have above other nations, viz., hardy to endure hunger, cold and hardships, and wonderfully swift of foot." If their discipline had only equalled their courage they would have proven the greatest soldiers in the world. Romantic Highland tales that conjure up a race of kilted giants were based on a relative few, such as Coll Macdonald of Barisdale, six feet four and so strong that he once caught and held a running deer and, another time, picked up a reluctant cow and heaved her bodily into a boat. "The gentry," allowed Burt, "may be said to be a handsome people, but the commonalty much otherwise; one would hardly think, by their faces, they were of the same species or, at least, of the same country, which plainly proceeds from their bad food." The average height of a Jacobite prisoner in 1746 was barely five feet four inches.

Nor, for that matter, was the diet of the gentry, albeit better than that of the common people, anything but spartan and monotonous. Here, for example, is a description of the diet of one mid-18th-century tacksman, varying little from day to day. Breakfast consisted of oatmeal porridge with milk or home-made ale brewed from barley and heather. This was interchanged with cabbage,

31

or kale, soup left "overnight" and bannock or an oatcake. The mid-day meal included sowans with milk, or oat-cakes and kale. Supper, served at seven P.M. in winter and nine P.M. in summer, was soup, sometimes with a bit of meat in it or, again, kale and oatcakes. The tacksman would eat with the servants who, in that era, were like members of the family and took their master's name.

Although their cows were poor producers, most of the year there was milk to drink and to make into cheese, until winter came. "In winter," wrote John Knox, "when the grounds are covered with snow and when the naked wilds afford them neither shelter nor subsistence, the few cows, small, lean and ready to drop down through want of pasture, are brought into the hut where the family re-sides, and frequently share with them their little stock of meal, which had been purchased or raised for the family only, while the cattle thus sustained are bled occasionally to afford nourishment for the children, after it has been boiled or made into cakes. This immoderate bleeding re-duces the cattle to so low a plight that in the morning they cannot rise from the ground, and several of the in-habitants join together to help up each other's cows."

The Highlanders were better herdsmen than cultiva-tors. A typical Highland farm was a cattle ranch with small strips of arable in the glen and great wild tracts of pasturage in the hills for the herds of small "black cattle," which might also be brown or red. Every June the herds-men left their "winter town" and drove their beasts up to the shielings in the mountain pastures to fatten on spring-fed grass, safely removed from the temptation of oat and barley crops growing in the glens. The herdsmen lived in rough stone huts, and kept moving on as the grass ran thin. The cattle, however weak and skeletal they had been in early spring, responded wonderfully, producing beef which Captain Burt pronounced "ex-tremely sweet and succulent." Summer at the high shiel-ings was the best time of the year. There were *ceilidhs*, songs, dancing and story-telling. The women and children milked the cows and made butter and cheese and the men, with one eye on their cattle, "stretched in Crowds basking in the sunbeams."

In September, before the autumnal storms, the fattened cattle were driven back to the glens and entrusted to professional drovers, who worked on commission, for the long trek to cattle fairs as far south as Craven in Yorkshire. It was not uncommon for 30,000 Highland cattle to be sold in England in one year.

Michaelmas, in late September, was the time of the great cattle drives; Captain Burt tells of coming upon such a drive. "The cows were about fifty in number, and took the water like spaniels; and when they were in, their drivers made a hideous cry to urge them forwards; this, they told me, they did to keep the foremost of them from turning about; for, in that case, the rest would do the like, and they would be in danger, especially the weakest of them, to be driven away and drowned by the torrent. I thought it a very odd sight to see so many noses and eyes just above the water and nothing of them more to be seen for they had no horns, and upon the land they appeared like so many large Lincolnshire calves." It was then that the *creach*, or cattle stealing, would be at its height, although the reivers called it "lifting," as if, said Burt, "it were only collecting their dues." Cattlemen frequently were obliged to pay tribute, or "blackmail," so their cattle would not be stolen, and captains of the Watch, a sort of home guard established to deal with such things as cattle theft, were accused, as Coll Barisdale was, of employing half their men to steal cattle and the other half to recover them. Although the cattle trade increased after the '45 rebellion, cattle lifting began to subside, but drovers remained the only Highlanders, apart from government soldiers, permitted to carry guns.

In the winter those cattle not sent to market were kept in the valleys, feeding on what they could find in the stubble fields since no hay was grown. Many died from hunger. Burt pitied the Highlanders their winters most of all, cooped up as they were in their "black houses," in the smoky light of peat fires, where they wove ropes of straw, harnesses of horse hair, and fashioned their brogues while the women spun wool and linen. "They have no diversions to amuse them but sit brooding in the smoke over the fire till their thighs and legs are scorched to an extraordinary degree and many have sore eyes and some are quite blind. This long continuance in the smoke makes them almost as black as chimney sweeps and when the huts are not water-tight, as is often the case, the rain comes through the roof and mixes with the sootiness of the inside, where all the sticks look like charcoal, falls in drops like ink. But in this circumstance the Highlanders are not very solicitious about their outward appearance." A generation later, in 1766, a writer for the smart, Whiggish *Gentleman's Magazine* in London, was less kind. "The common people are such in outward appearance as you would not take to be of the human species and in their lives they differ little from the brutes, except in their love of spiritous liquors . . . their faces are so coloured with smoke . . . their hair is long and almost covers their faces." The descriptions were remarkably like those of English peasants in the southern counties 400 or 500 years earlier.

But if winter was bad, spring could be worse, for often, and certainly in the recurring famine years, there was little or nothing to eat. The supply of oats would be running out, the cattle almost dead. "It is well known," wrote the anonymous author of *The Life of Archibald Macdonnell of Barisdale* in 1754, "that from the month of March to the middle of August some poor upon the coast having nothing but shell fish, such as mussels, cockles and the like, to support them. Poverty reigns so much among the lower classes that scarce a smile is to be seen upon their faces." The listlessness so often derided as laziness was caused by malnutrition.

One crop failure could mean the difference between subsistance living and famine. Cultivation methods had changed little since medieval times and remained so until the 19th century. The small arable strips which grew barley or oats or a bit of blue-flowered flax for linen were tended only a few weeks of the year, mostly during the ploughing and sowing of early spring and the autumn harvest. They grew potatoes in lazy beds and purple cabbage in the kale yards, working the ground with the *caschroim*, or crooked-foot spade, the awkward-looking wooden implement consisting of a six-foot handle and flat wooden head shod with iron. One man with a *caschroim* could open more ground in a day than two or three with ordinary spades. Their plough was a great heavy wooden contraption which took three men and a team of four horses to operate. Their garron horses, hardly bigger than donkeys, carried everything in panniers since there were no wheels or wagons.

As in other pastoral societies, women worked in the harvest fields. "They all keep time together by several barbarous tones of the voice," said Burt, "and stoop and rise together as regularly as a rank of soldiers when they ground their arms. Sometimes they are incited to their work by the sound of a bagpipe, and by either of these they proceed with great alacrity, it being disgraceful for any one to be out of time with the sickle." They also worked to music when fulling, or thickening, the newly woven plaids. "This is done by six or eight women sitting upon the ground, near some river or rivulet, in two opposite ranks, with the wet cloth between them; their coats are tucked up, and with their naked feet they strike one against another's keeping exact time." Burt got the impression the women worked harder than the men and recalled having seen "a Highlander basking at the foot of a hill in his full dress, while his wife and her mother were hard at work in reaping the oats." Men did the heavy work, ploughing in spring, digging for peat fuel and so on. Proper drainage was unknown, crops were usually insufficient to support the populations and grain was imported from the south, paid for from their cattle money.

Even if they had been better cultivators, there was little arable to farm. "From Perth to Inverness, and thence to the Western Seas," wrote Lord President Duncan Forbes in 1746, "no part is in any degree cultivated, except some spots here and there in straths and glens, by the sides of rivers, brooks or lakes, and on the sea-coast. The grounds that are cultivated yield small quantities of corns not sufficient to feed the inhabitants, who depend for their nourishment on milk, butter, cheese, & c., the product of their cattle."

Three-fifths of the land northwest of the Highland Line was moor and mountain, of which less than a quarter, and most of it in the east, was fit for cultivation. The estates controlled by the chiefs were vast, but land was of little value. Some of the territory owned by Lord Lovat around the Beauly estuary was good land, if wet and heavy, but on the farms owned by the Earl of Cromarty at Loch Broom in the west, for example, the percentage of arable to wild land was hopelessly low. At the hamlet of Ullapool, there were only 27 acres of arable and two of good pasture in a total of 1,600 acres, the rest being mountain and soggy moor. At Achnahaird on the Coigach peninsula a dozen sub-tenants struggled to make a living from 36 acres of arable and 12 of pasture. Less than one-half of the arable on any farm was under cultivation in any one season and much of that received too little sun and too much rain to grow healthy crops.

The lordly proprietors, the clan chiefs, rarely practised farming themselves but leased land to others. In the 18th century they had become, by and large, absentee landlords living in the comfort of Edinburgh, London or Paris. Describing the Lovat Fraser estates northwest of Inverness, the *Old Statistical Account of Scotland* reported: "The whole country, with two exceptions, consists of a variety of half-davoch [a land measure] lands, each of which was let or disponed by the Lovat family or their Chamberlain to a wadsetter or principal tacksman, and had no concern with the subtenantry; each subtenant had again a variety of cottars, equally unconnected with the principal tacksman; and each of these had a number of cattle of all denominations, proportional to their respective holdings, with the produce whereof he fed and clad himself and his whole family." Below the chief, in the hierarchy, was a pyramid of rentiers, tacksmen and wadsetters, and under them sub-tenants of varying status. A wadsetter was sometimes a laird, sometimes a tacksman, who had saved enough money to lend it to a chief or laird as a form of mortgage. The laird who mortgaged his land could reclaim it with cash at any time and then the wadsetter would become a tenant, or otherwise vacate the land and take his sub-tenants with him. If he stayed on as a tenant he joined the class known as tacksmen, or middlemen who leased farms in "tacks," or long leases, at relatively low rentals. They might work some of the land with their servants, but more frequently they farmed it out to sub-tenants on short one-year leases at rents which would ensure them a good profit.

"Some of these tacksmen or good-men possess these farms themselves," reads the Gartmore manuscript, "but in that case they keep in them a great number of cottars, to each of whom they give a house, grass for a cow or two, and as much ground as will sow about a boll (six bushels) of oats, in places which their own plough cannot labour, by reason of bush or rock, and which they are obliged in many places to delve with spades. This is the only visible subject which these poor people possess for supporting themselves and their familys, and the only wages of their whole labour and service.

"Others of them lett out parts of their farms to many of these cottars or subtenants; and as they are generally poor, and not allways in a capacity to stock these small tenements, the tacksmen frequently enter them on ground laboured and sown, and sometimes too stocks it with cattle; all which [the sub-tenant] is obliged to redeliver in the same condition at his removal which is at the goodman's pleasure, and for which during his possession he pays an extravagantly high rent to the tacksman. By this practice, farms, which one family and four horses are sufficient to labour, will have four to sixteen families living upon them." The "commonality" of sub-tenants supporting tacksman, wadsetter and, eventually, the landowner, included cottars, crofters, bollmen, steel-bollmen, pendiclers and mailers—their nomenclature changed with the region. A pendicler was a sub-tenant who supplied his own seed and cattle, as opposed to a steel-bollman whose stock and seed were provided by the tacksman. A bollman was a foreman on a tacksman's land; his name derived from the Gaelic *bo,* for cattle. A crofter was superior to a cottar although to an outsider there might seem little difference. Both rented a house, grazing rights and some arable.

The tacksmen were criticized for their role as middlemen: "The practice of letting many farms to one man," said Burt, "who again subsetts them to a much greater number than these can maintain, and at a much higher rent than they can afford to pay, obliges these poor people to purchase their rents and expenses by thefts and robberys." Originally a tacksman had been a son, brother or cousin of the chief, or landowner, and something of a warlord; as an officer in the chief's private army, in times of trouble he was expected to help by leading, or driving, his sub-tenants out to battle. By subdividing his land as much as possible, he not only increased his income but maintained the fighting strength of his clan. However, the tacksman's military role, which diminished through the years, ended after the battle of Culloden, and he became little more than a landlord, and sometimes not even that if a stranger appeared with a higher bid for the land he occupied. The chiefs no longer wanted men, but money, and began to increase, or rack, the rents, which had not been raised for generations. The paternal practice of excusing arrears of rent in the bad years was halted. Their ancient rights over their clansmen were rescinded with the passing of the Heritable Jurisdictions Act of 1747, dulling the chiefs' interest in their traditional duties.

On the Coigach estate of George Mackenzie, Earl of Cromarty, in the parish of Loch Broom, tacksmen were now sometimes by-passed and leases given directly to small tenants. In 1730 hardly two dozen crofters held leases directly from the Earl, but by the late 1740s this number had tripled. The practice of small tenants holding leases, singly or conjointly, was also adopted in the Lovat Fraser lands around Beauly on the east coast.

Living in a hamlet, or *baile*, the crofters worked the land in a system known as "runrig," from the Gaelic *Roinn-ruith*, or division. The arable was divided into long, narrow strips separated by margins of uncultivated land. Each tenant had his own rig, which changed hands from year to year so all could share the "infield," which was the best soil and could bear crops every year without lying fallow. The less productive "outfield" was farmed only every two or three years, after a fallow interval, and was for common use. The runrig ridges, which can still be seen in highland fields to this day, served as the only means of draining the soggy fields. At one time runrigs were shared equally by the tenants, but over the years it became common for one man to hold, say, a quarter of the farm while his neighbour might have only one-fifteenth. Rental might be paid in cash, in kind or in service, or a combination of all three. Burt cities a rent paid by one Donald Mac Oil vic ille Challum as follows: "Money 3 pounds 10 shillings 4 pence; butter 3 pounds two ounces; oatmeal 2 bushels one peck 3 lip; sheep one eighth and one sixteenth" (the other tenants presumably making up the shares with the remaining carcass of the sheep). Rent in kind was paid with cattle, chickens, grain, butter, cheese and woollen plaids.

The most onerous part of the rent consisted of services

39

that a landlord required from his tenants. "Extravagant services are still required and performed which the landlord would be ashamed to commit to writing," said the author of *The Highlands of Scotland in 1750*. These included sowing, tilling, harvesting, herding cattle and sheep, cutting and fetching peat—a time-consuming chore that required large crews of men—thatching and, indeed, almost anything a landlord had a mind to demand. In some cases the system was so abused that in the planting and harvesting months crofters had no time to do their own work. Servitude varied from region to region, from just a few days in the year as to much as four months for tight-fisted landlords would not pay for day labour if they could get it free. The writer of the 1750 report, a government surveyor touring the Forfeited Estates which had been seized after the 1745 rebellion, called the system slavery. He urged that service be written into a formal lease when the tenant took the land.

In many cases there were no leases; those that existed were of only a one-year duration. Since the burden of making improvements was on the tenant, rather than the landlord, the absence of a lease or shortness of it meant that improvements were not made. The 1750 report demanded that "a law be enacted to Oblige all Landlords among the disaffected Clans to give long Written Leases to their Tenants, none to be for a shorter Term than Twenty Years, and that every man who lives by Husbandry or Grazing in those Countries have such a lease from the landlord or his Steward. . . . By this means the tenants will Enjoy the Fruits of their own Industry and know the Sweets of Peace and Liberty; which will put it out of the Power of their Tyrant Chiefs to Induce them to Rebel against a Government to whom they will be indebted for everything they possess." Unfortunately this suggestion did not become law. It was adopted in some parts by the Committee for Forfeited Estates, but not to any great extent in Cromarty's Loch Broom estates or those of Lovat at

Beauly. The short-lease tenure was one of the reasons the people of the *Hector* emigrated.

Conditions varied throughout the Highlands. Travellers spoke of great differences from one glen to another; in one there might be hovels of turf while across the hill were thriving crops and good stone cottages. But by the 1760s the land was so remorselessly subdivided and overcrowded that it became increasingly difficult to make a living. The Aberdeen surveyor Peter May, sent to Loch Broom by the Forfeited Estates Commission to separate the land worked by the tacksmen from the land the tacksmen held from the Commission and leased to sub-tenants, found the job too much for him. "To do it distinctly is almost impossible, he reported, "as they are so interwoven with one another, and run-ridged on sundry farms with the tenants themselves, and these ridges are only patches that they dig up with a crooked spade, and so very small that there will be above 100 ridges in an acre scattered up and down like lazy beds of potatoes. Where they are at a size by themselves I shall measure them separately, but where they are intermixed as above there can be no such thing done with exactness."

Even with the land so divided, the author of the Gartmore manuscript reckoned there was work on the land for only half the Highland population and 28,000 men between the ages of 18 and 56 had no work. Men drifted to the Lowlands to work the harvest, as later they would go south to work in the mills during the Industrial Revolution. As the weak laws did not provide for the able-bodied, but only for "aged, poor, impotent and decayed persons, who of necessity must live by alms," troops of lusty beggars roamed Scotland. Nor did the uncertain food supply depress the birthrate, which rose during the second half of the 18th century. The times were bad and many did not get enough to eat and were left, as Thomas Pennant reported in 1772, to the care of Providence. "Hundreds thus annually drag through the season a

41

wretched life, and numbers unknown, in all parts of the Western Highlands, fall beneath the pressure some of hunger, more of the putrid fever, the epidemic of the coasts, originating from unwholesome food, the dire effects of necessity."

By that time new ways had appeared in the wake of the clan system, whose paternal safeguards had been swept away at Culloden after 700 years. "There was perhaps never any change of national manners so quick, so great, and so general, as that which has operated in the Highlands by the last conquest and the subsequent laws," wrote Dr. Samuel Johnson, after he and James Boswell made their celebrated journey through the glens in the summer of 1773. Johnson put the blame for this change not on the English government, but on the chiefs, whom he accused of "degenerating from patriarchal rulers to rapacious landlords." Although the people had always been poorly housed and badly fed, at least they had enjoyed some form of paternalistic security within the clan. This had been swept away and they were faced with a constant struggle to pay the rent. As Sir Walter Scott was to write:

> *Land of the mountain and the flood,*
> *Land of my sires! What mortal hand*
> *Can e'er untie the filial band*
> *That knits me to thy rugged strand!*

The filial band had been broken before Scott was born. There were no more chiefs over the vast lands first seized by the Jacobite rebels, then by the government, nor would there be for another generation until the lands were handed back to the repentant families who had once owned them. To fill the void after the annexation, the Commission for Managing the Forfeited Estates was created, with headquarters in Edinburgh. Its mandate was to bring a new social order and to make the Highlands more like the Lowlands and England. Nothing like this had been tried before. The redcoat and the bayonet would be replaced by a civilian government agent and a surveyor with a chain. The Commission ordered detailed reports on almost everything: agriculture, the nature of leases, the shaky state of education, the Kirk.

There are conflicting views on whether the Commission, in the end, improved or retarded the Highlands. Over a period of 30 years it tried to replace the old ways, devoting itself to planning improvements to agriculture, fishing, the manufacture of linen and afforestation. The Commission built roads and bridges, churches and schools and fought disease, thus adding to the population and further overcrowding of the glens. It did much good work, although its critics complained that many improvements never got beyond the planning stage. Its harshest critic, Lord Sydney, scoffed that Forfeited Estates were easy to distinguish because of "the bad condition they were in compared to other men's estates and for the almost total neglect of their cultivation." The truth as usual lay somewhere in the middle, but it is clear enough that the Commission failed to discourage large-scale emigration. By 1773, 20 years after the inception of the Commission, emigration had grown to proportions which Dr. Johnson called "epidemical fury," although compared to what was to come in the 19th-century Clearances, it was relatively mild. It was the Forfeited Estates of Cromarty and Lovat, and the neighbouring parishes tied closely to them, that sent Alexander Cameron and Alexander Fraser of Loch Broom and Beauly, and their neighbours, to board the *Hector* and sail to Nova Scotia.

CHAPTER THREE

The Forfeited Estates

During Christmas week of 1752, a horseman from Inverness arrived at the Rev. James Robertson's manse on Loch Broom with a notice that pleased the minister. Having seized 13 attainted estates of the Jacobite leaders shortly after the rebellion, the government had now passed an Annexing Act to nationalize those estates "for the purpose of civilizing and promoting the happiness of the inhabitants upon the said estates and other parts of the Highlands and Islands of Scotland, the promoting amongst them of the Protestant Religion and Good Government, industry and manufactures, and the principles of Duty, and Loyalty to His Majesty and His Heirs and Successors." The Cromarty lands in Loch Broom parish were henceforth to be operated by the government and the Loch Broom minister was requested to read the proclamation to his parishioners and explain, in English and Gaelic, the new laws, how rents would be assessed, how knitting and weaving industries would be established and how the children would be educated under the guidance of the Kirk. Since there was only one church and one school in the parish, which was 36 miles long and 20 broad, Robertson was confident the government would now build more. The proclamation was signed by Captain John Forbes, the government's Chief Factor for the combined estates of the Earl of Cromarty and of Lord Lovat of the Fraser clan, whose broad, rich lands lay along the east coast near Inverness.

In the Fraser country the proclamation was read in the parishes of Kirkhill, Kiltarlity and Kilmorack and it was in Kilmorack Parish, near the old Lovat market town of Beauly, 12 miles west of Inverness, that Captain Forbes proposed to set up headquarters. As Chief Factor he was expected to exercise "all the dignity, variety of interest, the Extent of power, which belonged to the government of a province." It was fitting that his base should lie at Beaufort, two miles from Beauly and hard by Dounie Castle, home of the Lovats since 1511 but now in blackened ruins since its sacking by Cumberland's redcoats in 1746. There on the banks of the tree-lined Beauly River, French-speaking monks had built a priory in 1230 and named the place "Beaulieu" for its pastoral charm. Captain Forbes found the community of Beauly much reduced by the recent troubles and had plans for rebuilding the village.

"It lyes," he reported, "in the centre of a very populous, fine country of excellent soil, but where the inhabitants are strangers to the right method of agriculture, manufacture and industry. There are several yearly fairs already held in and about this place, a mercate cross in it, and a great collection of poor people, who live in hutts and retail ale and spiritous liquors to the people who resort thither. There are very large, level fields of most excellent soil around it, fitt to be feued out for houses, gardens, etc., and there is already a courthouse, prison, which might be fitted up at a small expence [sic] . . . a village properly encouraged here could not miss to attract strangers of different professions and would, consequently, soon diffuse a spirit of trade and industry, as well as promote agriculture, thro' all this extensive country." Seventeen families, more than 100 men, women and children, lived in Beauly, raising potatoes, oats, barley and flax for linen and owning 60 cattle, 60 sheep and 30 horses. They were Frasers, Mackays, Grants, many of whom had been unable to keep up with their rent since the redcoats had carried off their crops and cattle. They had received no recompense despite the fact they had sent a delegation to London in 1750 to solicit aid in the name of the Clan Act which was supposed to provide two years of rent remission to peaceable tenants.

Beauly had been the social, if not the geographical, centre of the country of the Frasers, which stretched for 20 miles and lay in two unequal portions north and south of Loch Ness and the Ness River. To the southeast of the loch rose the massy brown hills of the Lovat Barony of Strath Errick whose mountains, according to a homesick soldier of the occupying English army, "are as high and frightful as the Alps in Spain." Strath Errick was home to almost 900 tenants of the Fraser lairds who shared the twisting glens and hills with their black cattle and with eagles and red deer.

North across Loch Ness and at its western end lay two Lovat enclaves, Portclair and Delcatack, in Glenmoriston, which had suffered, in its proximity to Fort Augustus, when Cumberland's Red army had harassed the glens. Homes had been set on fire, cattle seized, and those who did not flee into the mountains to live in caves were taken prisoner.

To Captain Forbes, accustomed to the rich green valleys of the Lowlands, for all he was Highlander born, the best of Lovat's lands lay north of the loch in the Aird, a gentle green plain where crops matured a fortnight earlier than they did in the west. In its southern reaches was the Barony of Lovat and just north again, across the peaceful Beauly River, lay the Barony of Beauly. Starting on the shores of Beauly Firth, with its sea birds and good fishing, the Barony of Beauly ran westward past Kilmorack Falls and into Strath Glass and Glen Strathfarrer, a wild country of heather and boulders, torrents and woods and mountains which stretched toward the Atlantic coast.

The three Lovat baronies provided livelihood for 500 families—more than 3,000 people—and it was the boast of Simon Lord Fraser, Eleventh Baron Lovat and hereditary Fraser chief, that he could raise 800 fighting men. Although obese and gouty by the time he was captured by the English and beheaded for treason on Tower Hill at the age of 79, Lovat was strong enough and handsome in his younger years when he set out to make himself "the greatest Lord Lovat that ever was." He was also complex and contradictory, a lapsed Catholic and "a fine-looking tall man and had something very insinuating in his manners and address," wrote one of his hired henchmen. He was capable of lordly gestures and gave banquets "in all the fullness and dignity of the ancient hospitality." His wine cellar, when the redcoats looted it, boasted 1,000 bottles. On the other hand he was capable of the tightest penny-pinching. He complained to his "Cousin Sandy," Alexander Fraser, a merchant in Inverness, of a leak in his new coffee pot and the next day wrote again complaining that his grocery bill was too high.

"I would change twenty merchants of the name of Fraser," he grumbled, "rather than allow myself to be imposed upon to my knowledge." But a few days later he sent Cousin Sandy a handsome gift of salmon from Beauly River.

Although he was a scholar with a fine library, he was accused of discouraging schooling among his tenants because he feared that a little learning would encourage them to seek greener fields. He was a believer in feudal ways but was one of the few chiefs who engaged in land improvement; poor people liked him for his easy-going jokes and little gifts as he went about his estates. He was a shrewd manager, although when Forbes arrived the Factor was critical of the bad farming methods of the tenants: the Frasers, Mackays, Chisholms, Munros, Grants, Mackenzies, Robertsons and people from other clans who lived in the scattered Fraser lands.

The Committee, or Board, of the Forfeited Annexed Estates commanded powers greater than those possessed by the hereditary chiefs they replaced. Composed of 28 Edinburgh officers of the Crown, judges and lawyers who received no stipend, the Board worked in six rooms in an old tenement in High Street, Edinburgh, owned by the Lovat Estate. On the ground floor was a china shop, which perhaps explains why the Board's offices were so oddly decorated, with several dozen "purple Dutch pigs."

From the beginning the Board's difficulties outweighed its successes. Time and again plans were aborted because of delays in royal approval, for after a burst of enthusiasm the King and the Duke of Newcastle lost interest. The Commissioners were busy men, moreover, and frequently meetings were cancelled for want of a quorum, so that on average they met once a month. At one stage their work was halted by "great confusion in the office accounts," and the Barons of the Exchequer in London threatened to take the whole Board to court for failure to keep proper records. The Commissioners rarely, if ever, visited the Forfeited Estates but frequently interrupted the work of the Factors by calling them to Edinburgh for consultation.

For all that, they did useful work on at least some of the 13 Forfeited Estates they administered, which stretched in scattered pockets from Sterling in the Lowlands up the eastern and western coasts as far north as Loch Broom. They initiated land reform. In concert with the Board of Fisheries and Manufactures, which shared several Commissioners in common, they provided employment for large numbers of unemployed. The growing of flax and the manufacture of linen was encouraged. Spinning and weaving schools were established at Beauly. In Inverness hundreds worked in the Board's factory which made cloth from hemp yarn. At Loch Broom they established a Linen Station, managed by John Ross, a merchant from Dingwall, about whom we shall hear more because of his role as leader of the people from Loch Broom who sailed aboard the *Hector*. When Ross' appointment to the Linen Station was announced in 1755, others who sought the job came forward to accuse him of having been a Jacobite in the 1745 rebellion but he was hired, nevertheless, by the government and became a man of influence at Loch Broom.

Some of the Factors of the Forfeited Estates, such as Captain John Forbes who was a landowner in his own right, were even-handed, efficient administrators for all their Whiggish prejudices. Some were Lowlanders who spoke no Gaelic and disliked the Highlanders. Their masters in Edinburgh, for all their earnest efforts, seem to have had difficulty in ridding themselves of the fashionable notion that the clansmen were ignorant and backward, rude children with no culture. The Commissioners themselves were part of the cultural elite of Edinburgh. Their efforts at improvement were largely controlled from above, with all the complications which burden such civil service committees. But slowly, improvements were made. Communities such as Beauly were restored to new life, the fisheries and coastal kelp-gathering industry were encouraged. The faces of many parishes changed although poverty was not eradicated. Dr. Samuel Johnson, arriving in the Highlands in the summer of 1773, found conditions quite different from what he had expected: "We came thither too late to see what we expected, a people of peculiar appearance, and a system of antiquated life. The clans retain little now of their original character, their ferocity of temper is softened, their military ardour is extinguished, their dignity of independence is depressed, their contempt of government subdued, and the reverence for their chiefs abated. Of what they had before the late conquest of their country, there remains only their language and their poverty. Their language is attacked on every side. Schools are erected, in which English only is taught."

There was no question that the change had been fundamental. On closer examination Johnson hazarded the opinion that the clansmen were now becoming acquainted with the use of money; "the possibility of gain will by degrees make them industrious." He did not live to see the glens depopulated, the clansmen displaced by sheep in the Highland Clearances during the passing of two generations.

In his early years at least, as Chief Factor on the Lovat and Cromarty Forfeited Estates, the dispatches of Captain John Forbes did little to alter the prejudices of the gentlemen reading them among the purple pigs in High Street, Edinburgh.

"Although soil is good in the Barony of Beauly," Forbes reported, "the people are generally employed in agriculture which they don't much understand, and in managing their cattle, but are for a great part of the year quite idle." He was alarmed at the extent of illegal moonshining: "14 or 15 stills and as many public houses . . . so that the whole of the people on the east part of this barony are employed in this pernicious trade." Three-quarters of the farms were so crowded and divided by runrigs they could hardly support their tenants. Barely ten per cent of the people spoke anything but Gaelic, English having gained ground only in hamlets close to Inverness, and more schools were needed. There was little manufacturing except for the spinning of flax.

Forbes reserved his harshest criticism for the people in the remoter reaches of the barony, such as Glen Strathfarrer, which had been a hiding place for Jacobite rebels and where "several thieves and persons of bad character did formerly reside and have not all left it yet." He urged upon the Commissioners the need for a church and a school as "the people are grossly ignorant and among them there are a great many Papists and scarce a person can be found who can speak one word of English."

From Beauly and the Lovat country he rode ten miles north to the ancient town of Dingwall and on into the small Cromarty barony of Newtarbat along the farther shore of Cromarty Firth. Here he found a population more to his taste. "The people [Mackenzies, Rosses, Munros] are sober, honest and tolerably industrious. It is to be observed that few of the inhabitants here were concerned in the late Rebellion, and it is a peaceable low country." They suffered, however, with the system of one-year leases, and "the granting of long leases under proper restrictions and conditions would have a good effect."

Riding west again through Dingwall and into the Cromarty barony of Strath Peffer, his good humour dissipated like the Highland mist. In this Mackenzie country he found "a narrow strath, the inhabited part not above three miles in length and one in breadth," the rents too high, the roads impassable, the people demoralized. "There are 12 maltsters, 12 brewers and 12 stills here which instead of being an advantage, has contributed, among other things, to render the people so poor and idle as they are at present, for it makes them neglect their farms, habituates them to drinking, & of consequence debauches their morals, breeds quarrels & subjects them to many fines." An "English school" and a school to teach spinning were needed, "as there are a vast number of children of both sexes on this barony, who are entirely neglected on account of the idleness & poverty of their parents." As elsewhere, farms were too small and their runrigs "interfere with one another in such a manner as makes it highly inconvenient for them all and impossible that they would thrive tho' the lands were sett at a much lower rent." Farms should have been divided "and as much given to each farmer as may

51

be supposed necessary to support his family by reasonable industry."

After investigating his districts in the east, Captain Forbes rode northwest 30 miles to the barony of Coigach in Loch Broom, up Strath Garve and through the mountains on the drove road until, far below him at the foot of Strath More, he saw the sparkling loch reaching away to the west and the white church of the Rev. James Robertson. Halting for refreshment at the manse, he found the minister in good health and "enjoying a yearly 44 pounds of stipend and a glebe of great extent, capable of grassing 40 milke cows." But the minister gave him no good news about the parish. People had not settled down again after the rebellion. There were reports of tenants harrying tacksmen's sheep, breaking down dykes, pasturing cattle in fields that did not belong to them and generally behaving in a lawless manner. Cattle thieves had come down from the northern hills that bordered the parish of Assynt. Education was lacking for there was but one school, 12 miles from the distant Coigach farmsteads. Less than 200 people, a tenth of the population, spoke English, so Robertson was obliged to preach in Gaelic.

At Ullapool—a name from ancient Norse, and then, as now, the largest settlement in the parish—Forbes found an inn, or change-house, and the families of 13 demobilized soldiers lately granted forfeited land by the government. Mackenzies, Sutherlands, Frasers, most of whom had been born in or near the parish.

"Coigach Barony," reported Forbes, "is very mountainous and rocky & will be 14 or 16 miles in length &, in some parts, 7 or 8 miles in breadth, & the soil of it is of various kinds & produces only some bear and some small black oats, but not so much as supplys itself, nor are the crops to be depended on because of the frequent rains to which the western coast is exposed. The principal product is black cattle, horses, sheep & goats & the pasture for these is extremely good and very extensive."

He heard that the local baillie had "apprehended a fellow in a tartan coat, whom he sent to Dingwall jail" for breaking the Dress Act, and although Forbes himself failed to find any law-breakers he observed that much of the barony was wild and remote and "very probably some fellows may presume to transgress where they can do it with impunity."

"Formerly," he wrote, recalling its Jacobite past, "it was a very disorderly place. The prevailing names are Mackenzies & Macleods and they are a very lazy, ignorant sort of people, but not at present addicted to thieving, nor so poor as the people of the barony of Strath Peffer." Besides the Mackenzies and Macleods, who made up two-thirds of the population, there were Rosses, Maclennans, Camerons, Macleans, Mathesons and others.

Coigach had been made a royal barony in the 16th century, which meant that it was a freehold estate on which the hereditary chiefs, Macleods at that time, administered through a baron court both civil and criminal justice and regulated such everyday occurrences as planting, herding, cutting peat and weaving cloth. By the 17th century the Mackenzies of Kintail had become the Coigach chiefs, largely by marrying into the Macleods who had come from the island of Lewis; the Macleods' resentment over their loss lived on to plague the Commissioners for Forfeited Estates in the 1770s.

Of the 28 farms in the barony, six were worked by "conjoint tenants," crofters who had banded together. A few, such as Donald Mackenzie's of Glastulich, were worked by a single tenant. With his wife and four helpers he was one of the fortunate of the barony, making a comfortable living on ten acres of arable and five of pasture, with 100 cattle, 30 sheep, 30 goats and 22 horses which he raised for sale. Most of the farms, however, were over-populated, with 60 families trying to scratch a living from 28 farms. At Ullapool, 80 people depended on 16 acres of potatoes, 12 goats and 56 sheep, and kept 64 cattle on the hillsides. Although the government had long since seized the land from the Earl of Cromarty, it was still leased out to tacksmen who, complained the Factor, "subsett the worst part of their farm to poor people at exorbitant rates and live rent free themselves."

With so many people on so little land, quarrelling was endemic and reached such a pitch at Dornie that the tacksman had tenants "removed for quarrels among themselves." Nor had the crofters any protection against the tacksman's whims. At Keanchulish, a tenant, even though he had paid his rent on time, was summarily "dispossessed to accommodate Hugh Macfarlane, Mackenzie of Achilty's groom." The minister's greedy nephew, Alexander Robertson, deciding he wanted the Langwell farm for himself, justified his grab on grounds that "the possessors are so poor, idle and ignorant, as well as contentious, that there can be no hope of their being ever able to improve the place." Rebuffed, he turned to another farm, whose tenants complained that young Robertson "looked with an eye of envy on their farms on account of the fine corn growing" and that he wanted their land to "support himself in a life of pleasure and dissipation." When another man of influence, Lieutenant Daniel Mackenzie, coveted the Achiltybuie farm occupied by the widow of Mackenzie of Achilty, he met his match. He alleged to the Board that the farm had been neglected, but Achilty's 16-year-old son Sandy insisted that the farm was fully up-to-date and challenged the Lieutenant to a ploughing contest to prove his point.

Most of the quarrels were between tenants and tacksmen. Tacks changed hands too often, the crofters evicted with each change although the Factors did make efforts to gain more control. Some of the sub-tenants had begun to fight the tacksmen, harassing them by turning cattle loose to feed in a tacksman's pasture and breaking down his dykes and walls. Poor people began to demand their rights, something they had never found necessary under the rule of their clan chiefs rather than a civil service board in Edinburgh. In his manse at the head of the loch, the Rev. James Robertson composed a warning to the Board of Forfeited Estates.

"Permit me to tell you," he wrote, "that several sub-tenants of Coigach have of late turned to be such bad neighbours of the Tacksmen that they refuse to keep their sheep or cattle off the grass or corn when the Tacksmen's cattle are in the hills at sheallings; that when they [the tacksmen] challenge them for this, and other acts of bad neighbourhood, they attack them with the most provok-ing and abusive language. Now, Sir, such insult from silly senseless men and scalding wives will sit very uneasy upon a man of spirit, let his temper never be so meek and peacable, and if you do not speedily command the peace I know what may be the consequence." The minister blamed his parishioners, the common people, as the trou-bles and ill-feeling stemmed, he claimed, from the crofters' refusing to volunteer their services to the tacks-men and going off to earn cash working in the herring fisheries around Loch Broom. "They loiter in idleness in some obscure hut drinking and eating the pennyworth they earned," he said, and when that was spent they begged from the tacksmen.

In the northern reaches of the parish there were reports of cattle theft, blamed on poor people from the parish of Assynt. John Macleod, the most notorious of the thieves, strode around "in full arms and in Highland clothes, plaid filebeg, etc. bidding defiance to the laws." Although he had a wife and children in Assynt, he lived with his old fa-ther in a remote corner of Coigach called Lochanganwich, where he was safe from the law. Assynt, in Sutherland-shire, although not one of the Forfeited Estates, was closely tied to Loch Broom parish through blood lines and, like Coigach, had once belonged to the Macleods before it was taken by Mackenzies. Poorer than Loch Broom, As-synt's emigration had commenced as early as 1763 when the people of Loch Broom were still merely considering emigration and hoping it would not be necessary.

Hearing such tales from the Highlands, the Committee for the Forfeited Estates began to consider land reform. Its mandate was political as well as economic; it had been established with a view to "demonstrating the lenity and compassion of the government towards the inhabitants and infusing them with a deep conviction of the Goodness of the present Royal Family." By giving the small-holders and peasants more independence and a better life, they sought to minimize the danger of another Jacobite rebellion. They sent the Aberdeen surveyor, Peter May, to Coigach to survey the farms—the first time this was ever done—and recommend improvements.

Both afoot and on horseback, May travelled the length and breadth of the barony, finding it a "very large country, being little else but high mountains and scattered woods, steep rocky places, a number of lochs in the valleys, and a great distance between houses." He complained of the incessant August rain and asked for a tent because "there is no such thing as sleeping in their houses in the summer time, they are so full of vermin." He kept careful notes in his neat and flowing hand and allowed that if the land were properly managed there should be no reason it could not support its inhabitants. "I have not seen a country where poor people might live more comfortably than here." He recommended that the farms be broken up and the land redistributed to eliminate tacksmen, so the tenants might hold leases directly from the Board of Forfeited Estates. The farms had become so congested and runridged that reform would be difficult. Although the Committee did try to change things, the wheels of far-removed bureaucracy turned slowly, and it would take 20 years before results were to show. By that time the tenants had deserted the land, some of them for Nova Scotia.

A typical example of these problems was the tack of Achnahaird. Held by tacksman George Mackenzie, it encompassed 54 acres of grain and was backed by 14 of fine pasture on the brae. The tacksman kept this prime land for his own use, leasing the poorer land—the rocky fields of Reiff out on the headland—to 20 families who had to make do with 36 acres of arable and 12 of pasture for the whole community. One hundred and twenty people lived there, descendants of the Macleods who had once owned Coigach before the Mackenzies. It was here that discontent became militant, brought to a head by Roderick Macleod, who was better educated and more determined than his neighbours.

Taking his complaints to the Board of Forfeited Estates, Macleod claimed the tacksman had doubled rents, imposed fines for no cause and had evicted four sub-tenants, three of them Macleods. He knew of ten families with runrigs "scarce sufficient to maintain one of them." The sub-tenants paid the tacksman three times as much for an acre of poor land as the tacksman paid the Board for rental of his choice land in the brae. In addition, the people at Reiff were expected to provide the traditional services—till the tacksman's land, cut his grain, procure his fuel, repair his dykes—at little or no recompense and at the expense of their own poor fields. "They are forced," said Macleod, "to undergo the hardest slavery and perform the vilest drudgery."

In his summation, the angry Macleod penned an indictment of the whole middleman system: "Thus a few persons enrich themselves with the spoils of, and with impunity to tyrannize over, numbers of other families that were in as good and often better circumstances and of a character at least as good as those very tacksmen before they were made such. . . . And he must beg leave to add, that the true source of Rebellions and Tumults, in the Western Highlands, is the slavish dependence in which the commons are forced to live, which leaves their properties and almost their lives at the disposal of their leading men, and it is more this day in Coigach than ever."

The tacksman, George Mackenzie, defended the tradition of demanding service from tenants by arguing: "Altho' a cottar or sub-tenant work one day in the month or week for his master, he very probably sits idle and basks himself in the sun for the greatest part of his time, half starved for want of victuals which the master always gives him in plenty when at his work."

All of this served to rouse the Commissioners in Edinburgh to enquire of their Factor what was amiss and why he did not correct it. The irritation expressed in the Factor's letter, writing to the learned lawyers in Edinburgh, is evident; he sided with the tenants:

"It is the custom in the Highlands and in the greatest part of the North, that when a tenant takes a large farm, he subsetts the skirt and worst part of it to poor people at as high a rate as he can, and makes them obliged to perform many services, and the rent and services paid by them is generally much higher in proportion than what is paid by the principall tacksman . . . that this is the case in Coigach I believe to be very true, and on't at all doubt that these poor creatures, the subtenants, are frequently oppress'd by these tacksmen, their masters . . . "

The tenants, he concluded, wanted an end to the tacksman system of rents and services and a termination "will be reasonable to do in terms of the Annexing Act as soon as the nature of the thing will admit."

The Commissioners agreed, ordering that as soon as "the nature of the thing" permitted, Macleod and his neighbours should be given leases direct from the Board and pay rents to Factor Forbes rather than to the tacksman. It was, perhaps, not entirely the Board's fault that we find Macleod still fighting for his rights ten years later. In fact, Archibald Menzies, General Inspector of the Board of Annexed Estates, blamed the tenants themselves for delays in land reform.

Menzies said the Factors had been at pains to divide the farms and improve conditions but had "been very much discouraged from pushing these articles by the licentious disposition of the tenants. Whenever a thing is not entirely to their mind they get an agent to draw up a long paper of complaints and grievances, which is laid before Your Honours . . . Things are come to such a pass upon these estates that no order of the Board, if in the least disagreeable to the tenant, can be executed without going through all the different courts."

By the 1770s, however, the slow machinery of the Board began to bring results and Roderick Macleod secured the tenancy he had fought for. Busy with the Lovat lands on the east coast, John Forbes appointed Ninian Jeffrey as deputy Factor to look after Loch Broom. A new church and a school were being built and conditions would improve still more, but for several of the families the improvements came too late. Even before 1772 they had thought of emigrating and the troubles that year confirmed their decision. They were not alone, as there were people on the Lovat Estates, in Assynt and other parishes who followed them.

CHAPTER FOUR

A Rage of Emigration

In August and September of 1773, Dr. Samuel Johnson, at age 64 gamely riding a Highland pony despite his bulk, visited the Highlands and islands with James Boswell. They had barely started their westward journey, down the Great Glen from Inverness to the isles, when they first encountered what Boswell, a Lowlander, was pleased to call a Highland "rage of emigration." At a small change-house in Glenmoriston, one of the green valleys so sorely ravaged by Cumberland and his redcoats in 1746, their host was one McQueen who had fought for Prince Charles at Culloden, married a laird's daughter, owned 100 sheep, 100 goats, 12 cows and 28 beef cattle, and complained that rising rents had him thinking of emigration.

"From him," wrote Johnson, "we first heard of the general dissatisfaction which is now driving the Highlanders into the other hemisphere; and when I asked him whether they would stay at home if they were well treated he answered with indignation that no man willingly left his native country. On the farm which he himself occupied the rent had in 25 years been advanced from five to 20 pounds which he found himself so little able to pay that he would be glad to try his fortune in some other place. Yet he declared the reasonableness of rising the Highland rents in a certain degree and declared himself willing to pay 10 pounds for the ground which he had formerly had for five." McQueen told Johnson that 70 men had left Glenmoriston for the colonies the year before.

When Johnson and Boswell reached the isle of Skye they found that what Johnson (not to be outdone in hyperbole by his acolyte) had called "this epidemical fury of emigration" had given birth to a fashionable reel called "America." The dancers would spin in widening circles until, like autumn leaves, or emigrants, they swept right off the floor in couples and small groups. "It shows," said Boswell, "how emigration catches till all are set afloat."

They also learned that 2,000 inhabitants had recently left the island, with 400 more soon to follow. Among them would be Allan Macdonald and his wife Flora, whose name, said Johnson, "will be mentioned in history and if courage and fidelity be virtues, mentioned with honour." Flora had been released after her arrest and sent home from London, a heroine to her fellow Jacobites and even to the English, but she and her husband, like so many of Prince Charles' followers, had fallen into debt after Culloden and would depart for North Carolina within the next year. Within five years they were to move to Windsor, Nova Scotia, where Allan commanded a detachment of troops, and where Flora herself lived for a year and a half before returning to London and then to Skye in broken health.

"There seems now," wrote Johnson in 1773, "whatever the cause, to be through a great part of the Highlands a general discontent." During the past five years a modest exodus had become a rising tide. In 1768 the tacksmen of Lord Macdonald of Sleat had sailed from Skye, with most of their tenants, to the Carolinas, where they had purchased 100,000 acres. In the year 1770 the *Falmouth* and *Annabelle*, which bore the first contingents to St. John Island, were but two of 54 emigrant ships leaving the Highlands—it had been a year of increased rents.

The savage winter of 1771-72 drove 1,000 Highlanders to North Carolina. Shortly after Captain John Macdonald of Glenaladale had carried more than 200 Roman Catholics to St. John Island, other members of the same vast clan Donald—the Macdonnells of Glengarry—sailed for the colonies with 400 people from Glengarry, Glenmoriston, Glen Urquhart and Strath Glass, all lands that had particularly suffered from the atrocities that followed the battle of Culloden. Sixteen ships departed in 1772 from the western coasts of Inverness-shire and Ross. "Many of considerable wealth have taken with them their train of labourers and dependants," wrote Samuel Johnson, "and if they continue the feudal scheme of polity, they may establish new clans in the other hemisphere."

Nothing in the past had equalled the emigration of 1773, the year of Dr. Johnson's investigations. The flow started early in spring, and by April 3 the Edinburgh *Evening Courant* was warning of "the unlucky spirit of emigration" and pitying those who "seek for the sustenance abroad which they allege they cannot find at home." Reporting that 1,500 had left Sutherlandshire in the previous two years, the newspaper measured out the mounting exodus, month by month. In June the newspaper reported that 800 had sailed from Stornaway, across the Minch from Loch Broom, and in July another 800 from Greenock, but it paid particular attention to the 425 people who sailed in August from Lochaber, Knoydart and Appin, the region which had stood as the backbone of Prince Charles' rebellion. "The finest set of fellows in the Highlands . . . at least

£6,000 in ready cash with them, so that by emigration the country is not only deprived of its men but likewise of its wealth." All told, 4,000 left that year, the most for any one year until the American Revolution stopped the flow in 1776; it was not resumed until 1783, and then under pressure of famine. They came from the shires of Inverness, Ross, Sutherland, Argyle, Perth and Caithness, and many from the islands—Skye, Lewis, Islay and the two Uists.

Precisely how many emigrated in the decade which ended in December of 1773 cannot be known as until that time no records were kept. However, during the two previous years ministers had made a half-hearted effort to record departures from eight Highland parishes, as requested by the government. Since only 3,169 departures were reported, the reports were obviously far short of the real total and some thought the ministers, fearing the government meant to halt emigration, had deliberately watered their returns. A more likely reason for such a low figure was the fact that for every emigrant ship sailing from regulated ports such as Greenock, Fort William or Campbeltown, there were many more leaving from some lonely sea loch. The only witnesses to these departures were kinsfolk and perhaps a piper playing that saddest of pibrochs—*Cha till mi tuille*—"We Shall Return No More," in defiance of the law prohibiting pipes as "weapons of war."

In the 12 years ending in 1776, about 23,000 Highlanders left for the colonies, according to accounts in contemporary newspapers, travellers' journals, letters and lists of disbanded soldiers who took up land. That this represented one-tenth of the total population of the shires—in particular, Inverness, Ross, Sutherland and Argyll—was bad enough. But the government's main concern lay in the fact that certain glens were being depopulated not only of the poor and homeless, but also of what the *Scots Magazine*, as well as the *Evening Courant*, called "people of property." Those were the years the tacksmen organized emigrations and people like Flora Macdonald and her husband sold their possessions to start anew in the colonies. The *Scots Magazine* claimed that emigrants from Sutherland, which had always been a poor shire, were known to have taken with them, between 1768 and 1772, £10,000 in cash, a great sum for the Highlands at the time. Emigration had become the fashion and, as the *Inverness Courier* reported, departures were not always sad. "Hands were wrung and wrung again, bumpers of whiskey tossed wildly off amidst cheers and shouts: the women were forced almost fainting into the boats; and the crowd upon the shore burst into a long, loud cheer. Again and again that cheer was raised and responded to from the boat, while bonnets were thrown into the air, handkerchiefs were waved, and last words of adieu shouted from the receding shore."

"To hinder insurrection by driving away the people," said Dr. Johnson, "and to govern peaceably by having no subjects, is an expedient that argues no great profundity of politicks . . . it affords a legislature little self-applause to consider that where there was formerly an insurrection there is now a wilderness."

Despite the wild suggestions for mass exile and clan suppression voiced by frightened men in London in the years following Culloden, the government had no wish in fact to rid the Highlands of its people; at least, not yet. It would be another generation or two before the vast influx of southern Cheviot sheep—"the four-footed clansmen"—gave rise to the Highland Clearances, mass evictions and mass emigration often aided by the government. For now, the government was inclined to agree with Dr. Johnson when he suggested "some method to stop this epidemick desire of wandering, which spreads its contagion from valley to valley, desires to be sought with great diligence." The Earl of Dartmouth, who had governmental responsibilities for the colonies, was so alarmed by rising emigration that in 1773 he set in motion legislation which prohibited land grants in Nova Scotia except for those made by the King ten years earlier. This prohibition was relaxed a year later and suspended entirely at the end of the American Revolution in order to accommodate the loyalists from the American colonies and the renewed emigration from Scotland.

Nor were most of the Scottish landlords yet eager to see the backs of their tenants. When Macdonald of Sleat lost many of his people to Albany in 1772, he had to entice replacements to Skye from the mainland and other islands so his rents would not cease, and he did not want to go to that trouble again. Some of the Mackenzie lairds went so far as to appeal to the government to use troops to stem mass emigration. When Lord Montrose, amusing himself in London, heard of the hundreds quitting his estates on the island of Harris, he hurried there to try to dissuade them. They informed him they would stay only if he reduced rents and refunded increases exacted during the previous three years. Since Culloden, and particularly after 1763, rent had risen between one-third and three times the previous rates in various parishes. "What is the cause of the present depopulation of the Highlands of Scotland by the emigration to America?" asked the Edinburgh *Advertiser.* "Answer: oppression by rising rents above what the lands can bear."

To the *Advertiser,* in its front-page commentary on January 8, 1773, the villains were the tacksmen and the landlords whom the tacksmen had served until the break-up of the clan system. The tacksmen, suggested the *Advertiser,* were leaving and taking their tenants with them to spite the great landowners. "Such of these wadsetters and tacksmen as rather wish to be distinguished as leaders, than by industry, have not taken leases again, alleging that the rents are risen above what the land will bear; 'but,' say they, 'in order to be revenged on our masters for doing so, and what is worse depriving us of our subordinate chieftainship by abolishing our former privilege of subsetting, we will not only leave his lands, but by spiriting the lower class of people to emigrate, we shall carry a clan to America and when they are there, they must work for us, or starve.' " The landlords encouraged emigration for two self-serving reasons, added the newspaper: so they could buy farms cheaply due to the scarcity of tenants, and so they would not have to purchase meal for starving tenants.

"It is not to be wondered," concluded the *Advertiser*, "that the poor natives listen to artful insinuations made use of by the first to encourage them to become their followers to this promised land, while the second countenance it, and the masters don't discourage them, or at least make no plans to dissuade them from it." The ordinary emigrants, "these deluded, brave and faithful people," went off to the colonies "little knowing that they are carried to market, like a herd of cattle, for the total emolument of their leaders . . . but of this they can form no idea till their arrival in America, when it is too late for them to repent."

Like the *Caledonia Mercury*, the *Scots Magazine* and so many other newspapers of the day, the *Advertiser* joined the government in trying to discourage emigration. A writer calling himself Scotus Americanus warned that Highlanders, speaking only Gaelic and used only to their ancient insularity, would encounter great difficulty adjusting to life outside the mountains and were "a race apart. They have ever shown the utmost aversion to leaving their country [although the facts show this was not the case by any means] or removing to happier regions and more indulgent climates."

Dr. Johnson, although no advocate of emigration, was not so sure. He described how the settlers already in the colonies were writing home to persuade others to join them, "for as their numbers are greater, they will provide better for themselves." Some of these letters, he said, were misleading and he recalled one signed "New Planter" which "claimed the climate of Nova Scotia put him in mind of Italy." There were those who, "after a voyage passed in dreams of plenty and felicity," found themselves cast into an uncleared wilderness, condemned to years of toil and poverty no better than the life they had left in the Highlands. On the other hand, when large groups of Highlanders went out to create their own settlements and stayed together they did not necessarily fare badly. "The accounts sent by the earliest adventurers, whether true or false, inclined many to follow them; and whole neighbourhoods formed parties for removal; so that the departure from their native country is no longer exile. He sits down in a better climate, surrounded by his kindred and his friends; they carry with them their language, their opinions, their popular songs, and hereditary merriment; they change nothing but the place of their abode; and of that change they perceive no benefit."

The great debate which set Dr. Johnson's conservative pen scratching had been enlivening the public press since the 1760s and would continue until the American Revolution halted emigration for seven years. Those favouring emigration included ministers of religion who argued that the alternative might well be starvation, either in the Highlands or while searching for work in Glasgow, Greenock or Edinburgh. The minority which championed emigration argued that there need be no fear of depopulation, for the birthrate was increasing—one reason being the recently introduced potato, a more dependable staple than oats, barley or the elusive herring of Loch Broom.

In a belated effort to find out exactly how many were leaving and why, the Secretary of the Treasury in London, John Robinson, had his customs officers record the departure of all emigrants, and from then on we begin to find detailed lists. When the *Hector* sailed for Nova Scotia, there was no official passenger list, just a bill of cargo lading. But by 1774 passenger lists were common and government agents sometimes interviewed people in some depth to discover their reasons for leaving.

An excerpt from interviews conducted aboard the ship

Bachelor en route from Sutherlandshire to Wilmington, North Carolina, gives a fair sample of the troubles and the hopes driving people to the New World.

William Gordon: 60, a farmer, with a wife, six children and the wives and children of two of his sons who had already settled in Carolina, gave four reasons. His sons had written begging him to come, he was paying 60 merks for land which had once rented for eight, he had lost his cattle in the severe winter of 1771 and he wanted to improve the lot of his children, "being himself an old man and lame so that it was indifferent to him in what country he died."

William Mackay: 30, farmer, married with three children ranging from eight to two years, one having died en route to the ship. His crops had failed, cattled prices were low, he could not afford bread for his family and had been "encouraged to emigrate by the accounts received from his countrymen who had gone to America before him."

William Sutherland: 40, farmer, married with five children, the youngest, nine, the eldest, 19, "left his own country because the rents were raised, as soldiers returning upon the peace with a little money had offered higher rents." The services demanded of him by the tacksman, "all done without so much as a bit of bread or a drink," were oppressive.

Elizabeth Macdonald: servant, 29, unmarried. Several of her friends already settled in Carolina had assured her she would get "much better service and greater encouragement in Carolina."

James Duncan: 27, farmer, married, two children, one aged nine months, the other five years old. Crops had failed, bread was dear and the price of cattle was such that one cow would buy only six bushels of meal. He could find no employment in Scotland but friends had written that wages in the colonies were good and the land was cheap.

John Catanoch: 50, farmer, married with four children 19 to seven years, had rented land from a minister, Alexander Nicholson, near Thurso, and besides the usual complaints of failed crops, costly bread, increased rents and appeals from friends already in the colonies, he said his landlord the minister had taken over his pastures to accommodate new tenants. As a result his cattle had died from want of grass and his arable was too small to support the family. Moreover, the landlord had demanded an intolerable 30 to 40 days of free labour every year.

William Sutherland: 24, married, his child left behind with relatives, had lost his cattle in the winter storms of 1771-72 and had been obliged to work so hard for the landlord in seed time and harvest "that he could not in the two years he possessed his croft, raise as much corn as would serve his family for six months." Having no money he proposed to hire himself out as a day labourer in America where, he had heard, "one man's labour will maintain a family of twenty persons." His wife would sew and spin.

Most of them had bitter memories of the Black Winter of 1771-72. In a country where every winter was the enemy, this particular one had been the worst anyone could remember, even William Macdonald who, at 71, was the oldest of the emigrants aboard the *Bachelor*. The winter had begun on September 2 with frost and sleet. The snow line crept down from the mountains to the crofters' doors, black ice formed on the lochs and the storms that blew in from the sea howled on into April. A cattle plague destroyed whole herds; usually, in other bad winters, only one in five had died. It had been a fell winter throughout the Highlands. In Loch Broom parish, Lieutenant Simon Mackenzie of Langwell saved only £20 worth of cattle from a herd worth £208. With the spring came famine.

In the parish of Assynt, Sutherlandshire, Thomas Pennant reported "crowds were passing emaciated with hunger, to the eastern coast, on the report of a ship being there, laden with meal. Numbers of the miserables of the country were now migrating; they wandered in a state of desperation; too poor to pay, they madly sell themselves for their passage, preferring a temporary bondage in a strange land to starving for life on their native soil." In a land of mountains, headlands, deep lochs and solitary glens he found "the people are almost torpid with idleness, and most wretched, their hovels miserable, made of poles wattled and covered with sods. There is not corn raised sufficient to supply the wants of the inhabitants."

The tacksman in charge of Assynt was Alexander Mackenzie of Ardloch, whose ancestors had owned land in Coigach. He estimated the population of the parish at 3,000—Macleods, Mackenzies and Mackays predominated—with little to offer the outside world but cattle, salmon and herring. The parish was so poor that when the minister scraped enough money to build a manse in 1771, he had to hire a mason from the south and import all the building materials, except for stone, from neighbouring Coigach and Inverness. Capt. James Sutherland, General Commissioner of the Sutherland estates and Mackenzie's superior, reported as early as December 1771 that Assynt tenants had been threatening to emigrate, and in the following year his letters to Edinburgh reflect a deepening alarm about the intentions of people in other Sutherland parishes as well. Because of the famine in the spring of 1772 he had great trouble finding enough grain in the south to feed his people; and arrears in rent, which had totalled £2,500 in 1770, had doubled in 1773.

Things were hardly any better in Loch Broom parish, although it was not so remote and poor as Assynt. Ninian Jeffrey, who was appointed Factor in Coigach, Loch Broom, in 1768, described the people as being "in so great want that they were eating the cattle that died and few or none of them had a bit of bread to eat." Many were sharing the oats and barley they had kept for their own meals with their remaining cattle. Jeffrey appealed for potatoes and seed grain but cautioned there were no horses left to fetch it. Forsaking the community quarrels that had so incensed the Rev. Robertson and the Factors Forbes and Jeffrey, the people helped each other and managed to survive.

In July 1772, 31 householders met to draft a petition setting forth their plight. Signing themselves "The United Inhabitants," they told their landlords, the Board of Forfeited Estates, that cattle were starving and although "the poor helped the poor," people were starving as well. They harked back to earlier years, to the brief boom in the selling price of cattle and corn in 1766-69, when they could pay their rent and feed themselves.

"But alas!" they continued. "Times are entirely altered as is most fatally experienced by your petitioners. Few or none of them but have lost a great part of their cattle and some their all. Besides this, their prodigious loss of cattle of all sorts, they expended all their corn upon these cattle so that they not only wanted bread to their families, but their land lays idle for want of seed. In this deplorable situation some of the Inhabitants had thought of transporting themselves and families to North America, but on mature consideration thought proper to make known their case . . . But such is the scarcity at present that most of the people are in a starving condition, the more so as their horses are so weak that they could not carry loads from the low country, and no ship appeared on the coast hitherto."

They asked the Board to reduce their rents, in return for which "the petitioners will drop all thought of going to America." Most signed the petition with initials or an X—Mackenzies, Macleods, Maclennans, Mathesons, Macleans, among them men who were to sail for Nova Scotia on the *Hector*, although at that time they had still not resolved upon emigration. The Board did nothing about the rents, but did send 600 bushels of meal and sold it to the people at cost price. Nor did things much improve. The autumn of 1772 was so wet and cold that harvesting, such as it was, was not completed until November, and to make matters worse the shoals of herring which usually ran through Loch Broom and which the people had counted on to get them through the year had mysteriously disappeared. They normally appeared every July, their arrival heralded by the gulls.

"It was a singular and remarkable fact," a Loch Broom historian wrote, "that the fishing always failed in the years of greatest scarcity." In the autumn the government sent another 600 bushels of bear and 48 of oats, but it was a dismal year and the people suffered great privation until the next year's harvest, in the autumn of 1773, began to bring some relief.

Ninian Jeffrey's correspondence with the Board makes painful reading. Like many Factors for the Forfeited Estates Board he was a Lowlander from Kelso, in the border country, who understood no Gaelic, complained that the Highlanders regarded him not as a Scot, but as an Englishman, and railed against what he perceived as their laziness and backwardness. But in the adversity of that year he proved to be not an unkindly man and did his best. By December 1772, he was warning the Board that the inhabitants were "in precarious state." The surviving cattle were too starved to take to market, seed grain was needed urgently—at the very least 600 bushels of bear, 600 of oats "of the lowest grain" and 270 bushels of potatoes. He managed to suppress his exasperation when the civil servants in Edinburgh, having only a vague notion of the geography of their distant estates, proposed to ship supplies to Dornoch Firth or Cromarty Road "as the most convenient port for Coigach." Patiently, Jeffrey remonstrated that this would never do, that the supplies were needed at Loch Broom, not on the farther side of Scotland.

On February 18, 1773, conditions remained perilous. "The winter has been so wet and stormy that scarce any of the people in Coigach has yet begun their labouring; and as few of them has provender to feed their horses it is with difficulty they are able to make out the labouring." By

June 9, 37 families had either given up their leases and departed or had sold their possessions in order to be ready for the first ship bound for the colonies. "The spirit of Emigration prevails at present in Coigach and Assynt and severals gave up their lands, but as there was not forty free days when they gave me the intimation I refused to take their land this year except Lieut. Alexander Macleod in Inverpooly whose intimation was early . . . " Their patience exhausted, tenants were simply breaking their leases and leaving. "The spirit of Emigration makes lands difficult to be sett [leased] at present rates," Jeffrey told the Board.

On the Lovat estates of the east coast, despite a relatively more easy climate, conditions had been almost as bad as those at Loch Broom and Assynt. A letter dated June 9, 1772, from Beaufort near Beauly, finds Capt. Forbes, the Factor, asking permission from the Board to purchase 2,400 bushels of meal from Aberdeen or Banffshire to be sold to the tenants in small quantities "and some given to the poor to prevent them from starving, most of the gentlemen of estates in that neighbourhood and in the Highlands finding themselves under the necessity of nursing their tenants upon this melancholy occasion, when the crop turned out so ill, and so many of their cattle perished for want of fodder in the severe winter and spring." Meal was selling at exorbitant prices and even then there was "not enough to be had for money."

On July 22 Forbes told the Board he had purchased meal for the people on the Lovat estates and also on the various Cromarty estates, "which had an extraordinarly good effect and prevented many from starving, but the other day a great body of the people assembled there and begged with tears in their eyes that [I] might bring more yet, otherwise some of them would starve." It would take between 800 and 1,200 more bushels to prevent starvation.

By the end of 1772 the people of the Lovat estates had joined those in Loch Broom and Assynt in discussions of emigration. For all its good intentions, the Board had failed to improve their lot and the burdens of rising rents, short leases or none at all, which made dismissal a constant worry, had been compounded by the Board's decision to take pasturage away by enclosing and cultivating large tracts of hillside which had previously served as grazing land for cattle. Even before the crop failures of the past year the tenants had been sinking into debt. In January 1773, 176 Lovat estate tenants gathered, much as the Loch Broom men had done, to petition the Board. Thirty-seven signed their names, the rest appending Xs or initials.

"We have lived upon credit till it is no more," they wrote, "by which we are at length brought to this fatal issue, that unless we are relieved we are apprehensive we must follow the same steps which our unhappy neighbours have pointed out to us, of quitting our farms, transporting ourselves and our familys to new and distant lands to find that Bread which our native country denies us. We mean not to offend, we humbly beg leave, with great deference, to inform your Lordships that we are advised the Rising of Rents falls not under the words or meaning of the annexing Act. We are told there are powers to diminish but not to augment. But it is your Lordships' sympathy and compassion on our circumstances, and not this, which we plead." They asked that rentals be reduced and included a document supporting their petition and testifying to their distress, signed by their ministers the Rev. John Fraser of Kilmorack and the Rev. Malcolm Nicolson of Kiltarlity.

Along with their fellow petitioners in Loch Broom they waited through the winter and into the spring, but there was no redress. As a result, when the black brig *Hector* arrived, those who could departed for Nova Scotia.

CHAPTER FIVE

Mr. Pagan and
Dr. Witherspoon

*When they find their labour cannot obtain their
support, after paying the rents of their land,
their conclusion is made in two words,* leave it,
*and go to that country where we believe there is
Ground for us all . . .*

AN INQUIRY INTO THE LATE MERCANTILE DISTRESSES IN
SCOTLAND AND ENGLAND, DEC. 5, 1772.

As the first cold mists of autumn of 1772 rolled up the
Clyde, John Pagan, sitting by the fire in the family count-
ing house in Glasgow, anticipated no difficulties in the
emigration scheme he had so carefully contrived and
which he was about to advertise in the *Glasgow Journal*
and the *Edinburgh Advertiser*. His notice was addressed

"To all Farmers and others, in Scotland, who are inclined to settle upon easy terms in the Province of Nova Scotia in North America."

"In order to effectuate the speedy settlement of these lands," Pagan promised unusually favourable terms. The first 20 families to apply would receive "in fee-simple, to them and their heirs forever" 150 acres for man and wife and 50 more for every member of the family, child and servant, "at the low rate of six pence sterling for each acre." In the older colonies to the south, land was going at three shillings an acre. To the next 20 families who applied, Pagan promised the same quantity of land for a one-time payment of a shilling an acre, and the third group would be granted land for one shilling and six-pence. The settlers would have two years to pay.

The price of transportation was reasonable—although it had to be paid in cash before departure—an adult or "full freight" ticket costing less than the price of a cow. For each full-freight passenger of eight years of age or more, a berth and food would cost three pounds five shillings, children aged two to eight would be accepted at half fare and infants under two would travel free.

So that no one might question the probity of the venture, Pagan explained that the famous Dr. John Witherspoon, the Scottish Presbyterian minister who had become "president of the college in New-Jersey, North America," was a partner in the enterprise, along "with some other gentlemen in that country. Dr. Witherspoon will take particular care that the strictest justice be done, and the settlers' different places appointed them with the utmost impartiality." The Governor of Nova Scotia would be asked for a charter for a Presbyterian church and the first minister to apply for a living there would receive 500 acres free, and the first school master 100 acres.

As soon as enough settlers applied, Pagan undertook to arrange for "a good and sufficient ship" and to supply each full-freight passenger with a weekly ration of three pounds of beef, four pounds of bread, four of oatmeal, "with barley-broth and burgue twice a week, and one Scotch pint of water each day." Although the usual passage took four weeks, Pagan claimed, since Nova Scotia was little more than half the distance to North Carolina, there would be sufficient food and water to last 12 weeks.

Altogether the advertisement, which appeared September 1 in the *Glasgow Journal* and September 18 in the *Edinburgh Advertiser*, was remarkably detailed, it failed to mention or clarify three points that were to bring much trouble later. Like many a real estate prospectus it tended to gloss the shortcomings.

While stating that the Pagan-Witherspoon grant included 20 miles of coastline where good fishing abounded and the soil was "very good for raising grain of every kind and stocks of cattle," the advertisement failed to mention that the land on which the emigrants would settle was miles back from the shore and lay under thick primeval forest. To the Highlanders, unused to clearing land, that forest was to look as thick as any jungle. With its brief reference to "about 20 families already settled upon the lands, and . . . a school of about 30 children," the advertisement gave the Highlanders an inaccurate impression of a well-settled community.

Nor were the Highlanders aware of the disappointing history of the grant. The Philadelphia Company had failed to attract sufficient settlers from Maryland and Pennsylvania and, threatened with loss of the grant for non-compliance with the settlement terms, they turned to Witherspoon and Pagan to recruit settlers from Scotland. Witherspoon had become involved with the Philadelphia Company through alumni or trustees of New Jersey College. He, in turn, had recruited Pagan and between them they purchased almost 40,000 acres of the grant for £225.

Witherspoon, 51 years old and a minister since the age of 21, had a lively past and was to have an equally lively future. A loyal Hanovarian in his youth, like most of his fellow ministers, he had been captured by Jacobite troops at the battle of Falkirk early in 1746. Although he was apparently only observing the campaign, some said he was actually leading a unit of Whig loyalists into the fray. Imprisoned in Castle Dounie, he escaped, in the best romantic fashion, on a rope of knotted blankets. After receiving a call to preach at Paisley near Glasgow in 1757, Witherspoon became known for his writings on morals and controversial church affairs—one of his pamphlets was so pithy that he became involved in a libel and defamation suit in which he was fined damages of £150. Such was his fame in 1768 that he was urged by Benjamin Franklin to become the first President of New Jersey College at Princeton and to lecture on philosophy, divinity, history and eloquence. Within a decade, on the eve of the revolutionary war, Witherspoon had also become known as an American rebel and, to the dismay of his Whig friends in Scotland, represented New Jersey at the drawing up of the constitution and was a signatory to the Declaration of Independence. Like his friend Benjamin Franklin, he dabbled in Nova Scotia land grants but found little time to do more than lend his name to the ventures.

Witherspoon's active partner in sending Highlanders to Pictou was John Pagan. The son of a sugar manufacturer, Pagan was a merchant and shipowner, a Burgess and Brother of the Guild of the City of Glasgow, a thriving business centre of 40,000 built on colonial produce such as tobacco. Pagan was associated with the firm of Robert Lee and Joseph Tucker, lumber merchants and shipbuilders at Greenock, 20 miles down the Clyde, which had still to be dredged to allow deep-draught ships to get up to Glasgow. With his nephew William and other kinsmen, such as Robert Pagan who had gone in 1768 to Falmouth (later Portsmouth, Maine) for Lee and Tucker, John was to build a Pagan business empire which would stretch out from Glasgow to New York,

Boston, Falmouth, Saint John, Halifax, Pictou and Quebec City. But that was mostly in the future, and now he was having difficulties.

He had appointed agents in the Highlands to accept applications for Nova Scotia land—Provost James Campbell in Inverary, Archibald Gray at Maryburgh on Loch Linnhe, James Macdonald at Portree in Skye, Dougald Mactavish at Fort Augustus in the Great Glen and Baillie Alexander Shaw of Inverness. Not only did these agents have little success, but after Pagan's advertisements had appeared, Baillie Shaw had also inserted his own notice in the *Edinburgh Advertiser* to complain that Pagan had used his name without consent. Shaw wanted nothing to do with the venture. This was particularly embarrassing because Baillie Shaw was held in esteem in northeastern Scotland, where he had served as an agent of the Board of Trustees for Fisheries and Manufactures in the promotion of the infant linen industry. Hard on Shaw's disavowal came more trouble. Pagan's advertisement had acted like a gust of wind on the dying embers of the emigration debate—it was now once more in full flame in the press. One writer mistook the simple purchase price for yearly rent and claimed Witherspoon and Pagan were out to rook the emigrants, who could do better at home. Another exaggerated the terrors of the Nova Scotia climate. Some questioned Witherspoon's motives as a man of the cloth.

In the *Edinburgh Advertiser* a letter from a correspondent signing himself "Well wisher to Old Scotland" was typical of the more thoughtful objections:

"Supposing them to have paid their freight, (which is indeed pretty moderate for so long a voyage), and to be safely landed in that bleak and foreign clime, far from their native country and their friends, the first thing that presents itself to them is a dreary tract of an uninhabited and uncultivated wilderness, entirely in the state of nature, full of marshes, and overgrown with prodigious quantities of useless timber and brushwood, which must be cleared away before the ground can be of the smallest use; and this will require immense labour and take up a vast deal of time. Now how are they to subsist in the meanwhile? It is impossible for them the first year to clear and cultivate as much land as will raise a quantity of potatoes or corn sufficient for that year's subsistence. Although the grounds were cleared to their hand, it may reasonably be supposed that the first season would be well neigh spent in building their houses and providing themselves in the necessary implements. In short, it might easily be made to appear that unless the settlers have money to buy cattle and provisions &c, they must inevitably perish for want of bread before any subsistence can be raised by their own labour."

The writer questioned Dr. Witherspoon's role. "Dr. Witherspoon being mentioned as one of the proprietors of those lands, some ignorant persons may perhaps imagine that he lives near that place; but that Reverend Doctor is Principal of the College of New Jersey, where he resides, and which is at least one thousand miles distant; so that whatever benefit they may promise themselves from his superintendency is entirely groundless, as perhaps he will not be there thrice, nor perhaps even twice, in his whole lifetime." There was, in fact, no evidence that Dr. Witherspoon went to Pictou even once.

Finally, "Well wisher" warned that no matter how reasonable the cost of outward passage, the tariff for people wishing to return home would be very dear, "so that they must either starve there, or subject themselves to the condition of banished felons, by drudging for others in some other part of the country for their daily bread." In the case of the *Hector* group, "Well wisher's" forecast was all too apt.

The pro-emigration forces rallied, and writing in the *Caledonia Mercury*, a "Bystander" argued that Nova Scotia's climate was no more disagreeable to hardy Highlanders than it had been to the French who had been living there in comfort for many generations. "Besides, Dr. Witherspoon hath access to know the soil and climate in that part of the province of which he hath obtained a grant; he is abundantly able to judge what is, or is not, a proper place for settlers; and it would be extremely hard to suspect that he would entice his country-men to settle in a land where they must either starve or live in misery. His reputation is at stake, and it is also his interest the colony may flourish."

Critics of the Pictou scheme, said "Bystander," had failed to suggest an alternative for the thousands of destitute farmers and unemployed weavers, tanners and labourers adrift in Scotland. "If such persons cannot find employment, they must, however, be maintained; if they are willing to emigrate, how can it be prudent to hinder them? If the *wise and humane* gentlemen I speak of are sure that Nova Scotia is an improper place for them, they, from humanity and sound policy, should either direct them to settle in a British colony, where their condition will be comfortable, or else they should immediately find out employment . . . and should also lighten the burden which most part of farmers in this country have borne for twenty years past. For if such a number of people cannot get employment at home, and are also intimidated from going abroad, they may probably become very turbulent neighbours in the country."

Darkly hinting that those opposing emigration feared losing their servants who made them rich, "By-stander" warned that "hunger is a powerful enemy to fight against; and though they have hitherto been peaceable it may push them on to the most unlawful and desperate attempts."

In January 1773, four months after Pagan had placed his advertisement, the argument still swept on. A writer signing himself "Veritas" declared "the country in general must certainly suffer by emigration" and urged the

government to settle would-be emigrants on the Forfeited Estates at easy rents. Failing this, someone should
at least point out to emigrants that they need not pay for
land in the colonies but could get it free by applying to
provincial governors.

There was even criticism from America, where by this
time the extent of Dr. Witherspoon's land speculation
was common knowledge. In 1770 he and the Pagans had
organized the immigration of 200 Scots to Boston in the
brig *Hector*. A year later he had purchased a large tract
near Ryegate, New Hampshire, and sold it to a company
of farmers from Renfrewshire in the Scottish Lowlands.
Now, in partnership with the Pagans, he was promoting
20,000 one-half acres of the Pictou land he had purchased
from George Bryan, John Bayard and Isaac Wykoff of the
Philadelphia Company, thus gaining controlling interest
in that flagging venture. Suggesting that Dr. Witherspoon might well be confusing God with Mammon, Dr.
Ezra Stiles of Yale College wrote that "the Doctor seems
to be taking Care of this World as well as for that which
is to come. Is he not laying a foundation for the Ruin of
some of his Children and Posterity!"

Stung by such criticism and convinced it was moti-
vated by old clerical feuds in which he had taken part,
Witherspoon penned a long letter—almost an essay—to
the *Scots Magazine* which, it seems, never printed it. A
man of immense enthusiasm, he had come to believe in
the future of a republican New World. So long as land
was not sold at a price higher than he permitted, he felt it
his duty to promote the emigration of Protestants from
Scotland.

"My having any concern in such an extensive undertaking was wholly accidental and unexpected," he wrote.
"I was invited and pressed to it, from a motive that was
not at all concealed, that it would give the people who intended to come out greater confidence that they should
meet with fair treatment."

Concerned, as was Pagan, that the controversy would discourage emigrants, Witherspoon said the charges against him narrowed down to this: "Migrations from Britain to America are not only hurtful but tend to the ruin of that country; therefore, John Witherspoon, by inviting people to leave Scotland and settle in America is an enemy of his country." This charge he claimed was folly because only 200 or 300 families were involved in his plans.

"It remains then, that he must be the enemy of the landlords, who may run some risk of being obliged to lower their rents. But is this a liberal way of thinking, to say a man is an enemy to his country, while he promotes the happiness of the great body of the people with a small diminution of the interest of a handful? I cannot help thinking it is doing a real service to my country, when I show that those of them who find it difficult to subsist on the soil in which they were born, may easily transport themselves to a soil and climate vastly superior to that."

Warming to his vision of a republican America Witherspoon continued, "I can never admit that the happiness of one class of man depends upon the misery of another, or that it can be any way contrary to the interest of the landholders in Scotland, that a few who find themselves pinched in their circumstances, or who have an active and enterprising disposition, should remove to America."

In Glasgow, the practical John Pagan had kept out of the argument and instead concerned himself with ways and means of attracting emigrants. Although they had been signing up in large numbers to migrate to established colonies such as North Carolina, where they often had friends and relatives, the response to his advertisement had been disappointing; in the early days of 1773 it had still amounted to little more than a handful of Lowlanders and a few names from around Inverness. To overcome such reluctance he had appointed John Ross of Loch Broom as his chief emigration agent. Ross had served for several years as an agent for the Board of Fisheries and Manufactures in promotion of the linen industry. He had worked for Pagan and Witherspoon once before, in 1770, when he had shepherded 200 Scots to Boston on the *Hector*. Since then he had returned to Loch Broom where he had set himself up in business as a merchant. Few knew the northern Highlanders better than the Dingwall-born Ross and, unlike his former colleague in government service, Baillie Shaw of Inverness, Ross had no qualms about using his contacts to further emigration.

Riding as far as Dornoch in Sutherlandshire to the north and Beauly and Inverness in the east, Ross had secured enough applications by March 5 to encourage Pagan to publish an advertisement announcing that the *Hector* of Greenock would "positively" sail for Pictou, Boston and Falmouth in New England between May 10 and May 15 and would load freight, as well as passengers. Assuming that his readers would have little idea where Pictou lay, Pagan appended a note explaining it was 15 miles from the Island of St. John, which had been attracting settlers in the past three years.

May 10 came, and then May 15, and still the *Hector* lay in the busy roads at Greenock. Nor had she moved three weeks later when entry No. 61 in the Greenock customs accounts for June 5 show her loading cargo: "In the *Hector* of Greenock, John Speirs Msr for Pictou Harbour in Nova Scotia—James Ewing and Mark Kuhill on British account—1 bale and 5 casks containing 100 pounds woollens, 400 pounds Haberdashery, 200 weight refined sugar manufactured by Mark Kuhill. All British." Much of this was destined for Boston where the *Hector* was to call after leaving Pictou Harbour.

By the first week of June, Ross had recruited enough emigrants to fill the ship—most of them from the Lovat estates in the east, from Assynt and other regions of Sutherlandshire and from his own Loch Broom parish. One June 3 he signed a contract* in Glasgow in which Pagan and Witherspoon gave him full responsibility for the Pictou venture. Not only would he organize the voyage, as he had done three years earlier on the *Hector's* trip to Boston, but he would also remain in Pictou to direct the colonization. The contract deeded to Ross "or his heirs or assignies or their Agents" 20,000 of the 40,000 acres owned by Pagan, Witherspoon and other partners of the Philadelphia Company, which had owned the grant since 1766. The contract stipulated that Pagan would have the land surveyed into lots ranging from 200 to 1,000 acres, would send out in the *Hector* that year a full year's supply of food which would be sold to the emigrants at cost and would guarantee the new settlers "every accommodation in the power of the proprietors untill they Build houses for themselves."

For his part, Ross undertook to settle "this year, a number of persons making up two hundred and fifty, or net two hundred and twenty full passengers." That presumably was the number he had already signed or felt he could sign. Ross was also required to pay the yearly token quit rent of £20 sterling required by the Nova Scotia government for the 20,000 acres. He announced that the *Hector* would sail within the month, taking on a dozen people, mostly Lowlanders, at Greenock, before proceeding north to Loch Broom to fetch the bulk of the settlers.

Toward the end of June, more than a month behind schedule, the *Hector* weighed anchor for Loch Broom, 300 sea miles to the north beyond the tangled isles and jagged mountains.

At the head of Loch Broom the Highlanders were already gathering; the hopeful, the adventurous and the

---

*See Appendix A.

merely discontented. There were Camerons, Grants, Frasers, Mackenzies, Mackays, Macleods, Rosses, Sutherlands; farmers, herdsmen, war veterans, a weaver, a miller, a laird's son, a widow, a piper, a blacksmith who had just escaped from jail, a scion of a wealthy family of bankers, one Roman Catholic family and children. There were Whigs and Jacobites but John Ross cared nothing for their politics so long as they had passage money and were likely to make good colonists. They came from the annexed estates of the Beauly Frasers, from Loch Broom and Sutherlandshire, Assynt parish, Laraig and Dornoch. They strode down the mountains with their piper playing as if they were bound for battle. A few climbed over the mountains from Gairloch and the south. Some arrived on horses, leading Highland ponies with panniers stuffed with belongings. Most walked, 40 miles from Beauly and beyond, carrying a few possessions on their backs and their babes in arms, over cattle tracks which had never seen a wheel. The people living at Loch Broom were more fortunate—the ship would pick them up in their own glen; there is a tradition in the Macleod families that the *Hector*, outward bound for Nova Scotia, stood to for an hour or two on the hither side of Horse Island down the hill from their crofts at Achavraie to take on passengers who were saved a 12-mile journey to the head of the loch where the others were taken aboard.

Wayworn and anxious, in families and small groups, the people from the north and south came down from the hills on the drove road skirting the river Broom to the green estuary where rough shelters had been set up against the rain. A few, it was said, stayed at the change-house at Ullapool run by an ex-soldier or with friends in the cottages at Ardcharnich, a short way down the loch. Those forced to camp by the shore felt no great hardship, for although the mountains kept their snow-tops, summer had come to Loch Broom and the local people were intent on hospitality which, said a writer of the time, "possesses the people of these parts. We scarce passed a farm but the good woman, long before our approach, sallied out and stood on the roadside, holding out to us a bowl of milk or whey."

There they waited for their ship and there the ageing Rev. James Robertson, who after all these years was still "The Mighty Minister" of Loch Broom and would be for a few years yet, held communion and prayed to God to bless them. There were so many he was forced to hold the service in the churchyard despite a steady rain and the story is still told that "between the tears of the congregation and the rain from heaven, the communion cup was never empty." Some complained in later years that, what with the spray and rain at sea, they were never dry from that day until they got ashore in Pictou Harbour. What the Rev. Robertson thought of losing so many of his parishioners is not known. His fellow minister Dr. Witherspoon had organized the venture, and if Robertson disapproved he gave no sign.

The ship was late—it was already July—and Captain Speirs was anxious to be off. The long-drawn business of ferrying the people from the wet shingle to the ships had begun, supervised by John Ross, the captain and his two mates. Amid the commotion, the crying of children, the crying of gulls, and shouts and goodbyes, the boats were rowed out to the *Hector* one by one, crammed with people in their Sunday best and the small piles of sacks, bags and wooden chests containing what few possessions they were able to take. The ship was still not quite ready to sail, for a new commotion broke out. The Mackay piper from Sutherlandshire, known variously as John or William, did not have sufficient money to pay his fare of three pounds five shillings. The people had come to depend on him to keep their spirits up during the voyage and after some discussion, in which several passengers agreed to share their food with him, Ross and the captain allowed the piper aboard.

Despite an agreement that she was to load staples for an entire year, she carried sufficient food only for the projected voyage.

The brig weighed anchor—the date has been passed down as either July 8 or July 10—spread her weathered sails and set off down the long loch in light winds and the evening tide, past the scattering of crofts at Ullapool, past Isle Martin where the herring boats lay, and the high fields of Polglass and Achiltibuie, and out beyond the Summer Isles. The last the passengers saw of land was the bulk of Rugha Mor above the crofts at Reiff where some of them had lived.

CHAPTER SIX

The Hector

There's a track upon the deep
And a path across the sea
But the weary ne're return
to their ain countrie.

THE EMIGRANT'S LAMENT

She was a Dutch-built ship, old even when John Pagan had acquired her many years before, and had once been in the smuggling trade, or so it was said. A Dutch ship answering her description is known to have been captured by the British navy off the Carolinas early in the 1760s. Registered at 200 tons burthen—the weight of cargo she could carry—her hold was about 83 feet long, 24 wide and 10 feet deep, and her length from rudder to stem post 120 feet. She was two-masted, the after-mast rigged with the large gaff sail which showed she was a brig, an ocean-going workhorse. The *Hector* carried no guns except for what small arms the Captain might have had in his locker. But in the hope she might be mistaken for a warship the owners had her black topsides painted with white trim to look as if she had four gunports on each side. This was a common practice to discourage privateers and pirates and any of His Majesty's naval ships intent on impressing merchant seamen into the navy.

Alone now upon the Atlantic, all canvas set and the Hebrides well astern, the *Hector* dipped and swayed and creaked along her southwest track to Nova Scotia, black hull glistening in spray and sun, her weather-worn grey sails a deceptive white against the blue of sky and sea. Like a seagull the *Hector* showed up best in flight, and from afar. John Pagan had given her a fine new Scottish name, a good skipper and a fresh coat of paint but he could not give her back her youth, and up close she was unlovely and her passengers had been known to complain that she was slow, wet and smelly. They picked slivers from her rotting hull with their fingernails.

Her crew consisted of sailmaker, carpenter, cook and a few seamen. John Speirs of Greenock was her master and would be for several months until she retired either in the breaker's yard or as a rotting hulk on Clydeside where she was condemned. Her first and second mates, both Lowlanders, were James Orr and John Anderson, who probably spoke no Gaelic. Apart from assorted freight in the lower hold, she carried nine tons of the most difficult cargo an 18th-century master could be called upon to transport—a full load of emigrants of whom 70 were children.

Except for John Ross and the three former soldiers who had fought in the colonies, none of the emigrants had been at sea before and had only the vaguest notion of where they were going or when they would get there. Not many spoke English. Their first misgivings came when the mate herded them down the walkway to the dark, stuffy cavern which was to be their home for many weeks. After the excitement and commotion of boarding, the children were tired and fretful. In the light from the open hatch and a few fish-oil lamps slung on the bulkheads, they were shown their beds—rough pine boards with two feet of space between the upper and lower tiers. They were free to partition their berths with old canvas or blankets, dividing bachelors from spinsters, family from family. As for those noisome stained and covered wooden buckets scattered here and there amid the bunks, only the children had to ask their purpose, nor did there ever seem to be enough of them. The sailors called them puke-buckets and tried to teach the passengers not to empty them to windward. The damp hold smelt of tar, old freight, brine-soaked wood and urine and there were no portholes. As the passengers hastened back up the gangway to the deck to take their first meal of barley soup and oat bread in the clean air and clear light of a northern Scottish summer evening, those few who had crossed the sea before, Ross and the old soldiers, may have wondered how these innocents would fare when rain and storm and heavy seas would pen them into that gloomy hold like cattle in a winter byre.

Among the children, 30 were less than two years old, most of them babies. Captain Speirs, who was also doctor, minister and law officer amid his endless other sea duties, had been called to a birth on July 3 when the ship had cleared Greenock on its first leg northward to Loch Broom. Margaret Fraser of Inverness, a widow of three months, had given birth to a daughter in a cubicle of sagging grey canvas. A member of the Grant clan from the hill country west of Inverness, she had married Hugh Fraser, presented him with two sons and two daughters and had signed up with him for the voyage on the *Hector* before Hugh became ill and died. Since her Sutherlandshire cousins, William and Ann Fraser, were intent on going on the *Hector* she was determined to go with them and thus it was she gave birth to little Jean aboard the *Hector*. There is no evidence that Margaret Fraser ever regretted her decision. Finding no means of livelihood at Pictou Harbour she walked 40 miles to the established township of Truro where she married a New Englander named Nathaniel Polly and raised a second family. Jean married David Page, a silversmith who came to Truro from Haverhill, Massachusetts, and had seven sons. Their descendants are scattered throughout North America. When Jean Page died at the age of 66, her tombstone proclaimed her the youngest *Hector* passenger and it stood in a Truro cemetery until 30 years ago.

Other than the birth there was little excitement on the *Hector* in the early days. The fine weather held and the old ship ran down her westing at a commendable five or six knots with so little fuss that nearly everyone was able to crowd on deck during the day to enjoy the fresh, clean air and sunshine, away from the evil-smelling hold. If anyone had told the master about the young girl and her mother lying down there with chills and fever, he might still have turned back for he knew the portent of such suffering. Soon it would be too late.

On deck the people lined up with jugs and wooden plates as the mates doled out the daily ration of one Scotch pint of water to every full-freight passenger and the week's ration of three pounds of salt beef, four pounds of bread and four pounds of oatmeal. Since one cook could not deal with 200 people, the women took turns cooking on little fires in sandboxes on the deck. They gossiped as they ate, compared their pasts and speculated on the future. Some had heard the Indians were ferocious, some had heard of a tree that gave both sugar and soap. They turned eagerly to the old soldiers who had known Halifax and Louisbourg and the wars against the French. A few tried their hands at fishing over the side and caught a cod or a halibut. From time to time John Mackay unlimbered his pipes and strode majestically up and down the deck playing a tune that drained the bitterness from thought of home. There was dancing and singing and story-telling, and wrestling among the younger men. It was almost a holiday mood.

If there were problems in those fortunate few days of sunshine and easy sailing, they lay in the usual complaints about lack of space in the hold or the daily allotment of sweet water. The days were warm, there was no milk for the children and one Scotch pint seemed hardly enough for drinking, cooking and washing. Some used sea water to wash their clothes. Each morning they were expected to clean around their berths. Occasionally the sailors spread canvas to catch a fleeting early morning shower.

Food seemed plentiful enough at first, although when people complained that the oatcakes were mouldy and threw them half-eaten into the scuppers, Hugh Macleod was known to pick them up and stuff them into a canvas bag he kept under his berth. He had learned frugality in a poor croft in the stoney parish of Assynt.

Sitting in a corner, his journal balanced on his knee, young William Mackenzie of Loch Broom noted all this down—the music, the dancing, Hugh Macleod saving husks of oatcake—and some of his observations were passed down by the Rev. George Patterson in his *History of Pictou County*, written a century later. But Mackenzie's journals disappeared—some say they were lost by Patterson's printer in the 1870s when he sent them to the print shop with his manuscript. Since no official passenger list was required by the government in 1773* (although such lists would be required from that year onward), as an old man Mackenzie reconstructed a list from memory in 1837, seven years before his death. A second list, more com-

*See Appendix B.

93

plete, was reconstructed by Squire William Mackay, a Beauly man who settled on East River.

William Mackenzie, who was not only one of the few aboard able to read and write but was also well-educated, had come for adventure. Eighteen years old, he was the younger son of Sir William Mackenzie, whose estate of Ballone on Loch Broom was named for an earlier Ballone which had been the Seaforth Mackenzie stronghold on Moray Firth on the east coast. William was not yet born at the time of Culloden, but had heard tales of those bitter times from his uncle, Colin, the same man who had fought in Cromarty's regiment as a captain and whose acquittal from a treason charge had been so hardly won by the Rev. James Robertson. Against his father's wishes— some say he ran away—Mackenzie had accepted John Ross' offer of the post of school master to the expedition, for which he was to receive a salary and a good piece of land. Although he never worked as a school master at Pictou, he was a useful member of the colony. One of the few possessions carried on the *Hector* which have come down to us through the years is his "gentleman's mirror." Another is Alexander Cameron's horn drinking cup.

William Mackenzie's good friend was Alexander Cameron, who also used the alias Murray, and who had seen the Culloden battle as a boy. Cameron was 44 when he sailed on the *Hector* with his wife Janet, one of the Rosses of Loch Broom, and their son Daniel. Like William, he was fluent in English. On the ship Cameron had met again with Alexander Fraser of Beauly, who had been with him in the throng of boys who had watched the battle at Culloden Moor. When the English troops had gone Fraser settled down at Beauly.

There he took up farming and married Marion Campbell, the daughter of a Jacobite landowner, and was prospering when he fell afoul of English law and thus became the first man to sign up with Ross for the *Hector* voyage. Along with his neighbours he had been augmenting his income with a whiskey still when the gaugers, or government excise men, seized the cart and horse carrying his barrels of whiskey. This was an outrage, and more so since the gaugers took the whiskey to an inn and proceeded to get drunk. When they stumbled off to bed, Fraser got a stable boy, who was also his relative, to lead the horse and cart out of the inn-yard in Inverness and drive them back in the night to Fraser's farm at Beauly. The next day Fraser took them to a neighbouring parish where he sold them, but he was determined, he said, to remain no longer in a country where he was subjected to such treatment. His wife and five children accompanied him.

Nor did Roderick Mackay, the hot-tempered young blacksmith from Beauly, take kindly to the gaugers. Coming across another such whiskey seizure, and indignant at such an invasion of the rights of property, he tried to rescue the whiskey and ended up in the Tolbooth jail in Inverness. As passed down by William Mackenzie and his friends and related by Dr. Patterson, Mackay's response on finding himself in prison was in the style of Sir Walter Scott's Rob Roy:

"His free-born spirit chafed under such restrains, particularly in a cause so good, and he was soon conceiving schemes to secure his liberation. Having ingratiated himself with the jailer he sent him one day to procure a quantity of ale and also of whiskey to cement their friendship. The jailer on his return, advancing into the cell with both hands full, Roderick stepped behind him and out of the door. Closing it after him, he locked it and carried off the key, which some say he brought to America with him. The first of these feats would have given him an honourable place in the hearts of his countrymen, but the latter, added to it, was sufficient to make him their idol forever." The key he brought from Inverness Tolbooth is now at the Public Archives in Halifax.

A thick-set strongly built man of 27, Roderick, or

"Rory," was the third son of the 73-year-old Alexander Mackay of Beauly. He had heard about Nova Scotia from his elder brother, Alexander, who had served there with the Fraser Highlanders between 1757 and 1763. In time all four Mackay brothers would go to Nova Scotia to settle, but for now Roderick was able to convince only his unmarried elder brother, Donald, to go with him. With his wife, Christina, and two children, Ann and John, he was now aboard the *Hector*.

Lest it should seem that only those in trouble with the law came from the Lovat estates, it would be hard to find a man of greater respectability than Hugh Fraser, a 32-year-old weaver from Beauly's neighbouring town of Kiltarlity, who carried with him a document from his minister, the Rev. Malcolm Nicolson.

"These do certify," the minister had written, "that the Bearer Hugh Fraser, Weaver, a married man who was born of honest parents in this Parish of Kiltarlity, where he has resided since infancy and behaved soberly and honestly free of any public scandal, so that now when he and his Wife and Family are to remove from our bounds we are at freedom to declare that we know of no reason why they may not be received into any Christian Society or Congregation where Providence may order their Lot." As the document is signed June 29, and the *Hector* departed hardly more than a week later, the weaver's family must have been among the last to embark since the journey to Loch Broom from Kiltarlity was long and hard. The reason for their tardiness seems to lie in the fact that at the last moment their son John, barely seven years of age, had come down with smallpox. Naturally they did not want to desert him, but finally Hugh and Rebecca Fraser decided to leave him with relatives and hastened with their son Donald and daughters Jane and Mary to Loch Broom. John joined them in Nova Scotia six years later.

From the old Jacobite country of Glen Urquhart, which had never recovered from the razing it suffered after Culloden, came the miller James Grant—known as "a peaceful man"—with his four children, Alexander, Margaret, Mary and Jane. At 48, he seems to have been a widower and established a grist mill at Pictou Harbour in 1790.

Of the three soldiers, all in their forties, Sergeant Colin Mackay and Donald Cameron had served in Nova Scotia and had fought the French at Louisbourg in 1758 and then at Quebec the year after under Colonel Simon Fraser, the eldest son of old Lord Lovat. Colin Mackay was born at Strathnaver in the far north of Sutherlandshire, but after the war he settled at Beauly where many of the 78th Fraser Highlanders were disbanded. On June 15, 1773, he set out for Loch Broom and the *Hector* with his young wife, Helen Fraser, and their one-year-old son Colin. Donald Cameron, his wife Mary Macdonald and their children John, Hugh and Mary were the only Roman Catholics aboard. Despite the initial intent of the Nova Scotia government to accommodate only Protestants, Cameron, as it happened, was the first of the group to get a grant of land in his own name, in February 1775. He was drowned years later in the East River of Pictou Harbour. The third soldier, Walter Murray from Sutherlandshire, had served in India and came to the ship with his wife Christy and infant daughter Elizabeth.

There were many from Sutherlandshire, particularly from Assynt, such as the frugal Hugh Macleod, and it was said there were 300 families trying to make a living from as many acres. Passing through that troubled land with its wild scenery, Thomas Pennant claimed, "I never saw a country that seemed to have been so torn and convulsed; the shock, whenever it happened, shook off all that vegetates."

Although there is reason to think the numbers may have been a little higher, Dr. Patterson in his history, written a century later from sources which have since disappeared, said three families had embarked at Greenock along with five young bachelors, and at Loch Broom 33 families and 25 unmarried men besides the agent, John Ross, had come aboard as passengers. The total number is stated in one account as 189, in another as 179, while Governor Francis Legge of Nova Scotia spoke of them, in round numbers, as 200. John Pagan's son Robert, accounting to the government in 1808 for the grant which Pagan had long since taken full control of, said the *Hector* passengers had numbered 190 (72 families in all), but did not give a breakdown. Whatever the exact figures, the names read like a roll-call of the glens; Frasers from eastern Inverness-shire, along with Munroes and Mackays; Mackenzies and Macleods from Loch Broom and Assynt; Rosses from the lower shores of Loch Broom and Maclellans from the head of the loch; Sutherlands along with Mackays and Macleods from Sutherlandshire. There were Chisholms, Grahams, Murrays, Mathesons, Douglasses, Macgregors, Macleans, Urquharts, Falconers, Stuarts, Macritchies, MacConnells, Lyons and Campbells. Although Macdonalds were the largest of the clans, there was only one Macdonald family aboard.

From the Lowlands had come Scotts, Sims, Mains, Wesleys and Robert Innes, whose father had died fighting for Prince Charles at Culloden. He had arrived at Loch Broom from Inverness with his wife Janet and son Duncan, seeking passage. Whatever his own financial state, his family was wealthy; his uncle George Innes of Stow was a Midlothian banker. Young John Patterson, one of the bachelors to board at Greenock, was the son of a ploughman who lived near Paisley. His mother was said to have married below her station and been disowned by her family. John had become a carpenter and, at the age of 25, was a moderately successful young man, building and renting out several houses at Quarreltown in the Paisley district. As he was the only emigrant aboard the *Hector* who owned profitable real estate, his departure from Linwood, where he left his parents, two sisters and a brother, has raised the question as to why he came. Perhaps like young William Mackenzie, the son of the Loch Broom laird, he sought adventure. A hint lies, perhaps, in the economic crisis in the Lowlands in 1772 which threw thousands of artisans out of work and raised the emigration level. In any event, Patterson did not sell his properties and continued to draw rents from them, and his life in Nova Scotia gave him no reason to regret his departure. He was clever, spoke both English and Gaelic, and at Pictou Harbour became a merchant, trader and builder of houses, bridges and mills. Fifteen years after his arrival he founded the hamlet which was to become the town of Pictou, as distinct from Pictou township and the other little communities which had sprung up. He became a Presbyterian deacon and a magistrate. The 19th-century Pictou County historian, the Rev. Dr. George Patterson, was his grandson, son of John Patterson's son Abraham.

So with this precious cargo, the *Hector* now sailed through night and day, sunshine and rain, dragging her log line to keep track of distance run since in those days, before the use of the chronometer made longitudinal navigation common, Captain Speirs relied on dead reckoning. The seas were often rough, people were seasick and when the grey fog rolled down and they could barely see the limp, dripping topsails they wondered, as such landsmen must, how Captain Speirs would find his way. It seemed a long time since they had seen land, the hills of Coigach sliding back into the evening mist. Few had any idea of the mysteries of the octant, back-staff, dividers, parallel rulers, compass or navigation by latitude, which were all the 18th-century master had to depend on. They fretted on those nights of lively winds when, as was the custom, the crew took down the sails, or most of them, and the brig was left to wallow on with hardly any way. They worried whether the food and water would last, and whether the old ship would dig her nose into the long waves and drown them all. But most of all they worried about the sick. Hardly had the seasickness begun to wear off than they were beset with something worse. Captain Speirs recognized the fevers, thirst and constant aches and pains in head and limbs as dysentery. He also knew that smallpox had broken out on the *Hector*.

At that time smallpox was still endemic, as common as measles if more deadly. In the Highlands it had carried off a fifth of each generation and its most fatal visitations were upon the children. In the dark hold of the *Hector*, not yet half way through her journey, it was the children again who must suffer now and there were more than 70. One, and then another, showed the symptoms—chills, fevers, backache, nausea and dizziness and, in a few days, the tell-tale spots that turned to pustules and left no doubt that this was smallpox. They lay on their straw-covered beds of pine boards, too weak to take anything but a sip of water, and there was nothing the parents could do but wait and hope the disease would burn itself out in four or five weeks. To the miseries of darkness, foul air, seasickness, homesickness and dysentery was added pain, and sometimes death. No details of their suffering have been preserved, only the bare facts, but many years later *The Times* of London, reporting an outbreak of disease aboard such an emigrant ship, described it thus: "After a few days have been spent in the pestilential atmosphere created by the festering mass of squalid humanity imprisoned between the damp and steaming decks, the scourge bursts out . . . Amid hundreds of men, women and children, dressing and undressing, washing, quarrelling, cooking and drinking, one hears the groans and screams of the patient . . ."

One by one, children died. Of necessity they were buried at sea, small bundles of coarse canvas pushed gently from the wet deck after the master's brief service of sea burial. Eighteen died, most of them children, and some families, such as Colin and Catherine Douglas' of Beauly, lost more than one. Adults suffered too; most of them recovered but Christina Macleod, the wife of Hugh

Macleod of Assynt, was to die soon after the ship arrived at Pictou Harbour. Hugh and their three daughters were left to make a life alone on the West River. The mother and daughter who were believed to have brought the epidemic aboard recovered and lived long lives.

It was not only the people of the *Hector* who were singled out that summer for such tragedy. In the brig *Nancy* with 250 emigrants from Sutherlandshire, 81 died before they reached New York. Fifty of the victims were children, and, as it happened, Dr. John Witherspoon was visiting New York when the *Nancy* docked and he preached a sermon on the tragedy in the Presbyterian church. As there were no health or safety regulations on these ships, 23 died on a 12-week voyage to North Carolina in a vessel with 450 passengers crammed into a hold no bigger than the *Hector's*. Under the Passenger Act of 1803, a space of 95 feet by 24 was required for 200 passengers, but the Act was usually ignored and often more people were crammed into a ship than would have been allowed in a slave ship from Africa.

The *Hector* sailed on in bad weather and good, and if the Pagan prospectus had suggested the voyage would last a month, Captain Speirs, from long experience, must have known it would last much longer. Ghosting through foggy calms, tacking against westerly headwinds, building up sail when he caught a welcome east wind—he had done it many times before on voyages to Boston and Philadelphia. And then, one foggy day in August, the seaman in the bows sounded with the leadline and found America, or at least brought up some Grand Banks mud from 60 fathoms. In a day or two the seabirds, which had deserted them a few days out from Scotland, were crying for food and the Highlanders needed no logbook to tell them they were approaching land. A week, ten days, two weeks at most, they were told, and they would be in Pictou Harbour. But then, as if they had not suffered enough, the storm struck.

It seems to have been something the *Hector* people, in their old age, wished to forget; John Patterson's grandson, the Rev. George Patterson, makes little mention of it in his history. "When they arrived off the coast of Newfoundland, they met with a severe gale, which drove them so far back that they were a fortnight before they were again as far forward." It was one of those autumnal hurricanes which harry the east coast every year.

Imagine, then, the black clouds building on the southern horizon, seas breaking, sails reefed until there was barely steerage way, and a great wind swooping down at nightfall, With decks awash, the hatch was battened and only the light of swinging oil lamps in the pitching hold; the strong, the sick, the moribund, thrown into each others arms among their slithering baggage of sacks and boxes. Amid the cries of the children they prayed, perhaps, sang hymns, composed themselves for death. On deck, lit only by the green lamp to starboard and red to port, Speirs and his men fought to save her in the breaking waves. The fact the *Hector* had to make up two full weeks of her journey suggests they got her head eased around, before the reefed sails could rip away, and ran out the storm under bare masts like a leaf in a millrace.

When the storm blew itself out the emigrants, believing themselves blown halfway back to Scotland, begged the Captain to turn back home for good and all. But he turned her bow southwestward, and crammed on sail, for his orders were to take her to Pictou Harbour; Falmouth, Massachusetts; and Boston. His chief worry was the supply of water and food. There was salt beef enough, but the bread had been spoiled by sea water. The drinking water, which had been looking as if it came from a scummy swamp, had grown green mould and only a few drops of vinegar could make it drinkable. Hugh Macleod, who had saved discarded oatcakes early in the voyage, now brought them forth from his sack and, with little but salt beef to eat,

Highland women, at left, grinding grain with a hand-mill, while those at right are fulling cloth. Commenting on this practice at Pictou in 1797, John Gerrond, poet and school teacher, said, "The people are generally clothed in a sort of blue cloth, which is dyed in the yarn and fulled or wauked, in the following manner: A number of people sit down in a ring, with their feet inwards, the cloth being in the middle, they then keep pushing with their feet, and in the course of an evening will full it a good deal . . ." (Scottish National Library, Edinburgh)

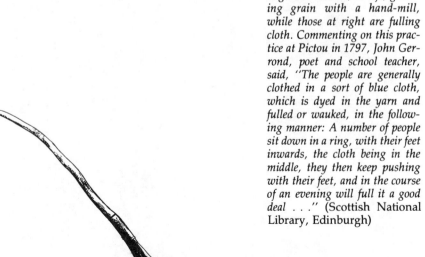

The caschroim ("crooked foot" spade in Gaelic) was the primitive hand plough with which the Highlanders tilled their small plots of land.

In summer the Highlanders would drive their cattle into the hills to the shielings where they built stone huts and spent the most pleasant months of the year. (Scottish National Library, Edinburgh)

A weaver's cottage in the Highlands—circa 1772—the sort of home the Kiltarlity weaver Hugh Fraser might have left to sail to Pictou on the Hector. *(Scottish National Library, Edinburgh)*

Small pockets of arable land along the shores of Loch Broom, where many of the Hector *settlers came from, provided inadequate sustenance among the hills and mountains. (B.K.S. Surveys Ltd.)*

Farming country on the Beauly River on the old Lovat Fraser Estate. Since the 18th century modern farming methods have been used, the land has been drained and trees were planted. Yet, this farm land has always been better than that of the western Highlands, such as Loch Broom. Arable land around Beauly was not enough, however, to support the growing population of the late 18th century and many tenants emigrated from this area to Pictou Harbour. (Crown Copyright/R.A.F. Photograph)

Edinburgh coffeehoute, (No. 1.) Sweething's-alley, or the wharf, will be duly attended to.

For PICTOU HARBOUR in NOVA SCOTIA, BOSTON and FALMOUTH in NEW ENGLAND.

THE SHIP HECTOR, JOHN SPEIR mafter, burthen 200 tons, now lying in the harbour of GREENOCK. For freight or paffage apply to John Pagan merchant in Glafgow, Lee, Tucker, and Co. merchants in Greenock; and in order to accommodate all paffengers that may offer, the fhip will wait until the 10th of May next, but will pofitively fail betwixt and the 15th of that month.

N. B. Pictou harbour lyes directly oppofite to the ifland of St. John's, at the diftance of 15 miles only.

Advertisement inserted in the Edinburgh Advertiser by John Pagan in 1773. (Courtesy Edinburgh Central Library)

To be SOLD,

THE Lands and Eftate of BAVELAW,

Dr. John Witherspoon, 1723-1794, Presbyterian minister of Paisley who became the first president of the College of New Jersey, later Princeton University. Dr. Witherspoon was responsible for bringing the Hector emigrants to Pictou Harbour. (Courtesy Princeton University Library)

A key to the 18th-century Tolbooth jail at Inverness. The jail is long gone, but the key which the Beauly blacksmith Roderick Mackay brought to Pictou on the Hector, *after making his escape, lies in the Public Archives of Nova Scotia.* (Courtesy PANS)

It was in clearings and cabins such as these that the people of the Hector *began their new lives in the virgin forest above Pictou Harbour.* ("A First Settlement," drawn by W. H. Bartlett; Courtesy Public Archives Canada C2401)

Pioneer homestead on Middle River where Alexander Fraser, the first to sign up for the Hector *voyage, built a new life. (Watercolour by J. E. Woolford, 1817; Courtesy Nova Scotia Museum)*

The town of Pictou in 1817, 30 years after its founder, John Patterson, purchased the land and began laying out his lots. Beyond the point of land at the right-hand side lies the place where the Hector *people landed, and across the water Alexander Cameron's Loch Broom farm and the mouth of West River. (Watercolour by J. E. Woolford, 1817; Courtesy Nova Scotia Museum)*

A Scottish farm on West River Narrows, four and a half miles above Pictou, 1817. It was here, on January 1 of that year, that the Rev. Duncan Ross founded the first agricultural society in rural Nova Scotia. The society imported seed grain, agricultural implements and Ayrshire cattle. On the flyleaf of their first minute book some unknown poet penned the lines: "Let this be held the farmers' creed/For stock seek out the choicest breed/In peace and plenty let them feed . . ." (Watercolour by J. E. Woolford; Courtesy Nova Scotia Museum)

A view of Pictou town in 1840 from the Hill on which Joseph Howe had stood a few years before to "seek a more expansive view of wood and wave, and try to form some definite notion of the general outline." He saw Mortimer's Point in the middle distance and "the beautiful tongue of land which stretches out into the Harbour." By 1840 the population of the town was about 2,000. (Litho by William Eager; Courtesy Public Archives of Nova Scotia)

Pictou County farm land, looking northwestward from Green Hill, which lies above Loch Broom between the Middle and West rivers. When this land was thickly forested, the first settler below Green Hill was the Hector *passenger Kenneth Fraser.* (Courtesy Nova Scotia government)

those who had thrown their bread away were glad to get it back.

Two weeks passed and they were into September, blue skies and blue seas and the sweet smell of spruce and fir blowing from the land on the west wind. Some time early in the month the *Hector* entered the Gulf of St. Lawrence and Northumberland Strait and, finally, crept past Pictou's sand-bar and into the wide and beautiful harbour. Tradition has it that the day was bright with autumn sunshine. The date was September 15. None among them left any record of how they felt as they lined the rails to stare at a shore which must have seemed as wild to them as Africa. Sailing cautiously up the wide harbour toward the point that lay near the entrance to West River, Captain Speirs anchored off what was to become known on the maps as Brown Point—or Brown's Point—named for the farmer John Brown who settled there. Before they got to Brown Point they would have seen in a little clearing Robert Patterson's new frame-house, the only one of its kind in the community. Just opposite them now was Dr. Harris' log cabin. Here and there in the bight of land which curved into West River they might have seen the scattered homes of John Rogers, James McCabe and a dozen other settlers, some of whom they could see hurrying toward them through the trees. "In honour of the occasion," wrote Dr. Patterson, "the young men arrayed themselves in their kilts, with *skein dhu*, and some with broadswords. As she dropped anchor the piper blew his pipes to their utmost power; its thrilling sounds then first startling the echoes among the silent solitudes of our forest."

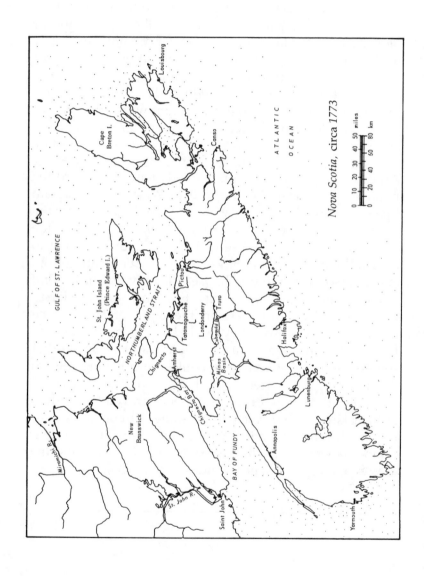

Nova Scotia, circa 1773

PART TWO

Nova Scotia

CHAPTER SEVEN

The Great Land Grab

*Lets away to New Scotland, where Plenty sits
    Queen,
O'er as happy a country as ever was seen,
And blessed her subjects, both little and great,
With each a good house and a pretty Estate.*

"NOVA SCOTIA, A NEW BALLAD,"
THE GENTLEMAN'S MAGAZINE, LONDON, FEB. 1750.

For a century and a half after Sir William Alexander had given his still-born Scottish colony a name, Nova Scotia was anything but Scottish. For two-thirds of that time it was under French control and after the British claimed it for good in 1713, under the Peace of Utrecht, it remained Acadian in population for another generation. The name bestowed so hopefully by the Scots had never quite died, however, and for want of a better one the English revived it, rejecting suggestions to use the simple English translation. But even when the majority of Acadians were expelled in 1755, the province remained Scottish in little more than name for generations. It was, if anything, an offshoot of New England, a fourteenth colony. Before the arrival of the *Hector*, the first Scottish emigrant ship to reach Nova Scotia since the early 1600s, the Scottish population numbered 173, most of them in Halifax where, in 1768, they formed a small chapter of the North British Society.

In England, government agents had stirred some interest in Nova Scotia when Lord Halifax founded his naval base at Chebuctou in 1749, peopled it with 2,000 English and a few Irish, Scots and Welsh and moved the provincial capital from Annapolis on the Bay of Fundy to the newly named Halifax. Next year the *Gentleman's Magazine* in London ran verses which sounded like a land agent's advertisement:

> *There's wood and there's water, there's wild*
> *   fowl and tame,*
> *In the forest good ven'son, good fish in the*
> *   stream,*
> *Good grass for our cattle, good land for our*
> *   plough*
>
> *Good wheat to be raised and good barley to sow.*
> *No landlords are there the poor tenant to tease,*
> *No lawyers to bully, no Bailiff to seize.*
>
> *But each honest fellow's a landlord, and dares*
> *To spend on himself the whole fruit of his cares.*
>
> *They've no duties on candles, no taxes on malt,*
> *Nor do they, as we do, pay sauce for our salt,*
> *But all is as free as in those days of old,*
>
> *When poets assure us the age was of gold.*

But apart from 1,000 Yorkshiremen who were to settle in Cumberland County in the north of the province in the early 1770s, English yeomen showed little interest and the Crown agents turned to the Continent "to all those German Protestants and other Foreigners, who shall desire to settle in said Province and are willing to become British subjects." They offered land rent-free for ten years and maintenance for a year after arrival. Almost 1,500 Germans as well as French and Swiss Huguenots came in the mid-1750s and settled south of Halifax at Lunenburg Bay, which they named after Lüneburg in Hanover. Some of the French-speaking Huguenots moved in 1771 to territory west of Pictou Harbour—to Tatamagouche and River John. About the same time as the Germans arrived, several hundred New Englanders came to Halifax, but apart from there and a few other toe-holds, Nova Scotia remained predominately Acadian.

For generations the French had built their farms, with cunning systems of dykes and drainage, beside the tidal Bay of Fundy, at Minas Basin and Chignecto Bay. They pushed up rivers to cultivate the marshes and clear and plant the southern exposures of the gentle uplands until there were nearly 10,000 "neutral Acadians," as they called themselves, living off what now was British land.

"The inhabitants of Acadia," wrote one of them, "are very industrious and resourceful in all things, necessity having compelled them to become so. They themselves make everything that is required in their homes . . . They are weavers, masons, carpenters, joiners, tool-makers; they make vessels for sailing along the coasts . . . " Above all they were masters of the art of dykeland drainage, learned by their fathers on the coasts of Europe and passed down to them, wherein they harnessed nature to their farming without the toil of cutting trees, pulling roots and hauling rocks.

The fame of their successful farmlands had spread to New England, and it was to New England that Governor

Charles Lawrence turned when the collapse of French power, first at Louisbourg and then at Quebec, made it safe to populate with English the marshes he had emptied of 8,000 Acadians by his act of expulsion. Although the Acadians had been peaceful enough, they had repeatedly refused to take an oath of allegiance to the British Crown. Suffering great hardship, the Acadians were rooted up and shipped away, most of them to the southern colonies where many ended up in Louisiana. Some fled into the woods, including those who had settled on the rich lands of Cobequid at the head of the bay where Truro now stands. Their homes were burned, their dykes left to the mercy of the autumn storms.

Thus, apart from Halifax, a few settlements such as Lunenburg, Canso, and the English forts at Annapolis and Chignecto in Cumberland County and the original bands of Micmacs, Nova Scotia in the late 1750s was a ghostly, empty place. In the latter part of 1758, Governor Lawrence inserted a seductive advertisement in the Boston *Gazette* inviting those New Englanders who found their own grants too cramped and rocky to come north to the ready-made farms seized from the Acadians and which he called, somewhat euphemistically, "the vacant lands."

Extolling the virtues of "100,000 acres of intervale farmlands," Lawrence said they had been planted for more than a century to wheat, oats, rye, barley, hemp and flax "and never fail for crops or need manuring." He also offered 100,000 acres of wooded upland above the marshes, "cleared and stocked with English grass [sweet hay], planted with orchards, gardens, etc." His description, although exaggerated, was apt enough as New Englanders knew well from the tales brought back by fishermen, traders and soldiers who had manned the forts at Annapolis and Chignecto or fought. Lawrence assured the New Englanders they would enjoy the same religious freedom as they had become used to in New England

and could govern themselves in local matters. Those New Englanders who had settled at Halifax ten years earlier had already seen to it that the province had a legislature with elected members.

Lawrence promised that each settler could expect an equitable division of arable, pasture and woodland, and although a quit rent of one shilling would be charged by the government on every 50 acres, this need not be paid for ten years. Initially, grants would be limited to 1,000 acres per household, with one-third of each grant to be cleared, planted or otherwise improved every ten years. Although the best land was on the Bay of Fundy and its offshoots, the offer also applied to other parts of Nova Scotia which had been divided into five counties: Annapolis, Cumberland, Halifax, Lunenburg and Kings. Nine "agricultural" townships were surveyed, each 12 miles square or about 100,000 acres, and there were also four "fishing" townships on the province's south shore.

Halifax, by now, had almost 1,000 New Englanders interlarded with the original English population and Governor Lawrence set out to attract another 2,500 New England families to settle in other parts of the province, particularly on the old Acadian lands. The New Englanders were willing. Those who were feeling cramped had been unable to push west because of the Indian wars and had been eyeing Nova Scotia for years; their response to the Governor was swift. "Very extensive tracts of vacated lands have been granted to industrious and substantial farmers," Lawrence reported to the House of Assembly in Halifax in August 1759. "Applications for more are crowding in upon me faster than I can prepare the grants."

Starting in the spring of 1760, hundreds of families came to settle beside the red tide-flats of Minas Basin, at Cornwallis and Horton Townships, at Falmouth on the Avon River or on the marshes at the head of the Cobequid and Chignecto bays. On the south shore, where townships had been laid out here and there on coves stretching from Chester around to Yarmouth, fishermen arrived from Nantucket, Cape Cod and Plymouth. From Boston and, particularly, Londonderry in New Hampshire were soon to come the first of those Scotch-Irish Ulstermen who were to make a mark on Truro, Onslow and Londonderry townships at the head of Cobequid Bay and on the later settlement at Pictou Harbour. All told, 500 families settled in Nova Scotia that year.

The following spring, Administrator Belcher in Halifax was to write: "The Inhabitants of the new Settlements are in general contented with their situation and, as the Winter has been moderate, more are coming early in the summer. They have built houses sufficient for their covering and have suffered no inconvenience on that account, nor have we lost by sickness among the new settlers above five or six persons. The greatest difficulty has been on account of provisions, for tho' we had agreed and have supplied them with provisions for a fourth part of the people, the others would have suffered had not Government allowed them a Transport to fetch provisions, by means of which they have imported at their own cost about 1,200 barrels from Connecticut." The total number of settlers from New England soon reached 2,000.

Unfortunately for the stability of the settlement, the land boom which developed was not confined to those anxious to work the land. Merchants in Boston, New York, New Jersey and Philadelphia, dreaming of profits from the commercial colonizing of great tracts of land secured at small expense, began to form land companies. They attracted men of substance such as Benjamin Franklin of Philadelphia and Dr. John Witherspoon, President of the College of New Jersey in Princeton, and also, inevitably, a cavalcade of colourful, if dubious, speculators such as Colonel Alexander McNutt. Since McNutt had such inordinate influence on the colonizing of Nova Scotia in the 1760s and 1770s and was regarded as a villain in the trials and tribulations of the *Hector* settlers, it is useful here to peer through the web of exaggeration, contradiction, hopes and failures of this spirited and, possibly, over-maligned land promoter to see what he was up to.

A Virginian, born of Scotch-Irish parents whose roots had lain in Galloway, Scotland, McNutt migrated from Londonderry, Ulster, in his youth and consummated his first land deal in his early twenties. By the time he was in his thirties he was working for Thomas Hancock who, as well as being uncle of the John Hancock who signed the Declaration of Independence, was Nova Scotia's agent in Boston. Not content with securing settlers on someone else's behalf, McNutt turned up in Halifax the summer of 1759 to hobnob with Governor Lawrence, whose sanguine temperament he shared. Since McNutt's stories were exaggerated, a better source of his early activities is a government paper which described them a few years later: "Colonel McNutt arrived at Halifax and applied to Governor Lawrence for Grants of Land for Himself and sundry persons, His Associates, and obtained a reserve of a large tract of Land for that purpose, which appears by a written engagement of Governor Lawrence's to have been one Township of Port Roseway [where Shelburne now stands on the south shore] and six Townships of the District of Cobequid, and on the Shubennaccada [Shubenacadie] River, with leave to settle Families on thirty-five rights (17,500 acres) on the Township of Granville [on Annapolis Basin]. In consequence in the Spring following he produced a List of Six Hundred subscribers, being persons of the Colonies who had engaged with Him to settle those Lands, but of those Six Hundred Subscribers, Fifty Families, only, came into the Province who were transported Thither at the expense of Government, had Lands assigned them in the Township of Truro and were supported there two years, with an additional expense to Government of building Forts and Barracks for their security. Troops were sent for their Protection and lately [1766] five hundred pounds of the Provincial Funds were expended for opening Roads of Communication from Halifax to those Settlements." These subscribers were McNutt's fellow Ulstermen from Boston and New Hampshire and included his brother, William, who settled in Onslow near Truro and designed the first Presbyterian church there.

Thus McNutt began a career of promising more than he could deliver. He was nothing if not bold. Although he had never advanced beyond the rank of captain in the Massachusetts militia, he claimed an honorary colonelcy from King George II and sported a dress sword he insisted the King had given him. Since King George II had died a year before McNutt made his first recorded visit to London, this may have been a figure of speech. He delighted in wearing court dress of gold lace, silver buckles, top boots and cocked hat atop a powdered wig.

In London he awed the Board of Trade with his grand schemes which included a request for a charter to "erect a City by the Name of Jerusalem" on the south shore of Nova Scotia where Shelburne now stands, across from the island where he once lived and which bears his name. With the help of Arthur Vance and William Caldwell who owned a shipping firm in McNutt's birthplace of Londonderry, Ulster, he offered to transport, mostly at his own expense, a then unheard of number of 8,000 Ulstermen to Nova Scotia, a population that would exactly compensate for the Acadians Governor Lawrence had evicted. In return, McNutt asked for 100 acres for himself for every 500 settled by the colonists. Since this was still several generations before the potato famine, the government rejected McNutt's offer on grounds that such an exodus would lead to depopulation of northern Ireland. But before the rejection he did have time to organize two shiploads, some 400 souls, whom he settled alongside the Scotch-Irish from New England in the townships of

Truro and Onslow, or out along the Minas basin at his township of Londonderry. These colonies, largely founded by McNutt or with his help, had been suffering such hardship and food shortage that in the spring of 1762 Lawrence's successor, Governor Jonathan Belcher, recommended to the House of Assembly that seed grain be sent to Truro and Onslow. He had become wary of McNutt's methods and had at first been less than helpful in settling the people McNutt had brought over from Ulster. He sent his Provincial Surveyor, Charles Morris, a New Englander, to report on the settlements and Morris' report, dated 1764, indicated that Truro and Londonderry were making progress but Onslow was still in sad condition:

"Onslow has about 50 familes," he wrote. "These are the most Indigent as well as the most Indolent people in the colony. Several families suffered severely last winter and some were famished. If they are not relieved this winter there will be a great danger of their starving or quitting the colony. They have but a small portion of stock, compared with the other Inhabitants of the Province, and there are very few people of any substance among them.

"Truro has about sixty families. These are Irish Protestants, mostly from New England, a very industrious set of people; have large stocks and tho' they have been settled but two years, will this year raise grain sufficient for their support, except a very few families. None of these settlers have as yet any grants of their land. About fifteen settlers, Protestants from Ireland, are settled on the north side of Cobequid Basin. These are industrious and doing extremely well considering they had neither money nor stock. Some little assistance they will want from Government. Justices have been appointed and Militia settled in these Townships." It was to be 1765 before the people on the Truro Township, 70 householders, received their grants for a total of 80,000 acres.

In the meantime, McNutt had gone to London to busy himself with new schemes. Having made an enemy of Governor Belcher he wanted to complain in person to the Lords of Trade about how Belcher had thwarted his efforts. All he wanted, said this man who sought to build a New Jerusalem on Nova Scotia's south shore, was that "every one might make their own way to Happiness, and that no person whatsoever of bad morals or guilty of any enormous Irregularity may ever be permitted to mar any office or power amongst the People."

His mood could hardly have been lightened when his partner in Philadelphia, John Hughes, wrote that businessmen whom McNutt and Hughes had encouraged to seek settlers for Nova Scotia were threatening to sue Hughes for breach of contract. Berating McNutt for going "home to Britain" at such a time, Hughes informed him that "several persons of Merit and fortune undertook at my Instance to engage Settlers for the Colony of Nova Scotia and have on the Strength of my Engagements and Letters procured Great Numbers to put themselves in a Posture for Removing this Spring and many are now and have been some time past on Expences to their Great Disappointment and Damages So that Some of them are determined to go Elsewhere. . . . But all threaten to Arrest me, and Some I believe will, and I make no Doubt will Recover Considerable Damages as many put themselves out of Business in the way of their Trades, and many others Sold or Gave up their little farms, being freely persuaded of the truth of our Information."

After learning that the difficult Governor Belcher had been replaced by Montague Wilmot who, in 1764, was planning to distribute great empty tracts of Nova Scotia's 10 million acres—mostly forest land—to speculators, McNutt prepared to corner the major share of the land.

Of the 16 companies bidding for the 16 available townships the next year, McNutt's name was associated with all of them. Some of the companies he had formed himself, but for others, such as the company of Benjamin Franklin, he seems to have acted merely as an agent. A letter from Philadelphia dated January 1, 1765, finds him promising Franklin "that I will use by Best Endeavors to have four Townships allotted in the Province of Nova Scotia." At that time a township consisted of about 100,000 acres or 12 square miles. One of the companies consisted of McNutt and his old business partners in Londonderry, Ulster, and McNutt appears not to have been bothered at all by such things as conflict of interest, for he informed the Nova Scotia government "that he did engage with several persons in Ireland, Pennsylvania, Virginia and other parts of His Majesty's dominions to provide land in this Province on the terms contained in his proposals, for the settlement of as many families as they could furnish."

Arriving in Halifax that spring, McNutt made a favourable impression on the open-handed new governor, who wrote to the Lords of Trade in London of "the late arrival of several persons from Pennsylvania, New Jersey and some of the Neighbouring colonies . . . in behalf of several Associations of Commercial people and others in good circumstances to view the country and examine the advantages the settlement and cultivation of it may produce. . . .

"Among the persons who have arrived here is Mr. Alex'r McNutt, who has frequently attended at your Lordships' board. His applications are of a very considerable degree and extent and he produces many letters from the Associations I have before mentioned, soliciting him in the most pressing manner to procure for them Tracts of Land for which they apply, and on such conditions as he had obtained at your Lordship's Board the 27th February, 1761, which conditions first induced the people in the distant colonies to form the design of making settlements here, and are the only terms on which they will accept the lands.

McNutt had lost no time in convincing the governor of

his indispensability. Governor Wilmot assured their Lordships that the settlers McNutt had landed in the past had been "of great utility and have qualifications as frugal and industrious people much above the generality of others." However, McNutt was demanding the same sort of terms he had solicited in London in February 1761. He took exception to the condition that his settlers would be obliged to clear a third of his land every 10 years not only because of the difficulty of doing so, but also because most settlers wanted to retain some wood and not denude their lands. He was also demanding 100 acres for every 500 given out to the settlers he procured. There was a long list of such conditions which were beyond the governor's mandate and he asked London for instructions. Not a man to waste time, McNutt proceeded to scout out the land.

There were other agents in Nova Scotia that hectic summer, but as "Mad Anthony" Wayne wrote at the time, McNutt had managed to convince Wilmot that he was "the only man that is capable of Complying with the terms of settlement, and Has done his Endeavours to make the Other Companies insignificant and not Equal to the Undertaking." In the spring McNutt was off in a schooner surveying the best of the townships. With him went Wayne, who was then 20 years old, a surveyor in the pay of Benjamin Franklin. It was later, as a brigadier in Washington's army in the revolutionary war, that his impetuosity won him the nickname "Mad Anthony."

The third passenger, the Reverend James Lyon, represented another of McNutt's many clients, the Philadelphia Company, which had appropriated that title although eight others also came from Philadelphia. "Parson Lyon," as Wayne called him, a graduate of New Jersey College, had renounced a budding career as a psalmodist in Philadelphia to become a Presbyterian missionary at Truro and Onslow. He was a founding member of the Philadelphia Company which, unlike the speculators who wanted land on the Bay of Fundy, sought territory east of Truro.

McNutt was interested in that region too, on his own behalf rather than the company's.

Throughout that summer of manoeuvre, argument and delay, Wilmot received no instructions from London as the 16 companies represented by McNutt pressed for better terms. On October 7 Wayne reported so much squabbling that there was "a Sort of a mess between the Councell and us and things Don't go as fast as I could wish." In the last week of October a compromise was reached. The companies accepted what concessions Wilmot was prepared to give, in return for agreement that if McNutt could wring better terms from the government in London, these should supersede Wilmot's terms. In a period of two weeks Wilmot signed away 2,540,000 acres in what has been described as a "veritable carnival of land-grabbing" and a "golden age of land piracy."

Beamish Murdoch, the 19th-century Nova Scotia historian, wrote, "Reflecting on the very large land grants sanctioned by Colonel Wilmot and his Council, I cannot help thinking it was an ugly year and the growth of the province was long retarded by the rashness of giving forest lands away from the power of the crown or the people in such large masses."

Almost half the granted land had gone to McNutt and his associates in empty townships stretching from the south shore of Nova Scotia to Pictou Harbour on the northeast shore, and deep into what is now New Brunswick. Within 40 years these companies lost all but 1,000 acres to the government because of their failure to meet the terms of settlement. Among those receiving land was Colonel F. W. W. Des Barres, a government surveyor, who claimed 20,000 acres west of Pictou Harbour, at Tatamagouche, where he settled a few of the French-Protestant Huguenots who had first gone to Lunenburg with the Germans but then moved on. They included deserving settlers such as the people at Truro who finally got title to the land they had been working for several years. Among them was young William Davidson of Aberdeenshire, Scotland, who to his surprise received a township of 100,000 acres at the mouth of the Miramichi River. He had been seeking only enough land to build a salmon fishing station, but the government would not divide the township and he got it all. He imported a few settlers from northern Scotland and some from New England.

Most of the grants, however, went to men of influence in the southern 13 colonies or in Britain—politicians, military officers, governors, such as John Wentworth of New Hampshire, and merchants, who sought to turn a profit from land which cost them a quarter of a penny an acre in those few cases where the government ever got around to collecting it. They could thank McNutt and his lobbying at the Board of Trade in London for such easy terms, but even McNutt could never get rid of the stipulations that the grantee had to clear and colonize the land within a set number of years. Where, for example, a grant totalled 200,000 acres the owners had to settle 250 people on it the first year and a like number every year for four years. McNutt spent so much time fighting those conditions he seems to have had no time to colonize the lands he won for himself that summer and in fact lost most of them for that same reason four years later. In a letter in April 1766 he accused Governor Wilmot and his Council of "sinister and selfish" views, of obstructing his plans and being partial to people in official positions in the allotment of the grants. In reply, Wilmot insisted "that the obstruction Colonel McNutt complained of from the Rulers of the Province since the death of Governor Lawrence had proceeded from his own intemperate zeal and exorbitant demands upon the Government, obstinately insisting from time to time upon terms of settlement that the Government were by His Majesty's Instructions unable to grant. In all other respects he had had that indulgence and kind treatment that any reasonable man could desire, not on account of his knowledge or ability but from a hope the

Government had that his zeal and application to make Settlements in the Province might be a means of inducing men of much more knowledge and ability than himself to become inhabitants in it.''

Despite his allegations of harsh treatment, McNutt had received grants under terms more favourable than those accorded others. The grants he received for himself were the choicest, as the Philadelphia Company partners learned to their chagrin when they ran their own surveys on the land they had been granted east of Truro township. For all its imposing size of 200,000 acres, their grant was largely worthless—trackless forest with no access to the harbour. Although they seemed to have had an idea, assuming they thought about it at all, that their grant bordered on Pictou Harbour, as originally allotted it fell considerably short of the harbour and the shoreline they so badly needed. The Pictou Harbour lands, they discovered, had already been allotted to others—the southeastern side to a Major John Fisher, the near or northwestern shore to none other than McNutt and his Ulster partners, 100,000 acres embracing the fine hardwood land on the northwest shore of the harbour and running far up the rivers at the harbour head. It was called the Irish Grant.

When, on top of this disappointment, the ingenious members of the Philadelphia Company found that their grant fell far short of the promised 200,000 acres, they complained to the government who agreed to let them make up the deficiency with ''liberty to choose the aforesaid quantity between Tatamagouche and Pictou.'' This they did, but all they were able to obtain of the harbour shore was four or five miles of alder swamp between Brown Point and the mouth of West River. McNutt kept the rest until the government forced him to give it up four years later for non-compliance with the terms of the grant, and it was four years after that before the government freed the land for bids from others. There were those who complained that McNutt was less than honest with the

Philadelphia Company, one of his associates, but the Company itself chose to look upon the matter as an honest error and let it go at that. There can be no doubt, however, that the Philadelphia Company's failure to gain proper harbour frontage set back the cause of settlement at Pictou Harbour for many years and severely hurt the people who arrived on the *Hector* in 1773.

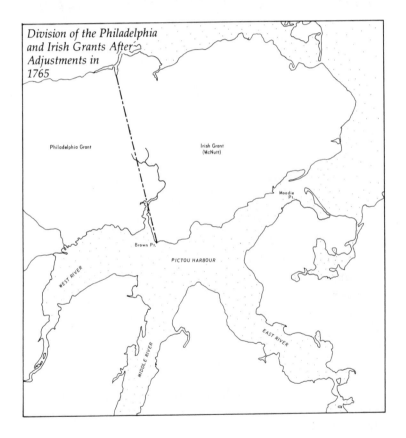

Division of the Philadelphia and Irish Grants After Adjustments in 1765

CHAPTER EIGHT

The Philadelphia Plantation

*. . . A pretty considerable share of Yankee blood
in them too, I tell you . . . and the breed is
tolerable pure yet, near about one half
applesauce, and tother half molasses, all except
to the Eastward where there is a cross of the
Scotch.*

SAM SLICK, THOMAS CHANDLER HALIBURTON

By the time the Philadelphia Company had redrawn the
boundaries of its grant to embrace a few miles of Pictou
Harbour, there was not enough time in 1766 to settle
anyone, let alone the required 250. In a letter to the government, the company complained of "very great disappointment on finding that a considerable part of the har-

bour of Pictou, *by some mistake in the survey,* was not granted to them as they expected, all of which, with many obstructions from the scarcity of money and the stagnation of trade . . . rendered them incapable of making any settlement this year, as intended." The company also complained that a man with the unlikely name of "Mr. Anthill" was frightening off potential colonists by telling them the grant was "rocky, barren and unfit for improvement." The government allowed an extension until June of 1767 to bring settlers to their land.

On January 26 of the same year, the following notice was posted at the London Coffee House in Philadelphia, wherein the Company made the best of "many difficulties":

"Whereas a grant has been obtained for a Tract of Land, situate upon Pictou Harbour and the Coast adjoining on the Gulph of St. Lawrence, in the Province of Nova Scotia, extending about Twenty Miles along the Coast, within Sixty or Seventy Miles of Halifax, the Metropolis of said Province and adjoining the Townships of Truro, Onslow and Londonderry, an improved part of the Country and from whence may be had cattle and Provisions of every kind at a moderate price. The Grantees have been at the Pains and Expense of sending three of their Partners, with sundry other persons, to view the said Land, and they have reported to the Company that the soil is fertile, intermingled with large quantities of Intervale or Low Bottoms, very rich and capable of being cultivated and improved with all kinds of Grains and Pasturage, and well Timbered with Black Birch, Maple Sugar Trees, Ash, etc. The said Harbour being one of the best on the Coast having sufficient Water for Shipping of any Burthen lying convenient to the Cod and Whale Fishing, and well floored with Oysters, Clams, and a variety of fish, especially Salmon and Rock Fish, and plenty of wild fowl.

"These are, therefore, to inform all sober industrious

persons that are desirous of becoming Settlers in that fine country that the Owners of said Land will dispose of it upon the following Terms, viz: To every Family consisting of Five Protestant Persons, Five Hundred Acres, and so on in proportion for a greater or lesser number in each family, at the rate of Five Pounds sterling for every Hundred Acres payable two years after their Arrival, and a yearly Quit-Rent of One Half-penny Sterling per Acre. They being obliged to Embark for the said Settlement by the Fifteenth Day of April next, and the Settlers shall have free liberty to make Choice of any part of the said Land, except such as is reserved upon Pictou Harbour for a town, in which the Head of each Family shall have an Half Acre Lot given them. All persons desirous of becoming Settlers may apply to George Bryan and Andrew Hodge in Philadelphia or Thomas Harris near Deer Creek in Baltimore County, Maryland, and be further informed and enter into Articles, and for their further Encouragement, two of the Company proposes going with them, to assist in making the Settlement, and will accommodate them with a proper vessel to remove thither, upon reasonable terms."

Unlike most of the land companies, the Philadelphia Company was making a determined effort to colonize. The Company consisted of 14 partners—judges, lawyers, merchants—men who had turned William Penn's "greene countrie towne" on the Delaware into the leading city of Britain's colonial empire. They included the Rev. James Lyon, who would soon move to Pictou Harbour; Edmund Crawley, who claimed 20,000 acres or one-tenth of the Philadelphia Grant for himself; the Rhea brothers, John and David, who dealt in drygoods; the Wykoff brothers, John and Isaac who dealt in real estate and slaves; Richard Stockton, graduate of New Jersey College at Princeton, lawyer, judge and, later, signer of the Declaration of Independence; George Bryan, lawyer and, later, Supreme Court Judge; William Symonds; Jonathan Smith, another New Jersey College graduate; Andrew Hodge from Ulster, who was an importer and leading citizen; and his son-in-law Col. John Bayard. There was Captain Thomas Harris, a Scotch-Irish Ulsterman who had been a farmer, inn-keeper and Indian trader before settling in Maryland to deal in land. His son Robert, another Princeton graduate, was the fourteenth partner. They were all upstanding, influential men, but Nova Scotia was nearly 1,000 miles away, almost a month by ship, and few people came forward to answer their advertisement. Three months later a second notice appeared, this time in the *Pennsylvania Chronicle* of April 25:

"The Owners of the Land at Pictou, in Nova Scotia, having hired the Brigantine *Betsey*, John Hull Master, being a double decked Vessel, almost new, and very well accommodated to carry Passengers, hereby give notice to such Persons as are minded to accept of their Proposals and settle said Tract, that the Brigantine will take them on board at Philadelphia any Day next week, and at Reedy Island on Monday and Tuesday the 4th and 5th of May; and then proceed on the Voyage without Delay. For further information apply to Andrew Hodge and George Bryan, in Philadelphia, and to such of the concerned as shall attend at Reedy Island, N.B. Passengers for Halifax will be carried at the most moderate Rates."

Late in April the *Betsey* sailed up the Delaware from her home port of Rhode Island. As a brigantine, she was rigged like a brig except that her mainsail was fixed fore and aft rather than square, so as to handle easier in the coastal trade. That she was small, less than 100 tons, mattered little since the Company had been able to attract hardly 40 settlers—only six families.

Accompanying them was the Company's agent and legal representative, Dr. John Harris, 28, the son of Captain Thomas and a graduate of medical school. With him was his wife Eliza, eight months pregnant.

Robert Patterson came, a native of Renfrew, Scotland, a bearded, stocky man of wide experience who had settled in Maryland near the Pennsylvania border to work as a surveyor after a career as a British army sutler. He was to become the Company's surveyor. With Patterson and his wife were their five children, the eldest nine, the youngest three months, and a few possessions which included an eight-day clock.

James McCabe was a Belfast man of Scotch-Irish descent. Although he was a Roman Catholic, he had obtained a place by taking it in the name of his Protestant wife Anne. They had six children.

John Rogers, a native of Glasgow who had lived in Maryland, came with his wife and four children.

Also sailing were Henry Cumminger, who brought his wife and "four or five" children, and a sixth family who moved from Pictou Harbour so soon after arrival that nothing is known about them, not even their names. The settlers brought three servants, two of them black slaves and one a convict who, according to the custom, was working off his sentence in the employ of Robert Patterson. Those were all the Company was able to attract.

The *Betsey* loaded staples to last the settlers a year or more, took on a deck cargo of 3,000 feet of sawn pine lumber for Halifax and, during the first week of May, she started on her journey. Within three weeks she arrived at Halifax where her skipper, who seems to have had an inaccurate notion of where Pictou Harbour lay, picked up sailing directions. Even then he somehow missed his bearings and was well on his way toward Newfoundland when a fortunate encounter with a Captain Owen on a southbound coaster put him right.

Wild, remote, unsettled from Canso around to Bay Verte on the Isthmus of Chignecto, the northeast coast of Nova Scotia was so little known, even in Halifax, that a few years earlier the Provincial Surveyor himself seemed unaware there was such a thing as a fine harbour at Pictou. "From Tatamagouche to the Gut of Canso," he wrote, "there is no harbour, but a good road [anchorage] under the Isle of Poitee [Pictou Island]. No inhabitants ever settled in this part of the country, and consequently no kind of improvement."

A century earlier the French explorer Nicholas Denys had reported that "the coast is nothing but a rugged mass, with the exception of several openings of different dimensions. The land round is low, it appears fertile, and is covered with fine trees . . . there is so great an abundance of all kinds of game that it is surprising, and if the game there is abundant the earth is not less beneficent." Perhaps because he was writing from memory in old age, Denys failed to mention the sand-bar at the mouth of what he called "Pictou River," which he said "begins right at the entrance and can be sailed seven to eight leagues within, after which you meet with a small island covered with wood; farther than that you cannot proceed without canoes." He found oysters "larger than a shoe and nearly the same shape, and they are fat and of good taste."

Ninety-six years after Denys had written those words, the *Betsey* poked her prow around the sand-bar and into one of the loveliest harbours her passengers had ever seen, a mile wide and bordered with trees—as Denys had described—"every kind of wood, oaks, maples, cedars, firs and pines." According to his Philadelphia instructions, the captain was to sail several miles up the harbour to Brown Point far ahead off the starboard bow. To the north lay the high land, thick forests of pine and hardwoods, in the Irish grant owned by Colonel McNutt; on the farther shore, equally empty, lay the grant claimed by Major Fisher. Under reduced sail, the leadsman at the bow tested the depth with his line and *Betsey* ghosted up the harbour into the twilight; rounding the point they realized they were not alone. Bonfires had flared on the shore. Dark figures crossed in front of the flames and they heard distant voices; fear of Indians caused the captain to sheer off to find a safer place to await the dawn. As the *Betsey* drifted in the dark, Dr. Harris and the women helped Eliza Harris in the birth of the colony's first child, a boy christened Thomas.

Looking through the captain's telescope at dawn, they saw the men waving from Brown Point were not Indians but half a dozen men dressed in the homespun of New England settlers, a welcoming party sent from the people of Truro who had heard of the *Betsey*'s arrival in Halifax. The bonfires had been an effort to guide the *Betsey* to safe anchorage. Among the young men who had hastened 40 miles through the woods were Matthew Archibald, John Oughterson, Thomas Troop and Ephraim Howard—New Hampshire-bred woodsmen unafraid of Indians or wilderness.

Supplies were ferried ashore and stacked among the alders, cooking fires lit and water fetched from the stream later known as Haliburton Brook. As they lay down to sleep beneath the trees that night, the settlers drew comfort from the shadow of the *Betsey* lying close offshore; but in the morning the *Betsey* was gone, with no goodbyes, slipping out of the harbour more silently than she had come. The captain was under orders to leave swiftly in case the settlers, dismayed by the immensity of the wilderness and the task before them, felt the urge to leave with her.

"Picture the loneliness of the little band," wrote Rev. George Patterson, "and [we] need not wonder that their hearts sank within them at the prospect of the toils and dangers before them." For here they found none of the rich, cleared land the New Englanders had laid claim to on the open marshes of the Bay of Fundy. "The more bitter, therefore, was their disappointment at the dreary prospect before them. After they landed, Mrs. [Robert] Patterson used to tell that she leaned her head against a tree, which stood for many a year after, and thought if there was a broken-hearted creature on the face of the earth, she was the one. As she looked upon her little ones left shelterless in the cruel wilderness, among savages deemed still more cruel, she could only cling to her husband with the cry, 'Oh, Robert, take me back!' "

As the company had promised, a townsite was surveyed along the shore and allotted by Dr. Harris and Robert Patterson. McCabe, the first to be assigned his half-acre townsite land, cleared it so quickly he was granted a second as an example to the others. McCabe's method was not to waste time chopping down trees, but, with a mattock, to scrape earth away from the roots, cut the roots and leave the tree to topple by itself. Among the roots he planted potatoes, however, since the ground was little more than a duff of decayed leaves, the potatoes harvested that autumn were but a few "weakly sprouts." It was fortunate the settlers had brought staples to keep them through the winter.

For more serious farming on their 500-acre grants, they had to go farther afield. John Rogers, known as a quiet, industrious "good man," chose what he called Rogers Hill several miles away, although, like the rest, he kept his cabin at the townsite for mutual support and security. The orchard on Rogers Hill planted from the seeds he had carried from Maryland still blossomed a century later. That autumn, armed with axes and a small compass, Rogers and the Truro settlers Thomas Archibald and John Oughterson blazed the first trail from Pictou Harbour westward through forest and hills to Truro on Cobequid Bay. Although it was not even a proper path, it was christened grandly "The Cobequid Road." Primitive as it was, the blazed trail symbolized contact with their nearest neighbours. By then some 680 people lived in the Cobequid townships, 300 at Truro, 245 at Onslow and the rest at Londonderry. Otherwise there were no settlers closer than Amherst on the Isthmus of Chignecto to the west and Canso to the east—a sweep of 150 miles along the coast of Northumberland Strait and around to the Atlantic—unless you counted small bands of Indians who began to make their appearance around the Pictou settlement.

There were signs that the French had once been on the coast, that they had established themselves at Tatamagouche and Merigomish and that working parties had camped at Pictou Harbour. On Haliburton Brook above the Philadelphia Company townsite, which later became known as the Town Gut, white pines had been felled with axes and between the stream and Brown Point the *Betsey* settlers found a cache or cellar roofed with rotting logs which they thought was the work of the French. Here and there they found a few rusted European tools, a sword and metal pots, and reasoned that the French had come there to cut the excellent white pine before the fall of Louisbourg had driven them from the coast, leaving their allies the Micmacs to make peace with the British in 1760 as best they could.

The Micmacs, probably less than 1,000, lived along the coast in villages of bark and hide. Some had moved a few miles west from their village at Merigomich to cultivate vegetable plots on the banks of the rivers above the harbour's head. The East River they called "the land of ducks," the Middle River "the straight flowing" and the West River was "clear water." The Miggumac, a branch of the Iroquois nation, were known on that shore as the Pectougwak, or "Pictou People," and many believe that Pictou was their descriptive word for the coal gas bubbles in pools and brooks, particularly around the East River in the coal-rich countryside. There were said to be remnants of Indian habitations by the East River and a burial site— a *Soogunagade*, or "rotting place"—where the river erosion had exposed human bones.

As recently as 1759, eight years before the arrival of the *Betsey*, the Micmacs had been on the warpath, raiding as far as Dartmouth across the harbour from Halifax and westward to Annapolis Royal. Two years after that the Pectougwak had concluded treaties with the British, a peace somewhat soured when the governor retracted his promise to give them their ancestral lands along the Northumberland Strait. The summer before the *Betsey* arrived, the Micmacs were still gathering in conclaves to demand that no white settlements be allowed; the uneasiness of the *Betsey* settlers was understandable. Sometimes when the men were away hunting, a few of the Indians would crowd into a cabin, frightening the women and children and demanding to be fed. But they were more a nuisance than a menace and some, such as young Patlass or Lulan, were helpful, particularly with the hunting. The bearded, square-cut Robert Patterson, a veteran who had begun to emerge as the natural leader of the colony, made friends with them and they also liked James McCabe, for both his easy-going humour and the religion they shared with him and which some had clung to even after the departure of the Roman Catholic French. They helped McCabe stake out his farm back in the bush and showed him the best land on the Philadelphia grant. When they had learned some English they told tales of the wars around the harbour, barely seven years before the *Betsey* people came, with maurauding Abenaki from across the Bay of Fundy, or Mohawks from the St. Lawrence Valley. They recounted how Mohawk raiders had attacked a band of sleeping Micmacs on Cariboo Island, just outside Pictou Harbour, by swimming from the mainland, but drowned when they misjudged the current in the dark. Another tale described how fierce Abenaki in two war canoes had caught some Micmacs fishing by torchlight and slaughtered all but two who had hidden themselves beneath a pile of seaweed. McCabe learned that they had known neither drunkenness nor much ill health, and he became skillful in the use of snowshoes and in locating the best hunting and fishing.

One *Betsey* family, unnerved by the wilderness, left for

Truro; the remaining five, hardly more than 30 people, settled in for the winter. In the spring of 1768 they planted potatoes, wheat and oats and began to acquire farm animals—cows, sheep, horses and oxen which were brought in by schooner. Two families from Truro came to join them and the Rev. James Lyon, feeling that the new settlement he had helped to found needed him more than Truro or Onslow, came to settle for a while near the brook which still bears his name. William Kennedy brought his family over the trail to build the first frame structure, a mill on Sawmill Creek at the head of the harbour. In recognition of this newest of 20 or 30 small settlements dotted about the province, the government in Halifax appointed Dr. John Harris justice of the peace at Pictou Harbour.

On January 28 of that year the Company in Philadelphia, still anxious to discharge its responsibilities under the grant, inserted another advertisement in the *Pennsylvania Chronicle* advising that a number of "good families" had settled in "Philadelphia Township" and any "inclining to become settlers on the said land, will meet with very great encouragement." Although the notice brought few settlers, it did bring Robert McFadden and Barnabas McGee, another Scotch-Irish Ulsterman, married to an English woman, and the next year Dr. Harris was heartened by the arrival of nine families including his elder brother, Matthew, with his wife, their six children and three black slaves—Die Mingo, Abram and Martin. In all, 67 people arrived in 1769, some from Truro, and four births were recorded, including a girl to John and Eliza Harris. There was further excitement with the arrival of James Davidson of Edinburgh, who not only began to farm but opened the first school in a cabin beside Lyons Brook. He gathered children into a Sunday school, one of the first in the British Empire.

There were also some losses. Thirty-six people, men, women and children, had left the colony, and there was one death, probably the wife of George Oughterson. And so the first burial ground was established. The community which Dr. Harris called Donegal, after his ancestral home in Ireland, straggled along the upper harbour from Brown Point to the mouth of West River. In two years it had solid roots, and by the end of 1769 there were 120 inhabitants—eleven families and two single men—and a few black slaves. They had acquired 6 horses, 16 bulls and oxen, 16 cows, 16 calves, 37 sheep and 10 pigs. Their harvest that autumn from the arable among the stumps and roots in the intervales and south-facing hills had produced 64 bushels of wheat, 60 of oats, 7 of rye, 8 of barley, 6 of peas and some flax for linen, as well as a good crop of potatoes which, with game and fish, was their diet. The colony was spreading out; Harris and Patterson got up on better ground by purchasing land from McNutt near Brown Point, where they built cabins and a company storehouse. Compared with McNutt, compelled that year to give his Irish grant back to the government for failure to populate it at all, the Company had not done all that badly. It had managed to bring out enough people to show good intent and keep its grant, but the partners in Philadelphia had by now decided the venture was unlikely to turn a profit.

Potential settlers living in the southern colonies, having learned the Philadelphia Company's land was not part of the famous marshlands of the Acadians, had shown little interest. Since 1768 such settlers had, in fact, shown more interest in the Ohio Valley, Kentucky and Tennessee, which had been closed by the Indian wars but was now re-opened by the Treaty of Fort Stanwix. Even the usually optimistic Benjamin Franklin, who had been granted land in that part of Nova Scotia which later became New Brunswick, was "convinced of the impracticability of exciting settlers to move from the Middle Colonies to settle in that Province, and even those who were prevailed upon to go to Nova Scotia, the greater part have returned with complaints against the severity and length of the winter." Captain Thomas Harris, a founder of the Philadelphia Company, travelling north in his old age to see how his sons were progressing at Pictou Harbour, became so discouraged by what he saw that he begged them to return to Philadelphia, but they had fallen in love with their wilderness lands and he returned to Philadelphia alone. He was the last of the Philadelphia Company founders to take much interest in the distant grant that most of them had never seen. Most were militant revolutionaries and when the War of Independence came they played an active part.

The drift of settlers from the Old Colonies to Nova Scotia had ended. It would resume only when the loyalists moved north after the revolutionary war, a decade later. Thus, in 1772, what was left of the original Philadelphia Land Company turned, almost as an afterthought, to Scotland for the emigrants they needed to hold their Pictou grant. Having heard of the Pictou grant through the New Jersey college graduates and trustees whom he knew, Dr. Witherspoon had joined the Company and brought in his Glasgow business associate, John Pagan. Through the efforts of these two, and particularly Pagan, the *Hector* came to Nova Scotia, rather than to the Old Colonies, and although the venture was not what the Philadelphia Company might have hoped for, the *Hector* expedition opened a new land for Scottish emigrants.

CHAPTER NINE

The Gloomy Forest

Oh, why left I my hame?
Why did I cross the deep?
Oh, why left I the land
Where my forefathers sleep?

THE EMIGRANT'S LAMENT

Wasted by illness and hunger, shaken by the storm, the people of the *Hector*, for all their brave show of salt-stained plaids, broadswords and bagpipes, can only have stirred the pity of the settlers who hurried through the woods to Brown Point to greet them. The ship was long overdue, for the original plans had been based on her arriving in the summer, when it would have still been possible for the newcomers to plant a crop of potatoes. Not only had the *Hector* departed late but the voyage originally expected to take a month or six weeks had taken eleven weeks in all, and ten from Loch Broom. Several of the passengers were still very ill, one or two dying, and one of the first boats ashore carried the body of Hugh Macleod's wife who was buried in the little cemetery.

The "Americans," as the *Betsey* settlers were called—for all they had been born and raised in northern Ireland or Glasgow—tried to help the emigrants with fresh food, sympathy and good advice but their own resources were lean and the harvest they were gathering from among the stumps was barely enough for themselves. "The arrival of such a number swept the place like a torrent of all the provisions it contained and left it nearly destitute," wrote Dr. Patterson. The *Hector* was to bring back supplies to last the winter when she returned from the southern colonies on her voyage back to Greenock, but for now the only food was that which the earlier settlers could spare.

From the start, the Highlanders found great adversity at Pictou Harbour. It was too late to plant any crops. Moreover, they had come expecting farm land—their own acres, at last—which at least *looked* like the arable land they had known in the straths and glens of Loch Broom and Assynt or the plains of The Aird south of Beauly. But here, except for a few stump-ridden patches at Brown Point and a mile or so away over toward Lyons Brook, there was nothing but the unbroken forest, and such a forest none had seen in their own denuded hills. They had been promised accommodation until they could build homes of their own, but again they were disappointed. When they saw the Indians watching them from the shelter of the forest they worried about the safety of their families, unaware that the Micmacs had fled at the sound of the pipes, and were fearful of these men in petticoats whose fierce reputation at Louisbourg had preceded them to Pictou Harbour.

At Brown Point, where the company agents Dr. Harris

and Robert Patterson had put up two or three log houses, including a store for the company's provisions, the Highlanders, helped by the Americans, began to build their own rough shelters. Except for John Ross and the two ex-soldiers who had been in Nova Scotia and Quebec ten years earlier, none had seen a log house or had the slightest idea of how to build one. They had no skill with a woodsman's axe, for their tools at home had been the hoe or the crooked spade, and the seasoned colonists from the south had to teach them how to fell big trees without killing themselves. The hardwood hills behind them were turning red and yellow, the nights sharp and chill, and they were warned to hurry in their work lest winter catch them without shelter. They had hardly started when one day Robert Patterson, the company surveyor, told them of good land he had surveyed for their use and invited them to come out to see it.

As he had done for the people who had come with him on the *Betsey* six years earlier, Patterson had surveyed land for the Highlanders and marked the lots out neatly as A, B, C, etc. The scanty harbour frontage, which had been left to the Philadelphia Company after Colonel McNutt's land grab, had long been occupied, and although McNutt had lost his grant in 1770 for failure to settle it, the choice land to the east toward the mouth of the harbour had been reserved for another speculator, a Lieutenant Richard Williams. To find land for the Highlanders, Patterson had gone back into the hills two or three miles westward toward the Cobequid Mountains—to Scots Hill, Hardwood Hill and Rogers Hill.

Marvelling no doubt at how their stocky, bearded guide found his way through such a jungle, the Highlanders followed him reluctantly through a primeval forest thick with deadfalls, silent with dark and gloomy groves of pine which soared 200 feet to shut out any light. Although the land had potential for seasoned settlers such as Patterson and his companions from

Maryland, for the Scots it was a fresh source of consternation and amazement. This surely was not the land they had been promised in John Pagan's advertisement. Where were the clearings? Where were the paths? They were fearful of getting lost, of wild beasts, of Indians, and had no idea how such a place might be turned into farm land.

"Never," wrote Dr. Patterson, "did there seem to be offered to men such an utter mockery." Seeing their dismay, and thinking it was the soil they did not like, the kindly James McCabe offered to show them choice land farther into the bush. They only looked at him helplessly and those who spoke English begged him to show them back to the harbour. There at least they might keep themselves alive by catching fish.

Nor were the people from the *Hector* alone among Highlanders whose reaction to the forest was one of dread. All their lives they had lived in wide, open vistas and what they had known as "deer forest" had hardly any trees at all. They were superstitious people prone to envisioning such dark places with a host of terrors, and for a generation and more their fear of the woods was a theme which ran through their folklore. Fifty years later the bard John Maclean, who settled up the coast at Barney's River (named for Barnabas McGee from Philadelphia), was to write *A-Choille Ghruamach*, "The Gloomy Forest":

> *Despair besets me in the gloomy wood,*
> *Bereft of joy, my thoughts can find no peace;*
> *This wilderness so hostile to our good,*
> *Has robbed me of all gifts I once possessed.*

The homesick poet-cobbler from Argyllshire eventually recovered and so indeed did the sturdy people from the *Hector*, but only after much bitter want. Now, in the autumn of 1773, considering themselves betrayed, they refused to settle on the uncleared backlands and their relations with their Yankee neighbours began to deteriorate.

Although the original population of the American colony had dwindled since 1770, there were still 16 families along the shore living in log houses 15 feet by 20, most of them between Haliburton Brook and Lyons Brook. The cracks between the logs were stuffed with moss and clay and the only source of heat and the main one of light was the fireplace. James Davidson from Edinburgh was still conducting school six days a week and teaching Sunday school on the seventh. The Rev. James Lyon of the Philadelphia Company had come and gone and the community had no minister. The settlers from Maryland and Pennsylvania were proud of what they had achieved in six years and were disappointed that the newcomers from the old country showed nothing but dismay. What Dr. Patterson delicately called "a jealousy" developed between the two groups. To make matters worse, John Ross had quarrelled with Dr. Harris and Robert Patterson, the two most influential men in the community, and although Ross stayed on as an ordinary settler he resigned his responsibilities leaving the Highlanders without a leader.

About the same time small groups began to drift away to the established communities around Cobequid Bay, walking with their families the 40 miles of blazed trail to Truro, a journey of two days and one night, more if there were children. Truro, 10 years old and thriving, consisted of nearly 150 families, mostly Scotch-Irish from New England or direct from Ulster. Truro had a Presbyterian church and a reputation for kindness and hospitality to strangers. There the Highland men hired themselves out as labourers and the women and children worked as indentured domestic servants, the children serving out their time until they came of age. Some moved to Onslow and others six miles north of Cobequid Bay to Londonderry, which had been settled by the Ulstermen brought out by Colonel McNutt.

William Matheson of Sutherlandshire took his family to Londonderry and did not return until 16 years later, when he settled at Rogers Hill in the very back country the Highlanders had at first refused. He was joined on the old Acadian dyke lands of Londonderry by James Murray and David Urquhart and except for Urquhart's daughter no one returned to Pictou. A few travelled on foot through the woods to Halifax, a naval base and garrison town with the wickedest reputation in the colonies, " . . . with its taverns, theatres, brothels and hard-living military men it was Sodom and Gomorrah as well," wrote a New Englander. "There are 1,000 houses in the town. We have upwards of 100 licenced houses [taverns] and perhaps as many without licence, so the business of one half the town is to sell rum and the other half to drink it." Donald Munro, a *Hector* passenger from Inverness-shire, went to Halifax to find work, married and returned to settle on East River. His grave was the first along the river which was to attract the majority of those *Hector* people who stayed in northern Nova Scotia.

Robert Innes never went back, but took his family to Windsor and then to Minudie in Cumberland County, where 1,000 Englishmen from Yorkshire came to settle. John Sutherland and 19-year-old Angus Mackay also walked the 80 miles to Windsor, described as "a fine township, and contains a deal of cleared land which seems very good." The gentry from Halifax kept country homes there and Governor Campbell, having banned horse racing in Halifax, carved out a race track around Fort Edward hill. Wheat, barley, oats and peas were growing on the marshland seized from the Acadians, there was a yearly fair and future plans for a market. Kenneth Fraser apparently tried out Londonderry for a time, then pushed on past Windsor for 10 miles to Horton, where he lived for 12 years before returning to Pictou's Middle River. He farmed there until his death at the age of 55, in 1792. He was one of the most religious men aboard the *Hector*, an elder of the church, and his gravestone at Alma read: "He lived and died in the faith of obtaining that crown of righteousness which the Lord the righteous Judge will give to all who loved His appearance." James Grant, the miller, settled for a while in King's County in the Annapolis Valley, and Charles Fraser in Cornwallis, but both were to return.

Those who stayed at the harbour that autumn felt great relief when they saw the familiar black hull of the *Hector* off Brown Point bringing provisions, before she continued her return journey to Greenock in ballast. This was food promised in the contract drawn up between Ross and Pagan before the expedition began, but as they lined up that frosty morning in front of the log storehouse at Brown Point to get their food, the people of the *Hector* received another shock. They were told that they had broken the terms of their contracts. They would get no food, said the Company agents, unless they either settled on the allotted land far from the harbour or were prepared to pay cash for the provisions. After all the settlers had been through, the attitude of John Harris and Robert Patterson, or of the Company whose orders they were following, seems almost unbelievable. We have few details, however, since there is no other evidence that shows these two men as cruel or wicked, it is possible they thought such a threat would cause the Highlanders to change their minds and honour the commitment to settle on the land laid out for them. If so, the agents had misjudged the Scots. Those who had money did, in fact, buy food for a while and the penniless sold clothes and belongings for food; but some were determined to use other means to get the food they felt was rightfully theirs.

Within days, Colin Douglas and Donald Macdonald, family men and former neighbours from Beauly and Kilmorack parish, entered the store and demanded that Harris and Patterson give them food. Both had reason to be desperate. Douglas had lost his two younger children to smallpox on the *Hector* and was determined his remaining children, Margaret and Alexander, would not die of hunger. Macdonald's youngest child, Nancy, had just become seriously ill and needed nourishment. Joined by the hot-tempered Roderick Mackay, the Beauly blacksmith, Douglas and Macdonald resolved to take the food by force.

Although Patterson and Harris were armed, the Highlanders seized the two agents and tied them up, hiding their guns in the woods. They measured out the food they needed, leaving a careful accounting of everything they took, intending to pay for it when they had the money; then Macdonald and Douglas shouldered the provisions and made off into the woods. Giving his friends time to get well away, Rory Mackay untied the indignant prisoners, told them where they could find their guns and then got away himself. Since the main settlement was far away no one there knew what had happened until the two agents came back.

The agents dispatched a messenger to Halifax, more than 100 miles away, to ask the garrison for help. Their account lost nothing in the telling. This was rebellion. The Highlanders had refused to honour their commitments, and now they were resorting to robbery and violence to pressure the leaders of the community, one of them a Justice of the Peace. Doubtless the officers in Halifax were surprised to hear there were Highlanders at Pictou Harbour, such were communications at the time. The older ones, with memories of the Jacobite uprising in their youth and the march on London, may have had a vision of a backwoods rising of the clans in Nova Scotia. At any rate, they agreed some punitive action was required, but not wishing to send their own men from Halifax they sent orders to the militia commander at

Truro to march on Pictou Harbour to deal with insurrection.

Fortunately for the Highlanders the militia at the head of Cobequid Bay was run by Scotch-Irish New England farmers stirred by the republicanism of the southern colonies and with no love for English officers of the regular army in Halifax. As it happened, the Halifax garrison commander, Lieutenant Colonel Hamilton of the 59th, had been having difficulties with the farmers on other matters. They had impudently refused to arrest and return deserters from his regiment who had straggled to Truro to partake of its hospitality, and when Hamilton sent a detachment to search Truro, Onslow and Londonderry for the men, David Archibald, a militia major and Justice of the Peace, "not only evaded and refused giving necessary lawful assistance but also countenanced and concealed the said deserters." Hamilton had demanded that the government suspend David Archibald "until he shall give sufficient satisfaction in respect of the matter charged against him."

When Hamilton sent orders to march on Pictou, David's brother, "Captain Uncle Tom" Archibald, a sensible man whose name is commemorated by Mount Thom near Pictou and who lived at Salmon River near the end of the trail which ran from Pictou Harbour to Truro, replied to his marching orders in most unmilitary fashion.

"I will do no such thing," he said. "I know the Highlanders and if they are fairly treated there will be no trouble with them." Colonel Hamilton wisely let the matter drop. The retiring governor in Halifax, Lord William Campbell from Argyllshire, having heard of the suffering of his fellow Highlanders at Pictou, had the government order the Company agents to give the Highlanders food. Although it took the people of the *Hector* a long time to do so, Robert Patterson claimed they repaid the company for every bit of food they had taken.

Upset by such goings-on and fearful of spending winter

in the wilderness, more families walked the long trail to Truro until only a third of the *Hector* passengers—60 or 70 people—were left in the rough lean-tos roofed with bark and branches. They spent a miserable winter at Brown Point learning the painful lessons of survival. They learned to dig up large quantities of clams and cover them with sand before the snow fell so they could be dug up during the winter as needed; they learned to fish through the harbour ice; to clothe themselves to protect their hands and faces from frostbite; to pile large stacks of wood beside their shelters to keep the fires constantly burning. These lessons were frequently costly. Metal utensils were practically irreplaceable and when a cast-iron pot cracked in the cold night when left outside with water in it, they lamented the loss but rarely left their pots outside again.

By Christmas week the snow was blowing through cracks and crannies in their lean-tos and by the last week of December there was a foot of snow. They received unexpected help from the Indians, who brought them meat from the hunt from time to time and showed them how to use snowshoes. The first child was born, a son for Alexander and Marion Fraser from Beauly, the first family to sign on for the voyage. David Fraser grew up to become a sea captain and fell into a series of adventures which included capture by Algiers pirates. There was one death. Nancy, the infant daughter of Donald and Mary Macdonald, did not live to see a Nova Scotia spring.

To augment their monotonous rations the men took to trudging to Truro on their new Micmac snowshoes to trade a few possessions or hire themselves out as casual labourers in return for a little flour or a bushel or two of potatoes which they carried home through 40 miles of snow. Even when the potatoes froze on the way, roasted in the ashes or sliced and toasted on the coals they were a welcome change from dried fish and salt beef. Years later when their lives were easier, the pioneers from the *Hector* would complain when they saw so much as a potato peel carelessly thrown away.

McCabe and the Indians taught the newcomers to hunt for deer and moose. The Scots learned to imitate the call of the female to attract the male within gunshot range and to run the animals down on showshoes when a crust had formed and the moose could be easily overtaken. James McCabe and his son John had become as skilled at hunting as the Micmacs and kept the Scots enthralled with tales both true and tall. In one episode they had shot a moose which, while helpless, was not yet dead, and as they were digging with their snowshoes to prepare a place for their fire the moose lunged to his feet and rushed young John who had time only to dodge behind a tree. The moose pursued him and kept running around the tree, but the boy, able to make a quicker turn, avoided injury until his father reloaded and shot the beast. On another occasion while hunting alone, John shot a large moose and having no flint to make a fire, he wrapped himself in the warm skin and went to sleep. In the morning he found the skin had frozen so solidly around him he could not move and it was some time before he could get his knife out and cut himself free.

Despite constant hardship, the naiveté of the Highlanders was sometimes humorous, even to themselves. Since it was winter they had seen no bears, but had been warned about them by the Americans. One day a Highlander, concluding that a strange-looking animal near the camp must be the dreaded bear, sounded the alarm and roused his neighbours. Surprised at finding that bears were so small, he fired nine shots before killing the beast. Examining it, the Highlanders hurt their fingers for no one had told them that bears had quills. When spring came they had ample opportunity to distinguish bears from porcupines. The only record of a bear attacking one of the *Hector* settlers concerned Alexander Cameron of Loch Broom. To escape he shinnied up a spruce which had no limbs for 40 feet. The bear caught the heel of Cameron's shoe in its teeth and started dragging him down, but 12 feet from the ground the shoe buckle broke and the bear fell to the ground, or so it was said. By the time the bear started climbing again, Cameron had reached the high branches, broke one off and struck the bear about the eyes as it climbed near. The bear fled soon after with the approach of help.

For some, the mosquitoes were worse than bears. One settler braved the winter only to flee the place in summer, calling the mosquitoes a plague from God. Less alarming were the Highlanders encounters with the flora. Having heard that sugar came from trees, one woman, pulling off bark and chewing it early that winter, was disappointed in the taste. The American settlers explained to her there would be no syrup for many weeks. By late February the snow had turned to rain, the streams began to flow and the harbour lost its ice. The Highlanders had survived their first winter. They learned that syrup really did come from maple trees, and when the sap stopped running they tied stout withes around the trunks and tried to squeeze out more.

In the chill of an early Nova Scotia spring those who had spent the winter on Cobequid Bay returned to join those who had stayed at the harbour to hunt for land. Like the Indians before them they found good alluvial soil several miles up the three rivers which run into Pictou Harbour. Since this land had once belonged to Colonel McNutt, whose grant had extended 20 miles up the rivers, and lay well outside the Philadelphia grant, they renounced the last of any formal ties with the Philadelphia Company and Pagan and Witherspoon. Like some of the Americans who came in the late 1760s, they became squatters. The first to take up land on the lower reaches of the Middle River was Alexander Fraser of Beauly.

The Scots would, in time, build homes beside the rivers, but during the first summer they merely began to clear the land. The Americans had taught them to make barrel staves and long shingles with axe and adze to sell to trading schooners which called at the harbour. Recalling the prices that timber fetched in Scotland, they invited a crew of expert hewers from Truro to help them prepare a shipload of square timber. They felled the great oaks and white pine close to the streams and rivers so as to float them, squared into "sticks" sixty feet long, and shipped the wood to Greenock in a rotten old vessel provided by Governor Walter Patterson of St. John Island. It was the first shipment of a timber trade which was to grow to such extent that within a generation 50 ships would call for timber at Pictou Harbour each summer.

Travelling from Truro to the Island of St. John in September of that year, Patrick McRobert gives the following account of Pictou. " . . . Not a house the whole way, nor any road opened, but only the trees marked where the road should be. This desart [sic] I traversed alone, being disappointed of a guide; kindled up a fire, and lay in the woods all night, and arrived next forenoon at Pictou. This is a very good and convenient harbour, formed by the junction of three rivers at about five or six miles from the coast or shore of the Gulph of St. Lawrence . . . This settlement is about seven years old, and mostly doing well for the time; the land is pretty good; they have good crops of wheat, rye, oats, and barley, on the spots they have got clear'd; potatoes and other roots thrive very well here, and one man has a fine little plantation of tobacco. There are about thirty families settled here, most of them from Scotland. They are very conveniently situated for the cod fishery in the Gulph of St. Lawrence; but as most of the settlers were very poor, they have only two sloops, and two or three shallops belonging to the harbour."

In fact the Scots, although helping the Americans to produce staves, shingles and lumber that summer, had produced little in the way of crops themselves. The Americans, although somewhat reduced in numbers by 1774, had produced four times more wheat than the meagre 64 bushels of 1769, had doubled their harvest of oats to 100 bushels and taken up crops of peas, barley, rye and flax from amid the rotting stumps. Enough land for pasture and hay had been cleared to feed 13 cows, 15 calves, 13 oxen, 25 sheep and a pig.

An administration had been established under Dr. Harris who, as Clerk of Pictou District, presided over Overseers for the Poor, Overseers of the Road (which was still only a series of blaze marks on the trees), Surveyors of Lumber, Clerk of the Market, Culler of Fish and a Constable. The Scots, as yet, held none of these posts and the harbour was still predominately a Yankee domain. Robert Patterson, whose tombstone tells us that he was "an honest man," had done well trading in guns and other goods with the Indians, and had bought a sloop to augment the two vessels owned by Dr. Harris. Patterson had been appointed Justice of the Peace and henceforth was known as Squire Patterson. Besides the Squire and the Harris brothers, the Yankee settlers included John Rogers, Abram Slater, Moses Blaisdell, James McCabe, John McCabe, Barnabas McGee; William Kennedy and Thomas Troop from Truro and some newcomers from Cumberland County who squatted on West River.

That autumn, a year after their arrival, most of the *Hector* people walked out to Truro, Onslow and Londonderry to wait out the winter. Food supplies were low and even those who had braved the first winter at Brown Point departed to earn their keep chopping fire wood and doing chores in the older settlements until the spring. But some remained at the harbour: the three bachelors, William Mackenzie, John Patterson and George MacConnell, also Alexander Ross, Colin Mackenzie and their families, and possibly others. Seventy-eight people, including the Americans, wintered that year in the log huts scattered among the evergreens and white snow between Brown Point and Lyons Brook—23 men, 14 women, 21 boys and 20 girls. James Davidson was running his school, although within the year he would move to Truro.

In the spring of 1775 the Highlanders came back with

the birds to build their homes. They had applied for government land grants and had been cheered in February by news that one of their number had received a grant 10 miles up the river the Indians called *Apchechkumoochwakade,* or Duckland, and which they themselves called Big River, or East River. Curiously, since government policy had been one of discrimination against Roman Catholics, the grant went to the only Catholic on the *Hector,* the soldier Donald Cameron. It is doubtful if he managed to fulfil the grant's conditions, which required him to clear three acres within three years, for every 50 granted, but he kept the land until his death.

Encouraged by the luck of Donald Cameron—although it would be eight years before they got similar grants—most of the people from the *Hector* were determined to get their land cleared, homes built and the settlements made permanent. An accounting* by Dr. Harris on November 8, 1775, showed 24 families and single men from the *Hector* had settled in, doubling the population. The Highlanders had won a foothold on the rivers and more were to come back each spring.

For Alexander Cameron from Loch Broom the choice of land was easy. While living the first winter in his lean-to on Brown Point he had eased the pangs of a homesick Highlander by looking out at the land just across the harbour which looked like his home parish in Scotland. That is where he and his wife Janet settled and raised eight children, and to this day the stubby peninsula which divides the West River from the Middle River is called Loch Broom, although any similarity to the Loch Broom of the Scottish Highlands might well escape the eye of a stranger. The man who had seen the battle of Culloden as a youngster, and claimed kinship with the lordly Lochiel Camerons, lived there in peace to the age of 103. In time, he was joined at Loch Broom, Pictou Harbour, by his

---

*See Appendix C.

young friend William Mackenzie, but only after Mackenzie had gone to Liverpool on Nova Scotia's south shore where he married Kazia Peach, whose father had come from New England and was a direct descendant of the Pilgrim Fathers.

George MacConnell and one of the two Hugh Frasers from Beauly—the farmer, not the weaver—claimed land 10 miles up the West River above the intervales farmed by James McCabe and Robert Patterson. Hugh Macleod of Assynt, whose wife had died on the *Hector*, also chose that river, as did William Maclellan.

Alexander Fraser, who with Alexander Cameron had witnessed Culloden, settled on the eastern shores of the lower Middle River and lived to the age of 75. As kinsman to the Lovat Frasers and husband of a laird's daughter, he had been comfortably off at Beauly, unlike the majority of *Hector* passengers, but on Middle River he was to know great hardship in the first few years. Having cast aside all ties with the Philadelphia Company and striking off on their own, the Highlanders were often hard-pressed for food. Fraser's son Hugh recalled how, having no food in the house, his father cut down a birch tree and boiled the buds so his family would have something to eat. Finding no nourishment in birch buds he then walked over to the harbour where Isaiah Horton had buried some potatoes and, in desperation, helped himself. When malicious neighbours told Horton what Fraser had done, the pious old Yankee said only that he thanked God the potatoes had been there to feed Fraser's family.

They went to Truro to sell their labour—Fraser's son, also Alexander, recalled that as a boy he once walked the 40 miles carrying his little sister on his back, the only food for the three- or four-day journey consisting of the tail of an eel. On another occasion, after returning from Truro with seed potatoes in the hungry spring, they had barely planted them in the lazy beds, round hollows four or five inches deep, and covered them with the hoe, when their hunger drove them to dig the split potatoes up again and eat them.

Like many of the children, Alexander Fraser's second son, Simon, had been "bound out" as an indentured servant at Truro. After finally scraping up enough cash for a cow, the family sent out the eldest son, Alexander, to buy it. Meeting Simon in Truro and finding him desperate to get out of his indenture, Alexander used the money to buy his brother's freedom. On arriving home his mother's first question was, "Have you got the cow?"

"No," said Alexander, "but I have brought Simon instead."

"Well, poor as I am," said Marion Fraser, the daughter of an Inverness-shire laird, "I would rather see Simon than a cow." The girl Alexander was to marry had been bound out as a serving girl in Truro and had to work there until she was 18 years old. These few incidents, told to Dr. Patterson by Alexander's fifth son and one of the last survivors among the children of the *Hector*, give an idea of what one family endured those first few years.

Others on Middle River were Donald Macdonald and Colin Douglas, who had seized the food in the Philadelphia Company's warehouse during the darkest days of the Highlanders' first winter.

Most of the Highlanders, however, were drawn to the rich soil on the East River intervales where Stellarton and New Glasgow now stand and where the first government grant had been awarded to Donald Cameron. Hugh Fraser, the Kiltarlity weaver of good character, settled there, as did Alexander Maclean of Loch Broom, and the old soldier Walter Murray of Sutherlandshire before he moved on to Merigomish more than 20 miles along the eastern shore. Colin Mackenzie of Gairloch moved there and lived to the grand age of 104.

The East River was the longest—40 miles from the harbour to its headwaters behind Sutherland's Mountain. From the harbour it was navigable for eight or nine miles and above the head of tide, above Stellarton and New Glasgow, lay the Upper Settlements which ran through some of the loveliest country in Nova Scotia. This was the land which became the home of the Mackays of Beauly, just as the Frasers had taken Middle River for their own. Colin Mackay, the old soldier, settled on Plymouth Intervale, amid the forest of spruce, hemlock and pine, and with his wife Helin he raised three sons. William Mackay, in his mid-forties when he arrived on the *Hector* with his wife Janet and four children, prospered there and was made a Justice of the Peace before his death at the age of 97.

In 1803 Lord Selkirk, on a visit to Pictou after setting up a colony of 800 people in Prince Edward Island, said Squire Mackay had built a fine stone house, kept 12 cows and 30 sheep, had cleared 100 acres and had the "manners of a true old Highlander." William Mackay told Selkirk that he had "difficulties" when he first arrived "from the impossibility of purchasing Provisions, but in one or two years they were independent—Any settler it is reckoned can in one year have potatoes enough—the next year grain is plenty—the third year to spare . . . Mackay settled at the head of tide mark as advised by the Bay of Fundy people for the sake of Interval land; the Highlanders have since settled up the River for, it is said, 20 miles farther."

Also living at the head of tide was Roderick Mackay, the Beauly blacksmith. Roderick, with his wife Christy and older brother Donald, set up the first forge above the site of Stellarton. They were later joined by brother Hugh and the eldest of the brothers, Alexander, who came out from Beauly with his family of seven in 1784. Alexander had fought at Louisbourg and Quebec and the family tradition is that he was the second man in the attacking force to set foot on the Heights of Abraham. He was reputed to be the strongest man in Wolfe's army.

There the men from Loch Broom and Beauly cultivated the river flats and built their cabins on high ground. Having learned the ways of the Americans, they built homes of logs hoisted one atop another with hewn logs for the floor, a door with wooden hinges and wooden latch, two small windows and a roof covered with bark and hand-hewn shingles. The chimney at one end of the house was built of rough stone up to the mantle piece, and above that were small logs of wood well plastered with clay. They made fire with the flint and dried spunk from old logs, and borrowed fire from a neighbour when their own went out in the night. Their chief farming implements were the axe, the hoe and the sickle and also the "crooked foot" spade they had brought from the Highlands. They carried their produce on their backs in creels made of thin wood, which would hold a bushel of potatoes. Their first crop was potatoes and it was some time before they could grow enough oats to supply their beloved porridge. They ate shellfish from the harbour and salmon from the river and, in place of the kale broth they had known in Scotland, made soup from nettles and the herbs the Indians taught them to trust.

Their hunger, at times, was such that Hugh Fraser re-called how his mother had once killed the only laying hen because there was nothing else to eat. She boiled it in salt water, because there was no salt to be had otherwise, and threw in herbs she had found in the woods to serve as vegetables. It was one of the hungry periods and they were soon ravenous again, but the children found the hen's nest "with 10 eggs in it" to tide them over until Alexander Fraser could find more food.

They wore the kilt on special occasions but otherwise dressed in homespun, like New Englanders, and wore moccasins in winter. They had trouble with the mid-winter cold. "However good your trousers are," wrote John Maclean, "they are useless without two pairs of stockings and hair-lined moccasins tightly laced with thongs . . . if I'm not careful my nose and lips freeze, and my ears are always in danger from the north wind with its biting bitterness."

Before they acquired sheep for wool, their pants and

shirts were of flax, grown, spun and woven at home. For those up the rivers whose transportation was the canoe in summer and walking the ice in winter, there were many drownings. Two of the Ross boys and a Maclean, their cousin, were drowned one afternoon when they went to rescue Mrs. Cumminger, who had fallen into Middle River when the ice gave way. The next day all four bodies were recovered. Canoes were big awkward dug-outs, hollowed from a large pine tree, and two or three of the *Hector* people drowned in canoe accidents.

But somehow most of them survived those early years, often with less sustenance than they had found at home in the Highlands, and even these meagre resources were sorely taxed with the arrival in the spring of 1776 of 15 families worse off than themselves. To the south the revolutionary war had started and the newcomers might be accounted among the early victims.

Although often called the "Dumfries' settlers," most of them had come from Kirkcudbright, Wigtown and Ayrshire in the southwest Lowlands, 67 in all, chartering the *Lovely Nell* in 1774 to carry them from the port of Annan to Georgetown Harbour on St. John Island. Unlike most of the *Hector* people they were relatively well-to-do farmers, educated in English. One of their leaders, Wellwood Waugh, and his half-brother William Campbell, were related to a landed family, the Lairds of Barnbarrock. Being rich enough to charter their own ship, they brought with them ample supplies, household possessions and, rare on any emigrant ship, a library of books. At first they had few serious worries, but one night disaster struck and from then on trouble would not subside as long as they remained on St. John Island. It was on the eve of the American Revolution, and the sailors from the Yankee vessels fishing and trading in the gulf had gathered in Georgetown before returning south to join the war. As a parting gesture before they sailed they got drunk and pillaged

Georgetown Harbour, carrying off the Lowlanders' supplies and furniture. That winter the people from Kirkcudbright barely managed to survive.

Their hopes the next summer lay solely in their harvest, for they had secured emergency seed from Nova Scotia. But a great plague of what they called mice, and some called lemmings, swept across the island. By August the rodents had left nothing to harvest. "That winter they would have perished," recounted Dr. Patterson, "were it not for a French settlement some miles distant, from which they received supplies, principally of potatoes, in exchange for the clothing they had brought with them from Scotland, until they scarcely retained sufficient to clothe themselves decently. From scarcity of food the men became reduced to such a state of weakness, and the snow was so deep, that they became at last scarcely able to carry back provisions for their families, and when, with slow steps and heavy labour, they brought them home, such was the state of weakness in which they had left their children, they trembled to enter their dwelling, lest they should find them dead, and sometimes waited at the door, listening for any sound that might indicate that they were alive." They were reduced to living on nettles, berries and the shellfish found along the shore.

After hearing there was food at Pictou Harbour across the strait, 15 families moved there. Later Wellwood Waugh remembered he had left St. John Island with only a bucket of clams to feed his family. Most of them settled on West River, four families on Middle River and two on East River. "Though these people arrived here in such destitution," said Dr. Patterson, "they were among the most valuable of the early settlers of this country."

The Lowlanders brought, above all, good farming habits to the community which, as simple herdsmen, the Highlanders lacked. Highlanders and Lowlanders complemented each other because, said the Nova Scotia historian

Thomas C. Haliburton who visited Pictou a generation later, " . . . to the frugality and industry of the Highlanders [the Lowlanders], add a spirit of persevering diligence, a constant desire of improvement, and a superior system of agriculture, which renders them a valuable acquisition to the Province."

With the slow swing of the seasons the lives of the Scots at Pictou Harbour began to improve. They planted oats and wheat in the good earth of the river flats at the head of tide and from the sale of barrel staves and square timber to traders at the harbour they could afford a cow or two. The American war had doubled the price of wood since it had cut off the British supply from the southern colonies. They salted and sold salmon which, on the East River, was so plentiful that a man was known to catch 15 barrels in a night, but they seem never to have acquired the habit of the Indians, or for that matter of their own people back in Loch Broom, of smoking fish.

As they gradually moved out from the harbour they found land along the rivers where the Indians had raised corn and bought the rights to use these little ready-made farms for next to nothing. Walter Murray, discovering that the Indians were starting to plant their traditional corn crop in the very soil where he had already planted potatoes, bought them off for £5. Donald Fraser, who had settled at the mouth of Maclellan's Brook where it empties into East River, used to say the Micmac Lulan was his "landlord," to whom he paid a bushel of grain every year for use of Lulan's corn patch, which was cheap at the price. Only occasionally, it seems, did the Indians resent the intrusion—for which, in the early years, the Scots must consider themselves lucky.

From the Highlanders' arrival that first wild winter, the Micmacs had adopted them, fascinated by the bagpipes, kilt and tartan, and although communication between the two was long a problem when neither spoke English, the Indians taught the Scots the use of the canoe to avoid hard travelling through the pathless woods. One Nova Scotia settler, the Yorkshireman John Robinson who had settled to the west in Cumberland, described the Micmac canoes in 1774 as "very ingeniously made, mostly of the bark of the birch tree, without either nails, pins, leather or hemp; instead of which, they sew them up with roots of trees, dyed different colours, and line them with ashwood slit thin . . . They are sharp at each end, about two feet in the middle, and will carry four or five men . . ."

They came to the settlements to trade fur for cloth, guns and rum if they could get them from the visiting schooners, brought gifts to the settlers and introduced the young Highlanders to their games, particularly wrestling. The Highlanders learned to be careful, however, for their visitors could be touchy. One man travelling up the Middle River was met by an agitated Indian woman who warned him to depart at once before her husband arrived, as he would certainly kill him. She was the wife of a young brave who claimed the Highlander had once tripped him unfairly in a wrestling match, an incident the Scot had long forgotten and presumably did not wait to discuss.

Roderick Mackay, after settling on West River, somehow fell afoul of the usually even-tempered Lulan. Years after Mackay and Lulan had buried the hatchet and become good friends, Lulan used to tell of how he had gone 20 miles to East River from his lodge at Merigomish with one of James Patterson's old trade rifles in his hand and murder in his heart. It was night and, skulking in the shadows, Lulan found the young blacksmith at the forge, hammer clanging, sparks flying and red fire dancing on his face. Seeing this fearful sight and fearing that Rory Mackay might somehow be the devil, Lulan, who liked to boast he had taken 99 scalps in the wars of his youth, turned and slunk off home. Short, broad-shouldered, in later years inclined to fat, Lulan lived to be 97, and won the gratitude of Scots throughout the district by saving John Patterson from drowning when the harbour ice gave way.

John Robinson, who often found the Micmacs rambling

through the woods in quest of game, described them as "a friendly, harmless well-behaved people, ready to do any little service for you they can, such as assisting you in crossing a river, directing you on the road, & c, but they cannot be prevailed on to assist in any sort of labour. They are stout and active, well made, of a yellow complexion, their faces and nose are broad, their eyes usually black, and their teeth remarkably white and have long black hair. They rub their bodies with bear's grease to prevent the muschetoes from biting them. They for the most part wear a piece of cloth, generally blue, something resembling a wide riding-coat, with a kind of sleeves, but have neither buttons or button holes: This they tie round them with a piece of the skin of some animal or the root of a tree. In general they wear neither breeches, stockings, or shoes; some indeed, wrap a piece of blue cloth around their legs, and others wear a kind of shoes made of mouse-deer's skin, which they call moggisons . . . The affection that reigns amongst them is somewhat singular, for when they meet after some little time absent they salute each other with a kiss . . . "

Although it was hard not be fond of such neighbours, there were moments of tension. The *Hector* passenger George Morrison, returning home one night, found that Indians had visited his house, forcing his wife to cook for them and refusing to let his children near their own fire to warm themselves. Rushing to their encampment he attacked the Indians with his fists with such fury that the entire astonished group decamped to a quieter neighbourhood. In Christy Mackay the Micmacs more than found their match. Not only did Roderick Mackay's wife refuse to cook for them unless she felt like it, but being a woman of firm temperament she scolded them when they overstepped the bounds of Highland hospitality.

Answering their greeting of "What news?" one day, she replied, "Ah, ah, great news! There is another regiment of soldiers arrived in Halifax and the Indians must now behave themselves."

But that was at a time when the American Revolution had almost everybody taking sides and the Indians, hearing that some of their brethren had been seized by the British far up the coast at Miramichi Bay, gathered in excitement at the harbour for a grand pow-wow. Some of the Pictou settlers, alarmed, petitioned Halifax to send in soldiers to guard them against "Indians and pirates." The soldiers never came, but in fact the Indians, having buried the hatchet years before, left it undisturbed.

The pirates, or American privateers, were another matter. At the beginning of the American war a muster roll "of the inhabitants of Pictou or Tinmouth capable to bear arms," encompassing all the harbour and as far east as Merigomish, listed 65 men, only a third of them men from the *Hector*. The majority of the *Hector* people were still living out in the western settlements, although many would return.

For the Scots at Pictou Harbour, the American Revolution was not so much a storm as a series of gusts which disturbed their lives from time to time. Other Nova Scotia settlements were in turmoil. On the south shore there was sedition and at Londonderry the member of the legislative assembly had run off to join the rebels at Machias, just outside the vague Nova Scotia frontier at the mouth of the Bay of Fundy. The New Englanders at Onslow refused to a man to take an oath of allegiance to the Crown, and at Truro all but three refused. At Cumberland, less than 100 miles from Pictou, there was open, armed rebellion. Warning that most Nova Scotians were rebels, Governor Francis Legge said he could trust no one but the Scots and a few hundred Yorkshire farmers who had arrived in the province. At least two-thirds of the population seemed intent on dragging the land they regarded as the 14th colony into the rebellion. But through it all the Scots remained obstinately loyal to an English throne they had little reason to love, for those who had grown up in the shadow of Culloden knew the cost of civil war.

Although only one or two of the *Hector* people took part in the American war, many Scots who later settled at Pictou saw service for the Crown. They served in the 82nd Regiment, the Duke of Hamilton's, composed of Highlanders and Lowlanders who garrisoned Halifax, and in the 84th, the Royal Highland Emigrants Regiment, which included veterans of the French war, emigrants who were promised land grants if they enlisted and large numbers of North Carolina settlers, such as Captain Allan Macdonald, husband of Flora the Jacobite heroine, who had in 1774 "begun the world again anewe" at a home in the Cape Fear Valley.

Allan Macdonald, one of the 3,000 Carolina Highlanders to join the first battalion of the 84th, was captured by the American rebels, and Flora herself was turned out of her home, deserted by her servants, robbed of her possessions and charged with treason. Traded for American prisoners, Macdonald came to Nova Scotia to command a company of the Highland Emigrants at Windsor. He brought his wife, then 55, with him, but she was ailing and complained of the unaccustomed cold. She spent the winter of 1778 at Fort Edward above the Avon River, and left Nova Scotia for home 18 months later, saddened that she had "served the House of Stuart in Scotland and the House of Hanover in America and lost both." Her husband joined her in Skye four years later when the Highland Regiment was disbanded.

The second battalion of the Highland Emigrant Regiment was raised in Nova Scotia mainly from Highlanders brought over from St. John Island by the Glenaladale Macdonald and by loyal Highlanders from Boston and Newfoundland. Archibald Chisholm from Loch Broom seems to have been the only *Hector* passenger to join the 84th. The second battalion was joined by more than 100 emigrants who had arrived on the ship *Glasgow*, and though they were called "volunteers," they were given no choice but to join. Ill-fed, unpaid, lacking uniforms at first, the second battalion of the 84th was for a while the mainstay of the Halifax garrison and a major part of the British army in Nova Scotia while the regular British regiments were off fighting in the southern colonies.

At Pictou Harbour the American settlers, except for Squire Robert Patterson, supported revolution, and bitterness developed between them and the loyal Highlanders. It was probably just as well the Highlanders had broken their contractual ties with the Philadelphia Company, whose partners were rebels. Dr. Harris and his brother Matthew were anti-British and in Philadelphia Dr. John Witherspoon, one of those most responsible for fetching the Highlanders to Nova Scotia in 1773, had become an ardent rebel leader. The Rev. James Lyon, the Philadelphia Company partner who had given his name to Lyons Brook before he returned to Onslow, had gone to Machias in the American territory at the entrance to the Bay of Fundy where he set up a Committee of Safety and tried to win General George Washington's support for an invasion of Nova Scotia. Washington, too busy elsewhere, declined but the militant Reverend Lyon was not daunted.

"I believe," he said, "men enough might be found in this country who would cheerfully undertake it, without any assistance from the Government . . . I confess I am so avaricious that I would go with the utmost cheerfulness."

The attack on Fort Cumberland by 72 New Hampshire men and 12 Indians from Machias, joined by 100 New Englanders who had settled in Cumberland and were led by Jonathan Eddy, showed Lyon was a man to be reckoned with. But after a 20-day seige the New Englanders were driven off, without bloodshed, by a detachment of Royal Highland Emigrants from Halifax and a company of marines. That was the end of invasion, but hit-and-run raids by Yankee privateers went on through the seven years of war.

The first privateer raid on the Pictou area came early in

the spring of 1776. The previous autumn a vessel carrying cargo from the West Indies to Quebec had become weather-bound at Merigomish Harbour and, abandoned temporarily by her crew who went overland to winter at Truro or Halifax, lay in the ice until spring. No one paid much heed when Daniel Earl, a Yankee, disappeared from home for several weeks that winter, but it was later learned he had gone to Machias to inform Lyon of the rich prize lying at Merigomish for the taking once the ice broke up. One day in early spring Squire Patterson's teen-aged sons, James and David, were cutting staves at Merigomish when they saw a ship come in. Before they learned her purpose they were captured by the privateers so they would not warn the settlers. Once they had got their prize free of the ice and into the strait, the privateers released the boys—accidentally breaking David's thumb with a marlin spike while taking off his manacles—and put them into a boat with a few biscuits and a jar of sugar to find their way back home. The boys got back to harbour safely to find on the shore a group of Highlanders who, having got wind of the privateers, had hastily assembled to do battle with every old musket and fowling piece they could lay their hands on.

The second incident, the next summer, was more serious. Dropping down the East River with a boatload of barrel staves for Captain Thomas Lowden's ship *Molly*, Roderick and Donald Mackay met a rowboat heading upriver, but being too busy to give it thought proceeded to the harbour and climbed aboard Lowden's ship. There, to their surprise, they met New Englanders, armed with rifles, one of whom tapped Roderick on the shoulder and told him he was a prisoner. With his customary impatience, Rory Mackay gave the man the back of his hand, whereupon the New Englander brought up his musket and said he was serious and the Mackays were prisoners of Yankee privateers. They were imprisoned in the hold.

The Mackays then learned how Captain Lowden, a sea

dog who had once commanded convict ships between England and Virginia, had been tricked. Invited to a social gathering ashore, the captain had gone unsuspectingly, leaving the *Molly* in the charge of the first mate. During the gathering in one of the settlers' homes the jollity had suddenly ceased and the other guests crowded around the indignant captain and took him prisoner. On signal, the privateers hiding in the woods rowed out to the *Molly* and imprisoned the mate and crew. Then taking the ship's boat a group of them—the ones who had passed the Mackays coming down—proceeded up the East River to plunder Roderick's forge of all the tools and iron they could find, for in the settlements such things were valuable.

When the raiding party returned that night, pleased with their day's work, they broke open Captain Lowden's stores and got drunk, forgetting to unload the rowboat which sank under its weight of iron. Hearing them carousing in the cabin, Roderick proposed to rush the stairs to the deck, seize the tipsy sentry and throw him overboard, while Donald stood guard with an axe at the companionway to hold the drunken pirates at bay. For Donald, as peaceable as Rory was impetuous, this was too bloodthirsty a scheme and he refused to take part; deeply disappointed, Rory Mackay complained later that had he been able to communicate with the imprisoned mate of the *Molly* (Rory still spoke no English and the mate did not know Gaelic), they would have retaken the ship that night.

The Mackays were released the next day and the privateers sailed westward to Bay Verte where they expected to rendezvous with the Yankee rebels in Cumberland County. When the Mackays raised hue and cry, Colin Douglas was dispatched through the woods to Halifax to alert the Royal Navy, and Captain Lowden commandeered a canoe and paddled across the strait to St. John Island where a British man-of-war was on station. The British warship followed the *Molly* to Bay Verte and found that the privateers, who had failed to make contact with the Cumberland rebels, had taken to the woods leaving the *Molly* abandoned. Several of the privateers got lost and perished from hunger and one, having eaten nothing but the leather of his boots for many days, limped into Truro and died.

Accusing the local Yankees of collusion in this treachery, the Highlanders made things so difficult for them that Dr. Harris moved away to Onslow, although some say he moved merely to give his wife Eliza a home in less remote surroundings. Wellwood Waugh, who came from an old Lowland Covenanter family, and thus had refused to take an oath of allegiance to the King, also moved and settled at Tatamagouche. Henceforth privateers were spotted off the coast, but either because they considered the Highlanders too poor to bother with or because their American allies had moved or did not want to anger the Highlanders, they left the place alone. The settlements to the south and west, Lunenburg, Liverpool, Annapolis, were richer targets and these they plundered until several merchants were ruined. Ironically, since many considered him a rebel sympathizer, Colonel John McNutt, the land speculator, was one of their victims at his retirement home at Port Roseway in southern Nova Scotia. He complained that *The Congress* privateer plundered his house of "Sword, Pistol, Firelocks, Powdr, Ball, Shot and Flints, Drawing Box, Writing Stand, with their contents, superfine scarlet and blew cloaths, books, silver spoons, silver buckles, plain, set and carved, gold lace, diamond rings, with a number of other articles." With his usual flair for large figures he totalled these at £1,300 and demanded compensation from the rebel headquarters in Philadelphia. "How I can be justly considered in a double capacity and treated as both Whig and Tory seems a Parradox to me," he said.

As for that other victim of the privateers, Roderick Mackay, the raid convinced him the war effort needed his personal attention. With his wife Christy and two children, he set out on foot for Halifax where he got a job as blacksmith in the naval yard. His first work was the forging of a tremendous chain to keep privateers away from Halifax's harbour. He stayed there 20 years, working up to foreman, before retiring on his East River farm. However, success never dulled his ardour. Strolling near Citadel Hill one day he berated an officer who had insulted a woman, whereupon the officer drew his sword and slashed the unarmed Mackay about the head. Telling the officer to meet him on the common within the hour, Rory Mackay withdrew to get his head bandaged and to pick up his favourite ash stick. The two met in combat and Mackay was so skilled with the staff that he disarmed the officer and, the story goes, "repaid him heartily for his cowardly attack." He bore the scars for the rest of his 84 years.

With the war drawing to an end the Nova Scotia government, recognizing the loyalty of the *Hector* settlers, finally confirmed their status by granting 35 families title to the lands they were squatting on. With all the coming and going of the past 10 years, and half the *Hector* people still scattered, there were still hardly more than 70 families in the Pictou area*—perhaps 250 people—but within another year or two the population would double.

The first to arrive by ship, from Halifax, were disbanded veterans of the 82nd Hamilton regiment, a mixture of Highlanders and Lowlanders—Frasers, Macdonalds, Mackenzies, Smiths, Scotts, Smalls—with a few Englishmen, including one who gloried in the name of British Freedom. They had been awarded 26,000 acres of the escheated Fisher grant, which started on the empty shore on the southeast side of the harbour and ran back to Merigomish. More than 200 officers and men had chosen land in a parade-ground lottery, but not being farmers, fewer than a quarter of them settled. Some did not even bother

---

*See Appendix D.

to visit the place. Some took a look and hurried back to Halifax to re-enlist. Others stayed only long enough to establish claims to their 150-acre lots and then sold them to established settlers for a paltry £4 or £5. Soldiers, as Governor Lawrence had once remarked, did not make good colonists and the words "sold out and went to Truro" are noted beside the names of many on the grant rolls. The site of a town, to be named Walmsley, had been surveyed for the soldiers by Squire Robert Patterson, but no town was ever built. Many of the soldiers who did settle, from Fraser's Point on the harbour back to Merigomish to the east, were hard-living bachelors, and about that time Francis Hogg set up his little grog shop in the woods, the settlement's first tavern. The older settlers, not averse to a drop or two themselves, were wont to complain that the veterans of the 84th affected the moral fibre.

Those who came in the second wave of post-war military immigrants—16 families from the disbanded second battalion of the Highland Emigrant Regiment, the 82nd—proved more tenacious. Camerons, Macdonalds, Frasers, Chisholms, Grants, they were Highlanders who had been promised 3,400 acres on the upper reaches of the East River and its tributaries. Since most of the rich intervale land in the valley where the Mackays settled had now been taken up, Donald Mackay guided their leaders, Big James Fraser among them, up toward the headwaters beyond Springville to the "soldier's grant." They were joined by other veterans of the 84th until their numbers doubled.

With the return of peace in 1783, the flow of Highland emigrants resumed, spurred by famine in the glens in 1782-83. In the shires of Inverness and Ross the crops had failed because of intense cold which had lasted until June of 1782 and had then been followed by rain and early frost in the autumn. A letter from Loch Broom on December 24 said, "The crop has failed much in Coigach having never riped fully, and some of it was damaged in the gathering.

The potato crop totally lost in the ground by early frosts."

During the summer of 1784 Roderick Mackay, now a blacksmith in the Halifax naval yard, welcomed eight families from Beauly and the neighbouring parish of Kirkhill. Among them was Roderick's eldest brother, the ex-soldier Alexander, still limping from the wounds suffered on the Heights of Abraham. He had brought with him a large family as well as his sister, Margaret, and her husband, John Robertson. Another brother, Hugh, was to join the growing clan of Mackays on East River.

By now, a decade after the arrival of the *Hector* people, there were 500 settlers around the harbour or in clearings stretching ten miles and more up the three rivers and out along the eastern shore to Barney's River on Merigomish Harbour. In the Highlands they had tended to live in farm villages; here their homes were separated by three or four miles of gloomy forest. The closest thing to a settlement was the straggle of log huts where the *Betsey* settlers had landed, between the jut of land at Brown Point and the mouth of West River. Across from that lay Alexander Cameron's farm and the new Loch Broom, and over on the south shore of the harbour the huts of the veterans of the 82nd Regiment.

Up the West River for ten miles, as far as George MacConnell's one-room cabin and his neighbour Hugh Fraser, were the homes of the Assynt widower Hugh Macleod, and for the first two miles from the river mouth the Kirkcudbrightshire people who had come over from St. John Island in the early days of the war. Lord Selkirk, when he travelled there, said it reminded him of "some Scenes in Swisserland." The people kept the ways of their native Lowlands: "The Girls wear Hats etc.; they will treat you with short bread, & in their Orchards is the Throle pippeen [apple]."

On the Middle River Alexander Fraser of Beauly now had 10 or 11 neighbours—Donald Macdonald, Colin

Douglas, Alexander Ross from Loch Broom, James Macleod from Sutherlandshire and Kenneth Fraser—the last two had returned from farms in the Annapolis Valley and taken up land three miles up the river.

The East River had become the most heavily populated, with the Mackays from Beauly, a mixture of people from Loch Broom parish and the veterans of the 84th Highland Emigrants. There was a growing settlement on Merigomish Harbour and, out in the bush at Rogers Hill, Scots Hill and Green Hill were a few loners. The Pictou district was now well and truly Scottish, and although living was still precarious—their cash crops mostly fish and lumber—the Highlanders had taken to urging their relatives at home to join them. They also asked John Pagan in Glasgow to find a Gaelic-speaking minister for them. A petition signed by Squire Robert Patterson, John Patterson the Paisley carpenter and Donald Mackay, Roderick's brother, recalled that "the Philadelphia Company made provision for and sent a minister, viz., the Rev. James Lyon, at the first settlement, yet he did not continue among us, which very much discouraged the people, and was exceedingly detrimental to the settling of the place." Pagan, who with Dr. Witherspoon still controlled the Philadelphia grant, passed along their request to the Presbyterian Synod. However, it would be two more years before a minister arrived.

CHAPTER TEN

A New Scotland

Then let them once but owre the water,
Then up amange the lakes and seas
They'll mak what rules an' laws they please.

LIBERTY, ROBERT BURNS

The Rev. James MacGregor, a tall, bearded young man of 27 years, came down the West River in Hugh Fraser's borrowed canoe on a fine Saturday morning late in July of 1786. The beauty of Pictou Harbour reminded him of a Scottish loch, but his first impulse was to turn around and go back to Scotland.

"When I looked round the shores of the harbour I was greatly disappointed and cast down, for there was scarcely any thing to be seen but woods growing down to the water's edge. Here and there a mean timber hut was visible in a small clearing, which appeared no bigger than a garden compared to the woods. Nowhere could I see two houses without some wood between them. I asked Hugh Fraser, 'Where is the town?' He replied, 'There is no town, but what you see.' The petition had the word *township* in it, whence I had foolishly inferred that there was a town in Pictou."

There would be no town for many years, but fortunately James MacGregor stayed. No one would contribute more to the alchemy—that mixture of freedom from old Highland ties, pride in land, democratic Presbyterianism and other factors—which would transmute backwoods Pictou. His first sermon, the next day, was on the text "The Son of Man is come to seek and to save that which is lost."

MacGregor, the son of a small tenant farmer who also worked as a weaver and whiskey moonshiner to put his son through school, was a Highlander from the Loch Earn hills in northern Perthshire. He had been raised in that dissenting branch of the Scottish Presbyterian Church known as the Anti-Burghers which refused all truck with the established Church of Scotland. He preached a muscular brand of democratic religion, strong on the Calvinistic work ethic and the need for education, which appealed to the pride of the people the English had scorned as backward. At Edinburgh University and the theology school at Alloa he had fully expected a call to preach in the Highlands and had schooled himself in Gaelic. When the General Associate Synod of Scotland, meeting in the spring of 1786, chose him to go to the wilderness of the New World, it surprised him greatly but he dutifully boarded the brig *Lily* at Greenock on June 4 with several other Highlanders bound for Pictou. He travelled from Halifax to Truro on horseback through the muddy narrow path and followed the blazed trail from Truro to West River on foot, and there Hugh Fraser offered to borrow a canoe and take him ten miles down to Pictou Harbour.

"Nothing but necessity kept me there," he said, "for I durst not think of encountering the dangerous road to Halifax again, and there was no vessel in Pictou to take me away, and even had there been one I had not money to pay my passage home." The petition from Pictou had promised the unusually handsome salary of £80 a year, but it would be 18 months before he received any recompense at all, save the simple food and rough accommodation supplied by his parishioners.

That Saturday afternoon at Squire Robert Patterson's comfortable home near Brown Point his spirits revived as he prepared for his first Sabbath service. "The squire gave orders to lay slabs and planks in his barn for seats to the congregation; and before eleven o'clock next morning I saw the people gathering to hear the gospel from the lips of a stranger . . . It was a truly novel sight to me to see so many boats and canoes carrying people to sermon. There were only five or six boats but many canoes, containing from one to seven or eight persons. I observed the conduct of some of them, coming from the shore to the barn, was as if they had never heard of Sabbath. I heard loud talking and laughing and singing and whistling."

He was a bachelor, always on the move around his parish, and as a keen observer and faithful diarist, his journals are one of the few sources describing how the Pictou pioneers lived. There was neither church nor school, "not a foot of road in the district," not even any merchants. Trading schooners called at the harbour from time to time except in winter, but money was so scarce the settlers bartered for staples and utensils with new-cut barrel staves, timber, fish, wheat, furs and maple sugar. There was as yet no grist mill, so they ground their grain, as best they could, with the handmills, or querns, they had brought from the Highlands. "This was the occasion of saving much wheat, for many a meal was made without bread on account of the trouble of grinding." Since a bushel of salt cost them a bushel of their precious grain they continued their war-time practice of boiling down sea water for salt, still unaware that only a few miles up the West River were natural salt deposits which would later be developed at Salt Springs. Tea was such a rare luxury that one woman, receiving half a pound as a gift, boiled it all up, threw out the brown liquid and proudly served the leaves.

At heart the Highlanders were still herdsmen, and given the little clearings they had made—so different from the broad grazing of the Highlands—they kept a surprisingly large number of sheep, 1,500 in the 1780s, as well as 356 cows and 450 "small cattle" which included pigs. Cattle, sheep and pigs were turned out to forage in the woods or along the shore despite the danger from bears. Although the *Betsey* people had acquired horses, the Scots had none until George MacConnell brought a small black pony to carry the mail to and from Halifax.

Their furniture, like their homes, was of logs as were their dug-out canoes and their coffins, as it was easier to hollow out a big tree to fit a corpse than to make boards with a pitsaw. Food was served on wooden plates and bowls or straight from the iron pot on the floor with everyone dipping in. MacGregor remembered evenings, as the guest of a remote parishioner, when his supper was one roasted potato. Except on special days when they might don well-worn kilts and plaids they had brought from Scotland, carefully kept and mended, the men dressed like their Yankee neighbours in linsey-woolsey shirts and long trousers, and in summer went barefoot. In winter they wore breeches, stockings and moccasins. They were partial to blue cloth, dyed in the yarn. The women wore woolsey both for petticoats and aprons.

There were more single men than women; women married in their teens and had growing families by the time they reached their twenties. One of the Yankee habits the young Scots women and men had taken to was the cosy, cold-weather practice of "bundling"—lying fully clothed in bed on a winter evening, the better to conduct their courtships. Men travelled prodigious distances to find wives and married on short acquaintance. Hearing that a ship with marriageable girls aboard had reached Halifax, three young East River men walked 100 miles to the city and were back with wives before they were much missed. James MacGregor, the busy minister who performed 144 marriages in his early years including one between a man who spoke only English and a girl who spoke only Gaelic, met his own wife only a few minutes before the wedding. Having failed to attract a bride by mail from Scotland, he took to courting Ann Mackay by mail. She was living in Halifax with her father Roderick, who had brought her to Nova Scotia on the *Hector* as a babe-in-arms. They were married in the spring of 1796 in Halifax and on the honeymoon trip back to Pictou by horse they made many stops to allow James to preach at settlements along the way. He and Ann were to build the first frame-house on East River where they had seven children before Ann died in 1810 following the birth of their fourth son.

Premature death among the women was not unusual. Their lives were hard, rearing their large families and doing a pioneer woman's work—spinning, knitting, making cheese and butter, preserving food against long winters and even working the crops when the men were in the woods. Although many of the men from the *Hector* lived long lives, into their eighties, nineties and, in at least two cases, beyond the 100-year mark, their wives frequently predeceased them by as much as 20 years. Several of the *Hector* men remarried and started new families. MacGregor remarried in 1812, wedding the widow of the Rev. Peter Gordon of Prince Edward Island, whom he had met in the course of his travels to the island.

Particularly in the first eight or nine years, when he was the only minister east of Truro, MacGregor travelled constantly to visit the lonely settlers. He used to tell of dangers he encountered in his travels, of escapes from drowning while crossing brooks and rivers swollen by rain and of losing his way in the forests. One such trip took him 400 miles to Passamaquoddy in what is now New Brunswick, a journey lasting two weeks each way.

"I had to learn," he said, "to walk on snowshoes in winter and to paddle a canoe in summer, and to cross brooks and swamps upon trees overturned or broken by the wind, and to camp in the woods all night—for there is no travelling in the woods at night when there is no road." Often there was no bed to sleep in at his destination and he would try to get some rest on the floor of some mean cabin, covered by his coat and old clothes provided by the family he was visiting. He sometimes complained of being kept awake by fleas.

One night he awoke in a lonely barn to find a man standing over him with a knife in his hand. On being asked what he was doing there, the stranger replied, "I thought you'd be afraid here all alone."

To which MacGregor said, "I am not alone. My Master is here with me." The stranger disappeared into the night. In the morning MacGregor found that his saddle bags had been cut open and learned that the stranger was a homicidal criminal.

But, for all the hardship, he loved his travels through the forests. "Many varieties of the pine, intermingled with birch, maple, beech, oak and numerous other tribes, branch luxuriantly over the banks of lakes and rivers," he wrote, "extend in stately grandeur along the plains, and stretch proudly up to the very summits of the mountain. It is impossible to exaggerate the autumnal beauty of these forests; nothing under heaven can be compared to its effulgent grandeur. Two or three frosty nights, in the decline of autumn, transform the boundless verdue of a whole empire into every possible tint of brilliant scarlet, rich violet, every shade of blue and brown, vivid crimson, and glittering yellow. The stern, exorable fir tribes alone maintain their eternal sombre green. All others in mountains or in valleys burst into the most glorious vegetable beauty, and exhibit the most splendid and most enchanting panorama on earth."

He was a poet and the hymns he wrote were sung in Gaelic by his congregations. People walked miles to hear him, and once he preached 37 sermons in three weeks, all of them an hour long and some two hours, as well as baptising many children. His fame as a Gaelic scholar was known in Scotland and when the publishers of a new Gaelic Bible asked him to go through it for mistakes he found 300. He was generous with what little money he had, gave poor settlers seeds he had intended to use on his own farm and, in one instance, gave a poor old woman his last £5 to buy a cow.

He could also be impatient and unforgiving. Once, when visiting a little settlement he considered particularly wicked, he told the people they did not deserve a minister but rather, he said, "You deserve Hell." He was active, wiry, "of ardent temperament" and great endurance and the people said they had never seen a man, raised in the Old Country, adapt more quickly to the wilderness life. For 40 years MacGregor travelled his parish and as far as Cape Breton, Prince Edward Island and New Brunswick, preaching the Bible and education.

He began his labours upon his arrival in Pictou as he meant to continue. "Towards the end of the first week I went up the East River to get acquainted with the people and be near the place of preaching next Sabbath," he recalled. Seventy families had settled around latter-day Stellarton where the good intervale land began and which all the men wanted for its good soil and ease of clearing. "Except for two families, the whole population was from the Highlands. But few of them, or those in other parts of Pictou, could read a word."

There had been no regular minister since the Rev. James Lyon of the Philadelphia Company had departed for Onslow almost 20 years earlier. MacGregor performed more than 160 baptisms in the first few years of his ministry, but sometimes felt impelled to refuse baptism because the people were so lacking in religious instruction. "Their singing and whistling, laughing and bawling, filled my mind with amazement and perplexity. I took occasion to warn them of the sin of such conduct."

The following Sunday he preached under a large elm tree on Alexander Fraser's land on lower Middle River and thereafter he preached outdoors every Sabbath until the autumn rains began. In winter he preached in homes, several services each Sabbath, moving, every fortnight, between the East River where he had taken lodgings with William Mackay, to the harbour settlement, then to the West River and the Middle River, renewing the circle until warm weather returned.

"The Upper Settlement of the East River, being unprovided with snowshoes, were excluded through the whole winter from all communication with the rest of the people as effectually as if they had belonged to another world . . . For six weeks in eight I was from home almost totally deprived of my books and all accommodations for study, often changing my lodging and exposed to frequent and excessive cold. But it had this advantage, that it give me an easier opportunity of visiting and examining the congregation than I could otherwise have had."

He found the settlers lacking in everything but rude health and the will to survive. Since the departure of the teacher Davidson from the Lyons Brook School ten years earlier, there had been little education of any kind. Occasionally neighbours might club together and invite an itinerant teacher, who was usually also a blacksmith or weaver, to spend a few months. "It was of no little discouragement to me that I saw scarcely any books among the people." Those few he saw were usually brought in by Lowlanders, such as Wellwood Waugh from Prince Edward Island, although he found that almost every household had a Bible even if those in the house could not read it.

He was disturbed by the depth of superstition, which he set out methodically to dispel. Accustomed to all manner of ghosts, kelpies, witches and fairies in their native glens—a witch had been burned to death in their own Highland region, at Dornoch, as late as 1722—they had little trouble transplanting superstition to the gloomy forests of Nova Scotia. The hoot of an owl, the cry of a loon or a wildcat all added to the original store of what the minister called their "absurd tales about ghosts, witches and fairies." He went out of his way to debunk the weird stories. When told the people had seen a ghost in a certain stretch of wood, he went there himself at night and did, in fact, see an object looming white in the darkness. When he investigated he found a huge disused hornets' nest. A more palpable ghost, he found, was a mad woman who made a habit of standing on a roadside stump at night wrapped in a white sheet. But there was one occurrence in Pictou Harbour, many years after his arrival, which even he was at a loss to fully explain. To most of the settlers it was witchcraft pure and simple and they would have it no other way.

On August 3, 1803, the ship *Favourite*, with her Captain Ballantyne, arrived at Pictou Harbour from Ullapool, Loch Broom, with 500 emigrants, making the passage in a record five weeks and three days. Barely had her passengers gone ashore when, for no visible reason, the *Favourite* sank to the bottom of Pictou Harbour, where her bones remained for years until they rotted.

"Such a strange occurrence might well excite enquiry as to its cause," wrote Dr. George Patterson 60 years later, "and as we have received from a most reliable and worthy old man, who when young was a passenger on board, a veritable account of the whole particulars, we shall give them as we received them.

"It appears that shortly before the vessel left, one man who came in her was out one evening looking after his cows when he saw a little creature like a rabbit going round to them and sucking milk from them. He immediately took his gun and tried to shoot it but found it impossible to do so. Suspecting the cause, he put a silver six pence into the gun and fired again, when the creature limped off, leaving traces of blood in its track. The next day he made enquiries if there were any person in the parish hurt, and sure enough found that one old woman was confined to the house by some injury she had received. He called on her residence but could not see her. On his engaging passage in the *Favourite*, she was heard to declare that with him on board the vessel would never reach America. In consequence of this the passengers applied to the authorities to have her confined until the vessel should arrive." They felt that in confinement at Ullapool she could not work her spell.

During her remarkably fast crossing, the *Favourite*, meeting a ship homeward bound to Loch Broom, sent word that when the ship arrived at Ullapool the *Favourite* would be safe at Pictou and the old woman could be set free. This message was relayed to the Ullapool authorities and the woman was released, with such consequences, it was said, that it was fortunate the *Favourite* had not been delayed by another day or two, for all hands would have been drowned. To James MacGregor's relief there was at least one passenger on the *Favourite*, a woman, who did not believe in witches. When asked what had caused the sinking, she said, "Oh they took the *ballast* out of her."

By his first summer at the harbour, MacGregor had stirred enthusiasm to such a pitch that the people volunteered to build not one, but two, log churches, each 40 feet by 30 with a gallery the young people could reach by a ladder. One was on East River above where the town of New Glasgow stands and the other more than ten miles away on land given by William Mackenzie near the shores of the harbour, at Loch Broom.

Four years earlier, in 1782, the itinerant "New Light" evangelist Henry Alline had stopped at "Picto" for 13 days and found but "four Christians in this place." Perhaps he preached the wrong branch of religion. Certainly he spoke no Gaelic, and few Highlanders spoke English. MacGregor had set off something of a revival and changed religious habits in the Pictou settlements where "many were found turning to the Lord." Dr. Daniel Cock, the Truro Presbyterian who occasionally preached to the Highlanders in English, spoke one day on the text "Fools make mock of sin." One Highlander, having trouble with the language, was heard to mutter, "Mr. Cock needn't have talked so about moccasins; Mr. MacGregor wore them many a time."

MacGregor's descriptions of his ministry in 1786-87, while his impressions were still fresh, give measure of his efforts to meet and understand his parishioners. "I was tired of winter before New Year's Day, but before March was over, I forgot that it should go away at all. The snow became gradually deeper, till it was between two and three feet deep.

"The ice was a great convenience during winter in all my travels, especially my visitations, as it removed all obstructions from water, and enabled me to go straight from one house to another, whatever brook, creek or other water might intervene . . . Before April was ended, the harbour was completely clear of the ice; and on the 6th of May, the day on which the elders were ordained, I saw the last patch of snow for that season. The boats and canoes were then launched and prepared for summer employment; for they were our horses, which carried most of us to sermon, and every other business. Now came on the spring work and every hand that could help the farmer had plenty of employment. From the beginning of May till the middle of June was the time for ploughing, and sowing the various kinds of grain, and planting the potatoes. But there were few ploughs in Pictou. All the later settlers had to prepare the ground for the seed with hand-hoes; for the roots and stumps prevent the use of the plough till they are rotten. The trees were cut down in winter, and crosscut, so as to be fit to be rolled in heaps for being burned. Rolling is heavy work, and often requires four to five men with hand-levers, on which account the neighbours gather to it in parties. The Americans are amazingly dexterous at this work, rolling huge logs along, launching them to the right or left, turning them round a stump in the way, or raising one end over it, and heaving it up on the pile. The ashes of the great quantity of timber which grows upon the land make good manure for the first crops—a most merciful arrangement of Providence for the poor settler, who has to sow and plant among stumps and spreading roots which often occupy one-third of the ground. The first two crops are generally good. No wheat was sown till the second week in May, nor potatoes planted till the first of June. Reaping was from the middle of August to that of November. The potatoes were raised in October."

He shared the poverty of his parishioners, but it was not so much the obvious hardships—the cold, fatigue and lack of food—that caused him to complain but rather incidental matters which detracted from his spreading of the message. "The want of mills proved a great impediment in my course of visitation," he wrote, "for it obliged every family to have a hand-mill for its own use. As soon as I sat down the mill was set a-going; and though it was but a hand-mill it made such a noise as to mar conversation, and most commonly kept either the male or female head of the family from all share in it. But for this circumstance I could often have visited two families for the one that I did visit."

He had ordained elders, or deacons, that spring, including Donald Mackay, Roderick's mild-mannered brother, on East River, Hugh Fraser on West River and John Patterson who, unlike the other *Hector* passengers, had continued to live near the Philadelphia Company settlers beside the harbour. Patterson had carried on his carpentry and was also a trader and lumber exporter. He had married

Ann, Matthew Harris' daughter from the head of the harbour. During the war he had returned briefly to his Scottish home near Paisley—perhaps the only *Hector* passenger ever to go home—to convert his properties into £80 cash. On his way back to Pictou he had come by way of Boston where he bought a large supply of New England primers which he sold at Pictou for some profit. In the 1780s he built a house northeast of Brown Point on 150 acres which had once belonged to the McNutt grant, and also purchased 100 acres of old McNutt land lying a mile to the east where, flanked by a hardwood ridge, the shore of the harbour curved toward the narrow entrance.

A few years after McNutt had lost his grant in 1770, it had been awarded to a retired half-pay officer, Lieutenant Richard Williams, who in turn had sold 10,000 acres to the Governor of St. John Island, Walter Patterson of Charlottetown. There is a story, with all the earmarks of the apocryphal, that Williams bartered this land to the governor in exchange for a fine horse. However he got it, Governor Patterson, who lost it later to the merchant family of Cockrans in Halifax because of debt, planned to build on it a town he wished to call Coleraine. When nothing came of the governor's plans, John Patterson laid out his own town and called it New Paisley. It seemed fitting that the choice harbour frontage which Colonel McNutt had denied to the Philadelphia Company and the *Hector* people should at last become the district town.

Except for a squatter's hut on the slope of the hill the land was uncleared when John Patterson began laying out his small building lots and cutting the winding trail along the boggy shore which became the main street. On the hill he cut a clearing and built a log house and down below he built a store. He also began to erect buildings for sale or rent, as he had done in his youth as a carpenter near Paisley. His first tenant was a publican, James Dunn, and then merchants and householders moved in, but his dream of a log hamlet called New Paisley died still-born when Lieutenant Governor John Wentworth, who had been asked to christen the town, decided to call it Pictou. The old Micmac name suited the settlers better than New Paisley or any other names which had been used or suggested for townsites in the past—Donegal, Teignmouth, Southampton, Walmsley and Coleraine. Since no less than three unrelated Pattersons were present at the inception of the town—John, Squire Robert and Governor Walter from Prince Edward Island—it is perhaps a wonder that no one tried to name it Patterson. Some time in 1788 John Patterson moved into his new home, the first in Pictou town.

Highlanders and Lowlanders, the Scots trickled into Pictou Harbour during the late 1780s, boosting the population of the district to 700. Then, during a few hectic days in September 1791, the population was more than doubled by the arrival of two ships, one of which we know was the *Dunkeld*, filled for the most part with Roman Catholics from the Western Isles, the first large number of Catholics to arrive.

No arrangements had been made to receive them, many were very poor and the *Caledonian Mercury* commentator may have been speaking of these immigrants when he wrote that autumn: "Every act is practised by the seducers to inveigle them thither. They represent that country to be in the most flourishing and most prosperous situation, provisions plentiful and cheap and wages high . . . But were they to think for a moment upon these illusory ideas, they could not fail of discovering the folly of such representations and the deceit of their seducers." It was about this time that suggestions were made in Nova Scotia to take steps to keep the province from being over-run by indigent settlers.

The people of Pictou Harbour tried to help the new arrivals, but there was simply not enough food and on September 23 the leaders of the Catholic immigrants appealed to Lieutenant Governor John Parr in Halifax. Explaining they had spent what money they had on their passage and winter clothing, the new immigrants begged the government for a year's supply of food "so as to enable them to subsist their heavy and numerous Families until by their unremitted labours they may be enabled to support them from the produce of such Lands as your Excellency may think fit to allot them in proportion to their Families."

Having thus put their case, the immigrants hastened to support it with both a threat of moving to the rebel states to the south and with none-too-subtle flattery of the English king. "Your Petitioner humbly hopes your Excellency will further give him leave to state that the Horrors of Famine and the dread of perishing through the Severity of an approaching Winter for want of a reasonable Supply of Provisions will unavoidably compel such of these poor People who are at present possessed of the means of removal to fly from the Province and take shelter in the United States where every possible Encouragement is given them. But from the ardent Desire of these valuable People (whose Loyalty has never been impeached) to live under the best of Government or the best of Kings, must again implore your Excellency to take their Case into your most serious consideration and to adopt such Measures as will secure these deserving People to this Government, and lay the foundation of a vast Influx of similar Settlers from Scotland the ensuing Spring, who will be forever lost to the British Government by their immediate Emigration to the United States."

Finding their plight much too serious for the Pictou residents to cope with, Parr wrote, "My heart bleeds for them and I am distressed to know what to do with them. If they are not assisted, they must inevitably perish upon the Beach where they are now hutted; humanity says that cannot be the case in a Christian Country." Since there was no government money for relief, Parr dug into his own pocket and sent them meal and salt herrings to carry them through the winter. Hearing of their suffering, the Rev. Angus MacEachern, who had just arrived in Prince

Edward Island from Scotland, hurried over to safeguard their welfare, spiritual as well as temporal, for some had turned up at James MacGregor's Presbyterian sermons, seeking Christian comfort where they could find it. With the spring most of them began to move eastward, often by canoe, along the coast to what is now Antigonish County, and even to Cape Breton. They settled both at Arisaig, where they built a log church, and at Antigonish Harbour, where other Catholics had settled earlier. They were joined, through the years, by thousands from the Highlands until by 1827 there were 11 Roman Catholic parishes in eastern Nova Scotia. But Pictou remained Presbyterian. After the death of Donald Cameron, the Cameron family, the only Roman Catholics on the *Hector,* also moved east to Antigonish County to join their fellow Catholics.

MacGregor, although he had tried to help them, was not displeased to see the Catholics move on for he feared their influence on his parishioners as much as Bishop MacEachern had feared MacGregor's on the simple islanders. In later years Dr. Patterson maintained that so little did the early settlers know, or care, about religious difference "that if a clever priest had come here at the time Dr. MacGregor did, the one-half would have become Roman Catholic." The Rev. James MacGregor called the Catholics who passed through the harbour "dangerous guests:"

"Much of their time was spent in naughty diversions, jestings which are not convenient nor decent, in telling extravagant stories of miracles done by priests, and absurd tales about ghosts, witches, fairies, etc. The minds of the Protestant Highlanders, being partly tinctured with these superstitions before the arrival of the Roman Catholics, were less prepared to resist their influence than the minds of more reasoning and sceptical Christians. They had been pretty much weaned from the remains which the first settlers brought from Scotland, but we have not got wholly over these bad lessons."

During the next year Deacon John Patterson's little hamlet, still redolent of new-cut wood and sporting a crude harbour-side wharf fashioned from three great logs, gained new status. Until 1792 the people had to walk all the way to Onslow if they had business with municipal authorities, as Pictou Harbour had only been an appendage of the District of Colchester, or Cobequid. Now the Nova Scotia legislature set up the separate District of Pictou, with the new village as its heart.

John Patterson was appointed Treasurer of the Court of Session, which ran the municipal, and most of the juridical, affairs, and as tax collector he received taxes in the form of wheat, logs, oats or maple sugar. He was awarded a contract to construct the first municipal building, a two-story stone and log affair. The lower story was a jail, and it is, perhaps, no reflection on James Dunn's tavern customers that Dunn was called upon to supply handcuffs and the stocks which were set up outside the jail door. No *Hector* passengers appear among the early prisoners, but seamen who visited the harbour did not take kindly to incarceration for their infractions and Deacon Patterson's account book tells of broken locks, "broak hinges and other damages" to his new jail. The local people who sat as lay magistrates on the Court of Sessions made by-laws suitable to the community and held wide powers in municipal administration, roads, bridges, matters of law infringement, and were empowered to solemnize marriages. They licensed Peter Grant, whose father lived above the harbour, to open a school.

The Pagans, who had bought out Dr. Witherspoon to become practically sole owners of the old Philadelphia grant, brought out a contingent of 66 families, mostly Scottish, to settle on the grant which had by now been deserted by most of its original settlers. In an effort to avoid escheatment, the Pagans reversed the old policy of merely renting land to settlers, and for the sum of £257 passed over title to 7,306 acres to the 66 families, who cleared

1,600 acres in 10 years.* Although the Pagans eventually
lost their grant, the new settlers were allowed to remain.
The Pagans estimated they lost £700 in their efforts to colonize the Philadelphia grant, but met with no success
when they sought reimbursement from the provincial
government. Although there is no evidence that John
Pagan, who later settled in Quebec City, spent time at Pictou Harbour, his sons made up for that by taking an active
part in community affairs. Robert Pagan, who married a
daughter of Squire Robert Patterson, the Philadelphia
Company's long-time agent, was lay magistrate in the
Court of Common Pleas and Lieutenant Colonel in command of the 400-man Pictou Militia, of which his brother
Thomas was a subaltern.

Of all those associated with the *Hector,* no one had as
much impact on the community as did John Patterson.
Lumberman, shipbuilder, landlord, farmer, tax collector,
he put aside his ledgers and day book on the seventh day
to take up Bible and Shorter Catechism to labour for the
Lord. When it came time to build a church in his town, it
was John Patterson who loaned the money. When he died
in 1808, the year the Pagan or Philadelphia grant reverted
to the Crown, the man who sired the thriving village as
well as 12 children of his own was called "The Father of
Pictou."

The long years of war in Europe which began in the
1790s hastened the growth of Pictou's timber trade and its
offshoot, shipbuilding. Captain William Lowden of Dumfries in the south of Scotland, having settled on lower East
River and then having moved to the village, set up a shipyard, windmill and log house, the lower story of which
was his home and the upper his storehouse. Before the
church was built religious services were held in the house.
In 1799 Lowden built the 600-ton *Harriet,* the largest vessel
launched in Nova Scotia in the 18th century. John Dawson
and the Copeland brothers, Alexander and Thomas, also

*See Appendix E.

Lowlanders from Dumfries, built houses and began trading along the coast with schooners. Hugh Denoon, who came from Red Castle on Beauly Firth where both his father and brother were ministers, set himself up in the shipping business, became a customs collector and a magistrate and organized immigration schemes which were to bring thousands of Highlanders to Pictou Harbour—sometimes, as we shall see, with unfortunate results. Apart from John Patterson, few of the *Hector* passengers engaged in commerce, as they had little experience. One exception was William Matheson, whose father had settled at Londonderry but then moved to establish a farm at Rogers Hill. Young William borrowed £20 and became a pedlar, before selling the family farm, moving to West River and exchanging goods for timber and country produce which he sold in Pictou. Also, George MacConnell opened a tavern on West River.

But the merchant who was to tower over the others was a penniless young newcomer from the eastern fringes of the Highlands, Edward Mortimer from Keith, in Banffshire. John Patterson, his rival in business, used to remind Mortimer of how he had arrived at the harbour in 1788 at the age of 21, on a trading schooner from Halifax. "I dinna ken whether ye had twa shirts, but I ken ye hadna two jackets." He was tall, broad-shouldered, heavily built, and had a business capacity to match his ambition. With a few years of successful trading behind him, he had purchased Mortimer's Point, as he called it, northeast of Brown Point, and opened a store, married one of Squire Patterson's daughters, built ships and traded throughout the southern Gulf of the St. Lawrence. He became one of the richest young men in Nova Scotia, Chief Magistrate of Pictou, and in 1799, at the age of 32, he was elected Pictou's first member of the Legislative Assembly in Halifax where, until his death at the age of 52 in 1819, he hastened the growth of Pictou. He was known as the "King of Pictou," a bluff and hearty man whose wealth came from the timber trade and later from coal.

Timber enriched Pictou for 30 years and when the pine ran out the coal, whose escaping gas bubbles had given Pictou its Indian name, became the major export. Coal had been discovered at the back of the farms of the Rev. James MacGregor and Squire William Mackay as early as 1798, but at first it was dug only for local use. The Squire's son John Mackay, known as "The Collier," got a licence to export in 1807, and although he himself went bankrupt the later discovery of one of the great coal basins of the world pushed the East River settlements into the Industrial Revolution.

Since the summer after their arrival John Patterson and his companions from the *Hector* had been exporting square timber, but Edward Mortimer made Pictou Nova Scotia's biggest timber port. The Highlanders had become lumberers and the great 200-foot white pines and oaks which had terrified them in the autumn of 1773 were now a source of cash. Contracting with Mortimer each autumn, gangs of Highlanders took to the woods with food and rum to build crude camps and spend the winter felling and squaring trees and hauling them by oxen to the streams and rivers which would float the logs down to Pictou Harbour and the waiting timber ships. The Rev. MacGregor chided them for neglecting their farming, since in their eagerness to make money they spared time for only a hasty spring planting. He also scolded them for heavy drinking when he learned that 400 puncheons of rum imported from the West Indies had been consumed by lumberers and heard Edward Mortimer's reckoning that it took one gallon of rum at a cost of eight shillings to produce one 25-shilling "stick" of square timber. Yet the lumbermen, freezing in their rough winter camps or on the wet spring river drives, were only indulging a love for liquor exhibited by the whole community.

"The habitual use of liquor was common among all classes," Dr. Patterson observed. "The minister took his dram as regularly as parishioners. The Elder sold liquor.

No respectable person thought of sitting down to dinner without the decanter at one corner of the table. The poorest would have felt hurt if a friend called and he had no liquor to give him. No workman was employed without his daily allowance . . . no bargain consummated without a dram. On all occasions of public concourse, liquor flowed freely and scenes of family interest, births, burials and bridals were consecrated in a similar manner." Dr. Patterson found it remarkable that men who drank so much all their lives lived to such old age, imbibing *usquebaugh* in their younger days in the Highlands and rum when they came to Nova Scotia; but it was, he added, a "tremendous evil," and before the middle of the 19th century Pictou became famous for its powerful temperance movement.

Apart from weddings and the occasional *ceilidh*, there was little enough excitement at the harbour, unless an emigrant ship came in. Then everyone would run to the shore and some people would canoe down the rivers, for there were usually relatives aboard. There was great anticipation in the summer of 1801 when they learned that their neighbour Hugh Denoon had organized two shiploads to sail from Fort William and Loch Broom with people from Loch Broom parish, Beauly and the eastern Inverness parishes of Kilmorack and Kiltarlity.

Early that year Denoon had travelled the Highlands, from his native Beauly Firth to Loch Broom, soliciting emigrants with visions of bountiful farm lands and trees that provided a family with sugar, soap and fuel. He chartered two vessels, the *Dove* and the *Sarah,* at Fort William where customs records indicate he had signed up a total of 625 passengers. There was some dispute about Denoon's own figures, which showed too few passengers on one ship and too many on the other. There is, to this day, considerable confusion over how many people Denoon managed to cram on those two ships.

The *Dove,* the smaller of the two at 186 tons—not quite

as big as the *Hector*—carried 275 people; her passage, although squalid and uncomfortable enough, must have been uneventful since it failed to attract much notice from the chroniclers of the time. But the *Sarah*'s crossing was a nightmare, even in an era of terrible emigrant crossings.

At 350 tons the *Sarah* was considerably bigger than the *Dove* and although, according to Fort William Customs, she carried 350 people, of whom 144 were children, Dr. Patterson maintains in his history that she actually carried "700 souls, though two children being counted as one, and infants in arms going free, they were reckoned as 500 passengers." She was but halfway to Nova Scotia when she was stopped and boarded by sailors from a British man-of-war. It was wartime and the navy was kidnapping able-bodied landlubbers and turning them into sailors. The navy men had seized 25 of *Sarah*'s young male passengers and were about to sail away with them when Denoon, who had a persuasive tongue, managed to bluff the commander into believing that he was a government agent and that the men were needed in Nova Scotia; thus he won their freedom.

But no sooner had they escaped the press gang when an epidemic, both smallpox and whooping cough, broke out aboard the *Sarah*. By the time she reached Pictou Harbour 47 passengers had died. The survivors had been at sea for 13 weeks, two weeks longer than the voyage endured by their kinfolk on the *Hector*, and it was to be longer still before they could join their friends and relatives. At the harbour they were quarantined for weeks on a narrow spit of land and no one was allowed to approach them. Listed on the passenger manifests as farmers, tenants, labourers, these newcomers from Beauly and its neighbouring parishes, from Loch Broom and parishes to north and south, moved up the rivers to settle or back into the bush, enlarging older settlements or carving new ones. One of them, said Dr. Patterson, was to kindle the first fire on Mount Thom (where the *Hector* people had refused to settle because of the thick forest) on New Year's Eve, December 13, 1801. "His wife, as she gazed through the partially open roof at the waving tree tops overshadowing them, and within, at her shivering little ones clinging around her, thought of the comforts she had left behind in the old land, and declared her wish to be back in Scotland, if it were even to be in a jail."

With over-population in the glens resulting from the increased birthrate in the second half of the 18th century, and with the clearing of glens by landlords converting estates to huge sheep runs, large numbers arrived at Pictou in the next two years. Summing up that movement of people Robert Brown, Sheriff-Substitute of the Western District of Inverness-shire wrote, "In the year 1801, a Mr. George [sic] Denoon, from Pictou, carried out two cargoes of emigrants from Fort William to Pictou consisting of about seven hundred souls. A vessel sailed the same season from Isle Martin [Loch Broom] with about one hundred passengers, it is believed, for the same place. No more vessels sailed that year; but in 1802 eleven large ships sailed with emigrants to America. Of these, four were from Fort William, one from Knoydart, one from Isle Martin, one from Uist, one from Greenock. Five of these were bound for Canada, four for Pictou, and one for Cape Breton. The only remaining vessel, which took a cargo of people in Skye, sailed for Wilmington, in the United States. In the year 1803, exclusive of Lord Selkirk's transport (800 to Prince Edward Island) eleven cargoes of emigrants went from the North Highlands. Of these, four were from the Moray Firth, two from Ullapool, Loch Broom, three from Stornoway, and two from Fort William. The whole of these cargoes were bound for the British settlements, and most of them were discharged at Pictou."

"Many of them," said one of their descendants, "who thus commenced in the woods in destitution, afterwards became independent and left their families in comfortable circumstances and had reason to bless the selfishness of the Lairds and Dukes who had turned them out of the little holdings, possessed of their fathers for generations, and pulled the roof trees from off their humble homes."

By 1803 there were 3,000 people at the harbour and in settlements which stretched for a radius of 12 miles from the village of Pictou. Thirty years after the arrival of the *Hector* there was a look of permanence about the homesteads. Lord Selkirk, having settled Scots in Prince Edward Island and curious to see how the older settlement was progressing, commented on the East River folk of Pictou: "The old settled Highlanders, even those of 10 or 12 years date, have in general cleared as much as they want and do little more—having not ambitions of making money so much as living comfortably. Many of the older settlers are now building, or have got, neat framed houses." Painted frame-houses with split pine shingles were still somewhat rare, however, and there were many homes of squared or unsquared logs with roofs of birch bark or boards. Most had board floors and large cellars to keep potatoes safe from frost.

Knowing a Highland crofter's hunger for owning his own land, they were proud possessors of 300 or 500 acres, much of it uncleared, but nonetheless their own. On East River, the most heavily populated area, Roderick Mackay, the blacksmith, had come back from Halifax to farm 350 acres near his brother, Donald, who was now married and owned 450. Their older brother, Alexander, who had fought at Quebec, settled near them and their sister and brother-in-law, the John Robertsons of Kilmorack, had homesteaded farther inland to become the first settlers of Churchville. The Mackays built up their family fortunes on the upper river, and old Alexander's son, Alexander, won fame as the strongest, fastest man in the county.

There are many stories about him. One is about a bull which had gone wild and was shut up in a barn where none dared approach him. Alexander Mackay was sent for and standing by the side of the door he ordered that it be opened. As the bull rushed out, Alexander seized it by the horns, threw it on its back and held down the struggling beast until it grew quiet. Another time he chased and caught a caribou calf, to the surprise of the Indians who considered the caribou the fleetest animal in the forest. He tamed it and traded it to Squire William Mackay for a heifer. Squire William got the better of the bargain, for he sent it as a present to Governor John Wentworth who rewarded the Squire with a grant of 2,000 acres. Alexander lived to be 97 and when in his nineties could still mow his swathe of hay with the younger men.

Over on Middle River, Alexander Fraser, the *Hector* passenger who had been at Culloden as a youth, had achieved the independence he could not have in Beauly. He and his sons had received grants totalling more than 500 acres and in a petition requesting more acres, which were granted, they allowed as how they "now have certain comforts." The days were gone when their only neighbours on the river were Indians and there was no food except what they could gather in the forest.

It was in that year on September 24, 1803, that Alexander Fraser, the first to engage passage with the *Hector* in 1773, kin to the Lovat Frasers of Beauly, husband of the daughter of an Inverness-shire laird, died at the age of 75. He had sired seven children, including five sons, of whom two were born at Pictou. He had paid dearly for his independence in the early years but he laid firm foundations for a thriving family in Pictou County. From them were descended the Frasers who developed the Rocklin area and who were prominent in the development of the county.

Alexander's son, Alexander, who had come on the *Hector* as a child, occupied the family farm after his death. He became a church elder and was accounted among the more affluent of the settlers; his will in 1828 shows he possessed 520 acres which he distributed among his children.

Since business was still largely barter, he bequeathed no cash money but did pass down to his sons his three suits of "body clothes." Another of Alexander's sons, Simon, married Catherine Cameron, daughter of Alexander's old companion at Culloden, Alexander Cameron. Alexander Fraser's son David, the first child born of the *Hector* settlers at Pictou, served for more than 20 years as a sea captain and was father of John Fraser, who was for many years Pictou's only lawyer.

By 1803 there was a dependable food supply. No longer was it necessary—and had not been for many years—to walk out to Truro for potatoes to sustain them through the winter. Their staple diet of potatoes, herring, mackerel, coarse bread, butter and cheese was often augmented with beef or a pig salted down for the winter. They wasted nothing, from the snow-white tripe to the scrubbed intestines, which they stuffed with spices and minced meat for sausages, to the fat which they melted into yellow cakes for candles. Visitors found their diet had improved so much that children of eight or ten years were as big as boys and girls of 15 or 16 back in the Highlands. They were also more vigorous. According to Walter Johnstone, a settler who wrote a few years later from Murray Harbour, Prince Edward Island, across the Strait from Pictou, "I was told by a teacher from Scotland that the children here would learn as much in school in three months as they would do at home in twelve. At the age of ten years they have the freedom of speech, and the fortitude and boldness, of a Scottish boy of twenty."

They made clothes from their own fine quality wool produced by their lean, long-legged white-faced sheep, and from the flax grown in increasing quantity. The creak of the treadle and rumble of the spinning wheel were heard in every cottage.

Religion now played a larger part in their lives, and in many homes there was family worship twice a day. The Rev. James MacGregor had done his work well. A passage from his journals describes his methods: "I sat up many nights, almost the whole night engaged in religious conversation, sometimes rejoicing with those that rejoiced, and sometimes weeping with those that wept. The work of grace was apparently increasing."

Steeped as he was in John Knox's Book of Discipline and the idea of basic education, each time he conducted a baptism MacGregor instructed the parents to educate the child. "I found it easier than I had thought," he said, "to rouse the Highlanders to attend to the education of their children, so far as to read the Bible." At his own expense he imported Bibles from the British and Foreign Bible Society and devotional literature in Gaelic. He encouraged the settlers to establish one-room log schools.

The Rev. Duncan Ross had arrived in 1795 from the parish of Tarbat in the Cromarty country of Ross-shire to assist MacGregor. Young Ross, who settled on West River, had quite a sense of humour. He used to say of his preparation for the Pictou ministry that he had been lectured for one season in heresy and one season in superstition and then banished to the backwoods of Nova Scotia. He did, in fact, run into superstition among the Pictou settlers and when he preached a common-sense sermon on the subject of witches when his congregation wanted him to preach hell and brimstone, he lost several of his followers. "Mr. Ross was a man of a very clear and logical mind and strong natural powers," said Dr. Patterson. "He could scarcely be called a popular preacher but by intelligent persons his pulpit ministrations were highly relished for their clearness, variety and solidity of matter . . ." His style was an excellent balance to that of James MacGregor and between them the two secessionist Highland ministers formed the Associate Presbytery of Nova Scotia at a meeting in Robert Marshall's barn on July 7th, 1795.

John Gerrond, an itinerant Dumfries-shire poet, who lived among them for a year in 1797 working as a blacksmith and part-time school teacher, found the Scottish settlers in robust health and "extremely hospitable both among themselves and to strangers" and possessed of a sense of independence equal to that of their democratic Yankee neighbours. At Pictou there were neither lairds nor tacksmen to regulate their lives.

Down at the harbour the village was growing, although John Mackay, who had arrived as an 11-year-old on the brig *Sir Sydney Smith* in 1805, recalled his disappointment at finding "nothing at Pictou that could with any propriety be called a Town. There was one blacksmith shop, one tavern, and two or three small grocery shops . . . The East River at this time was certainly wild enough. The site of New Glasgow with the exception of a small log shantie at the bank of the river, was then a perfect wilderness . . ." There were, in fact, 18 buildings in Pictou village at that time and there would be soon be a fine frame church complete with belfry. John Mackay was to become a magistrate and 60 years later he wrote of "marvellous changes": "The whole face of the country is changed. In place of the four log churches, there are now over forty, each of which will accommodate 500 to 900 sitters on an average. I can count nine churches from the windows of my room. The old canoes are replaced by a steamer which runs twice a day between New Glasgow and Pictou." Mackay said that in 1805 itinerate teachers would come into his neighbourhood during winter and thus he learned to read and write. "Books were scarce and money not easily got by the likes of me; yet I managed to get some good books some way. From the Rev. MacGregor I borrowed many books; among the rest an encyclopaedia in two large volumes. I read it all and mastered a good deal of it, and made it my own." He was barely in his twenties when he started teaching in a log schoolhouse on Maclellan's Mountain behind East River, and later in the village of New Glasgow.

Like most villages, Pictou in 1805 had its local characters, among them the Micmacs Lulan and Patlass. Patlass, who had learned to play draughts and had become the waterfront champion beating all comers, had the Micmac's dry, ready wit. He enjoyed apeing the town officials, particularly the constable. On one occasion a sea captain had brought ashore a fighting cock and put it to battling a bird belonging to a townsman. Watching the struggle from the crowd for a while, Patlass suddenly seized one of the fighting cocks and walked off with it. The captain called to him to come back, but Patlass replied, "Take him to jail, fightin' in the streets." Patlass was drowned off Middle River Point in 1827, the same year his friend Lulan died, at the age of 97. Both had befriended the Scots from the start and had helped to teach them survival in the wintry woods of Nova Scotia.

Patlass and Lulan had adapted to European ways, but in general, while the Scots flourished, the Micmacs declined. Since the arrival of the whites, alcohol, smallpox and tuberculosis had taken a sickening toll. Logging and farming had driven away much of the game they had depended on for food. In the early days they had frequently given up their small plots of arable to the settlers for a pittance, and even on their reserves they were not safe from encroachment when the government gave the Scots the right to buy land on the reserves. Certainly some efforts were made to help them, led by the Rev. James MacGregor, for one. There were attempts to teach the women spinning and knitting and to educate the children in the white man's culture. In 1828 the settlers at Pictou organized the Indian Civilization Society, although it appears to have achieved little permanent good. By the 1840s there were fears they would die out completely by the end of the century, and in fact the Micmac population estimated at nearly 900 in 1775 by Dr. Harris had dwindled to something like 250 less than 100 years later. Those who remained continued their seasonal occupations—fishing in summer and hunting and trapping in winter, engaging in a little farming and making baskets for sale in Pictou town. By 1877 Dr. George Patterson noted that "of late there has been an improvement among them," and in fact the prophesy that the people who had helped the Scots gain a foothold at Pictou Harbour were a "doomed race" was not literally true. They did survive, though their traditional way of life was seriously altered and impaired. But after those first few years, when they had brought the settlers food and taught them to use canoes and snowshoes and to hunt and fish, the Micmacs played little part in the development of Pictou.

There were times, even when they had become established, that the Scots had all they could do just looking after themselves. In 1815 a plague of rodents, similar to those which had swept Prince Edward Island 40 years earlier, destroyed the crops before disappearing as mysteriously as they had come. They burrowed in the ground and ate the potatoes and were known to destroy an acre of grain in three days. They fell into the sticky troughs of the maple sugar makers and got into the cottages where they ate the bindings of the Bibles.

The settlers had not yet recovered from "the year of the mice," when they suffered "the year without a summer." "In August ice was formed half an inch thick." wrote Dr. Patterson. "Indian corn was so frozen that the greater part was cut down for fodder. Indeed almost every green thing was destroyed." It was a time of hunger such as the older people of the *Hector* had known in the Highlands in 1772.

But still the new settlers came from Scotland. In the years 1815-1820, following the Napoleonic wars, 20,000 Scots sailed for British North America, 1,500 to Pictou. Finding the harbour lands and the lower river intervales already occupied, they pushed on deep into the country, giving Highland names to little communities, such as Gairloch, Glengarry, Lairg, Beauly, Culloden and Lochaber, or bestowing hopeful names such as Garden of Eden. The Highland Clearances had begun.

Far up the rivers the new settlers had to learn to pioneer as the *Hector* people had done, cutting out farm land in the "bullying forest." "Many a labour I'll be involved in before I can secure a living" lamented the bard, John Maclean. "I'll be worn out by my work before I get any yield from it and before I cut a clearing so I can plough. Piling tree trunks on bonfires has strained my every muscle and all of me is soot-black."

"The poor wretches who are shoved into the back woods are making the greatest efforts of industry," wrote Judge Stewart of Prince Edward Island in a report on Pictou, "and notwithstanding all their privations and sufferings are wonderfully patient and persevering . . . the more I hear of my countrymen here the more I admire that Caledonian spirit . . ."

They learned, as best they could, from the earlier settlers, the *Hector* people and others, and adopted Yankee ways. Few had money and everything they used was home-made—hoes, barrels, yokes and soap. They made their clothes from wool that was carded, spun and woven from their own sheep, or hackled, spun and woven from the flax they grew.

The settlement of New Glasgow, across the East River from where the Mackays and others of the *Hector* had founded what became Stellarton, was thriving by now, on swampy land which had been covered with spruce, hemlock and pine. It had been named by Donald Mackay, a blacksmith who set up his forge there, and a surveyor's map of 1816 shows it was occupied by half a dozen families. Farther up the river the *Hector* passenger had opened a grist mill, as the people of the Upper Settlement had begun to raise large quantities of grain. James Grant had been one of the many *Hector* people who, after wandering for years in other parts of the province, had come back to the district. Described as "a quiet peaceful man," he died at the age of 97, in 1822.

The farmers on West River formed an agricultural society—the first in Nova Scotia—to improve farming methods and livestock, importing cattle from Ayrshire from where many West River settlers had come. The Rev. MacGregor, who would later establish a similar society on East River, was impressed by the farming skills of the Lowlanders but not, it seems, by those of his Highland neighbours, although they learned in time to raise impressive crops of wheat, oats and potatoes.

"Being emigrants from the mountainous parts of Scotland, where their fathers were little occupied with either ploughing or reading," MacGregor complained, "they had not much opportunity of being acquainted with agriculture before they came to this province, and ever since the ignorance of the English language has prevented them from profiting equally with others by the advantages enjoyed here." He complained of quarrels among the *Hector* settlers, which were usually over land boundaries which had been badly drawn in the 1780s. Even the vast acreages of the New World had apparently not stopped the bickering learned on the Forfeited Estates in Scotland where the tiny pockets of arable land were continually at issue.

MacGregor himself became involved in such a quarrel while boarding with William Mackay who, for all his reputation for hospitality, was seen by MacGregor as "a man of lofty and obstinate temper." Whether over land or something else, William Mackay had begun to quarrel with his neighbour and relative, the ex-soldier Colin Mackay, and MacGregor tried to make them stop by refusing both admission to the sacrament of the Lord's Supper. While Colin apologized, William refused and MacGregor found he had made an enemy for life. Nor was he able to reconcile the quarrel between William Mackay and another *Hector* passenger, the Roman Catholic Donald Cameron, whose religion appears to have isolated him from at least some of his Presbyterian neighbours.

When MacGregor had arrived at Pictou in 1786 there had been no minister or priest of any denomination on the entire north shore of Nova Scotia. But by 1803 MacGregor, whose energy had taken him to communities through all that area, had been joined not only by the Rev. Duncan Ross on West River, but also by a young man who settled at the harbour to build successfully upon MacGregor's early work.

The Rev. Thomas McCulloch arrived at Pictou Harbour on a cold November day in 1803, clutching in his arms two educational globes, one geographical and one astronomical—a portent of where his interests lay. He was 27, the same age as MacGregor when he had arrived, and was bound not for Pictou but for Prince Edward Island. When two church elders from the village, Robert Pagan and John Dawson, met him he had just discovered there would be no boat to Prince Edward Island until spring, so the elders asked him to minister to the village of Pictou, which had no clergyman of its own, until such time as he could proceed to the island. By spring, McCulloch had become so engrossed in the religious and educational needs of the town he decided to remain.

The son of a master print maker in the cloth trade at Fereneze in the Parish of Neilston, Renfrewshire, McCulloch had entered Glasgow University to study medicine but switched to theology at Divinity Hall, Whitburn. In Glasgow University, with its aura of David Hume and Adam Smith and its polymath search for moral common sense, McCulloch had acquired a love for liberal education that was to serve the Pictou people well. Whereas the simple Calvinist Highlander James MacGregor, steeped in John Knox's ideals of a church and school in every community, saw education as religion, McCulloch went further.

MacGregor claimed, in his Sabbath sermons on Sin and Salvation, that "without knowledge people can be neither good Christians nor good citizens."

Said McCulloch, "A liberal education is valuable, not so much on account of the information which a young man picks up at college, as for the habits of abstraction and generalization which he imperceptibly contracts in the course of his studies. These enable him to discriminate, arrange, and classify his knowledge; and thus to accelerate his subsequent improvement with ease and certainty." Both were Anti-Burghers and improvers, and between them they stirred the latent intellect of the children of the *Hector* people and brought a wondrous flowering of knowledge to the backwoods of Pictou County in the 19th century.

Aided and abetted by old Highland pioneers who could barely sign their names and backed by the merchant Edward Mortimer with both money and his considerable influence in the Nova Scotia legislature, the tireless McCulloch began to plan an institution of higher learning which would feed the Scots hunger for advancement. His visible target was the obvious need to train local ministers since it was difficult to obtain clergy from the Old Country. He opened a grammar school and with the help of MacGregor began to collect funds for a college. A subscription signed by East River settlers reads: "We are persuaded that such an institution would have a powerful influence to promote the interests of society both by disseminating general knowledge, correcting the vices of youth and instilling in their minds the principle of virtue."

In 1816 he founded his higher seat of learning called Pictou Academy, rather than College, because the government had not licensed it to grant degrees, but it otherwise aimed at standards set by universities in Scotland. He erected a modest, two-story wooden frame building with tower and steeple, and as Principal his first address was on "The Nature and Uses of a Liberal Education."

The Academy offered a four-year course which included Latin, Greek, Logic, Moral Philosophy, Mathematics, Algebra and Natural Philosophy, most of which McCulloch taught himself. He built a library, an array of scientific apparatus and a museum for scientific study which attracted a visit by John James Audubon to McCulloch's collection of wild life specimens and minerals. Aside from this heavy workload McCulloch preached twice a day in the new church. He established a Divinity class to educate local ministers, but since the Academy was non-sectarian his religious teaching was outside the college.

"I was one of his first students," wrote Jotham Blanchard, "and have often seen him, at 8 o'clock of a winter morning, enter his desk in a state of exhaustion, which too plainly showed the labours of the night . . . " Such were McCulloch's standards that no one was surprised when John Logan Murdock, whose father was a shoemaker, went to Glasgow University in Scotland with three classmates to study for the Master of Arts degree and all four were awarded M.A.s without need of further study. McCulloch found time to write uplifting editorials in the *Colonial Patriot*, established in 1827 as the first newspaper outside Halifax (apart from one at Shelburne which failed after just a year), and the *Stepsure Letters* which, under the guise of humour, poked fun at the foibles of the Pictou pioneers in a way contrived to make them mend their ways.

Dressing his 20 students, recruited from log homes within 12 miles of his Academy, in the flowing red gowns of Glasgow or Aberdeen, McCulloch, as MacGregor before him, fired the community with respect for learning. "There is no British colony improving with such rapidity as this and learning bears a proportion to other things," he wrote to a friend in Scotland. "With respect to family affairs I may add that I have now eight children and we have food and raiment. I undergo considerable fatigue but upon the whole enjoy a degree of worldly comfort and also of respectability I could not have aspired to in Britain."

Writing of McCulloch's Academy in his *Historic and Statistical Account of Nova Scotia*, T. C. Haliburton said, "It is rapidly spreading around it a spirit of education. Its people now are filling many respectable offices with credit to themselves, and what the province wants exceedingly, it is furnishing a race of qualified school masters."

MacGregor, when in his sixties, put his sense of

achievement into one of his inspirational poems, "Education," which doubtless reads more gracefully in Gaelic:

> *The Gael were ignorant, blind*
> *Education was scant in their midst*
> *Their knowledge was so shallow and backward*
> *That their loss they could not comprehend,*
> *They did not believe in gain or advantage*
> *To give prime education to their children,*
> *Though they might perceive*
> *It was this that gave the Sassanach a*
> *chance . . .*

But, continued MacGregor, after the coming of education the life of the Highlanders changed:

> *Now Highlanders will lift up their heads,*
> *They will no more in bondage remain;*
> *They shall have the high learning of the*
> *English,*
> *And Intelligence without stint.*

Despite a tough constitution, by 1828 MacGregor's hard life had taken such a toll that he suffered a stroke. His right side was paralysed, his memory affected and for the third time in 40 years he missed a Sunday service, but he recovered enough to go on reading the Bible to his parishioners in their homes. He would carry his own candle to read by so he would not have to use theirs. He still preached occasionally but on February 28, 1830, he delivered his last sermon; he suffered another stroke the next night and died two days later at the age of 71.

According to Dr. George Patterson, who on his mother's side was grandson of the Rev. James MacGregor (as well as being grandson to the *Hector* settler John Patterson), 2,000 people attended MacGregor's funeral. The tombstone read: "When the early settlers of Pictou could afford to a minister of the gospel little else than participation in their hardships, he cast in his lot with the destitute, became to them a pattern of patient endurance, and cheered them with the tidings of salvation . . . He lived to witness the success of his labours in the erection of numerous churches, and in the establishment of a Seminary, from which these churches could be provided with religious instructors . . . as a public teacher, combining instruction with example, he approved himself to be a follower of them who through faith and patience now inherit the promises."

A few years later the community lost McCulloch when, in 1838, he became the first Principal of Dalhousie College in Halifax where he served until his death in 1843. The academy would never be the same after his departure, but by establishing a school where a Scots lad could obtain an education for £20 a year, McCulloch made Pictou a source of future doctors, lawyers, ministers, teachers and administrators, totally out of proportion to the size of its population or the station in life of most of its settlers. The Academy continued McCulloch's work for another generation and among its students was another great educator, J. W. Dawson, first Principal of McGill University in Montreal.

Most of the Academy's students had come from the 60 log schoolrooms and 25 Sunday schools throughout the district—many of them started by MacGregor—and 11 of them on East River which over the years sent 300 ministers into the world. The people who lived in the 15-mile stretch between Churchville and Kerrowgare gave 35 clergymen to the Presbyterian Church, along with a provincial Governor, a Chief Justice and a Premier of the province.

By the 1830s, the 40-year-old town boasted 200 buildings, a population of 1,500 and a thriving export trade in shipbuilding, coal, fish and still, to some extent, in timber, which they used to pave their streets. It was, claimed the Scots of Pictou, the most important town outside of Halifax. When the politician Joseph Howe, then editor of the

Novascotian, came riding up to investigate, he found many handsome homes, crowned by Mortimer's house on the point and "some large and commodious stores . . . it has certainly progressed in a manner very creditable to the zeal and perseverance of the original settlers . . . "

From the hill above the town, which had been cleared for fields and gardens, he gazed south beyond the town to the whole township and its population of 10,000 Scots. Within five years the district, still part of Halifax County, would become a county in its own right, 50 miles wide and 20 deep with an area of 1,000 square miles.

"The waters of the broad Harbour are spread out like a mighty mirror before the eye," wrote Howe, "bounded on the left by the high land which stretches away towards M'Lellans Mount, Merrigomish & c and on the right by the woodland that lies between Pictou and the river John; while the East, West, and Middle Rivers, the folds of which are lost in the foliage of the trees and the undulations and irregularities of the land through which they flow, seem, as they wind away from the opposite shore of the harbour, like vast and beautiful veins, passing through the very heart of the country—the happy medium of circulation for the animating and sustaining tributes of Agriculture, Manufactures and Commerce . . . "

Riding back up the rivers, for now there were roads, Howe was struck by the Highlanders' "extravagant desire" to own large tracts of land. In the Highlands, land has meant wealth and status. "The habits of thought and reflection created by such a state of things," wrote Howe, "are not to be shaken off when the emigrant arrives in a country where land is of comparatively trifling importance [and] we have known many instances of serious embarrassment . . . " There was the case of the settler who, rich in land but nothing else, had sold 250 acres for £2 eleven shillings and seven pence. Another sold his land for a suit of clothes so he would have something decent to wear while seeking work at Truro.

Howe found the place abuzz with radical politics and

only half in jest he called Pictou "that abode of patriots" and "that cradle of liberty." The Highlanders had not escaped feudalism for nothing. They were now true Canadians, as Bard John Maclean of Barney's River, the poet of "The Gloomy Forest," affirmed:

Canada is our country,
The new land of freedom and plenty,
A good land in which overlords
Do not expel us from the glens.

Captain William Moorsum, author of *Letters from Nova Scotia,* also came riding up from Truro that summer and from the heights of Mount Thom he paused to admire the view toward the northeast.

The white buildings of the village of Pictou glistened in the sunlight and far beyond lay blue Northumberland Strait and the low-lying shore of Prince Edward Island. Riding down the West River Valley he found it cultivated for 15 miles from the upper-most settlement to Loch Broom, on Alexander Cameron's farm by the harbour. He described the district as "peculiarly Scotch," as well he might, with "keen-looking fellows" standing in knots in the streets of the village discussing "in broad Scotch or pure Gaelic" the topics of the day. There were buildings of stone as well as wood, some of them three stories.

"Thirty years ago," he mused, "the whole extent was little better than a wilderness and Pictou but a melée of miserable huts. In a few years more its character will, in all probability, be still further changed. The Highland bonnet which slouches like a nightcap over the eyes of the present generation of settlers will be worn out and replaced by a hat of native straw plaited by the hands of their children." On the back road he met a fine old man of more than 80 years, "walking stoutly along the road clad in the veritable costume of his ancestors except that his hose were of plain grey worsted." The old man spoke hardly any English and might well have been one of the people from the *Hector.*

By that time the patriarchs of the *Hector* were dying off.

When Hugh Fraser, the Kiltarlity weaver who had come with such good credentials from his parish minister in Inverness-shire, had died at the age of 86 four years earlier, only 12 of the heads of families who had come on the *Hector* were left to follow his remains on foot to the cemetery. It had been only two years since Squire William Mackay of Beauly, Justice of the Peace at East River, "went to bed in his usual health and was found dead about half an hour after" at the age of 97. Roderick Mackay, the headstrong blacksmith who had carried the key of Inverness jail to Nova Scotia, died in 1829 at his East River farm at the age of 83, having fathered descendants who were to include famous men, a Lieutenant Governor of Nova Scotia among them. Young William Mackenzie, who had resisted urgings to return to Loch Broom, Scotland, to claim his inheritance as the son of a wealthy laird, lived on into the 1840s, dying at the age of 90 at his farm at Loch Broom, Pictou County, where he was known among his neighbours as "The Peace Maker."

For Alexander Cameron the road from Culloden had been long. The Loch Broom boy who had witnessed the battle of 1746, which had ended an ancient way of life, and sailed to Pictou Harbour on the *Hector* at the age of 44 to build a farm at Loch Broom, Nova Scotia, died at the great age of 103 on August 15, 1831. He left a widow, eight children, 63 grandchildren and 21 great-grandchildren, and there are Cameron descendants in every Canadian province and scattered throughout the United States. Within his lifetime he had witnessed both the seeding and the flowering of Highland life in the new Scotland.

APPENDIX A

Contract drawn up between John Pagan and John Ross, June 3, 1773, setting forth Ross' responsibilities as leader of the expedition and the rights of the settlers going to Pictou Harbour on the Hector.

Scottish Record Office: Register of Deeds: McKenzie Office, vol. 220 (1776):

| In presence & | 6th Nov^r | Copy Contract between John |
| Da Rae Ad^{te} prop | 1776 | Pagan and John Ross |

This Contract between John Pagan merchant in Glasgow as one of the proprietors and having power from and taking burden on him for the reverend Doctor John Witherspoon & the other proprietors of a Tract of Lands in the Province of Nova Scotia in North America Commonly Called the pectew [?pecteu] Lands of the one part and John Ross merchant in Lochbroom in Ros shire of the other part doth witness that the said John Pagan in Consideration of the Obligations of the said John Ross herein after written doth by these presents Bind and Oblige himself and the other proprietors of the said Tract of Land and his and their heirs Executors and successors at their own Cost and Charges to Cause Survey Forty thousand Acres of the said Tract of Land where the said John Ross or his heirs or assignies or their Agents shall Chuse in so far as not already Granted and possessed by others and to lay off or divide the same into Lots each Containing from two hundred Acres to one thousand Acres by strait Lines drawn through the said Tract of Land at proper Distances parelell to each other, and to put the said John Ross or his heirs or Assignies or his or their Agents on his or their Arrival in Nova Scotia in possession of Twenty thous^d acres of the said fourty thousand acres to be Chosen by the said John Ross or his foresaids from the whole of the said fourty thousand Acres in this manner he or they may take either the one side of each line or every alternate Lott on both sides leaving the Lotts of the Proprietors as large as those of the settlers and observing the same rule on every Considerable Stream or publick road And the said John Pagan Binds and Obliges him and the other proprietors of the said Tract of Land and his and their foresaids on their own Charges to Grant Convey and make over in full property to the said John Ross and his heirs or assignies forever the foresaid twenty thousand Acres of Land to be Chosen as aforesaid with Liberty to fish in the rivers in and on the Sea Coast belonging to the said Tract of land, But under the Burden of a yearly quitrent pay^{le} to the said proprietors or their heirs or assignies of two shilling lawfull Sterling money of Great Britain for each one hundred Acres of Land the said John Ross or his foresaids shall be putt in possession of in Consequence of these presents Commencing the payment of the said Quitrents at the same with the Quitrent payable by the proprietors of the said Tracts of Land to his Majesty the King, and hence furth to Continue forever, And to Grant Subscribe and Execute in the most formal valid and habile manner all Deeds of Consequence and other Deeds and writts necessary for that purpose provided alwise that the said John Ross or his foresaids be obliged to settle on the said Twenty thousand Acres of Land this year a number of persons making up two hundred and fifty or net two hundred and twenty full freight passengers, and the said John Pagan for himself and the other proprietors of the said Tract of Lands Engages that one years provision for all the passengers to be sent out by the said John Ross this year in the Ship Hector John Speirs Masters shall be found at first Cost the persons to whom the same are furnished paying ready money therefore, and the new Settlers are to have every accommodation in the power of the proprietors untill they Build house for themselves. In Consideration whereof the said John Ross Bind and Obliges himself and his heirs Executors and Successors to settle on the said land such Number of persons as may be sufficient to make up two hundred and fifty and not under two hundred and twenty full freight passengers and to pay the said proprietor of the said tract of Land or their foresaids the said Quitrents of two Shillings Sterling for each hundred acres he shall be put in possession of as aforesaid Commencing at the time before mentioned and payable yearly thereafter and both the said parties Oblige them and their foresaids to fullfill perform and observe their several parts of these presents under the penalty of two hundred pounds Sterling to be paid by the party failling to the party observing or willing to observe and besides performance And they Consent to the registration hereof in the Books of Councill or any other Competent Court herein to remain for preservation and that Letters of Horning on a Charge of six days and all other Execution necessary may pass upon a precept to be Interponed hereunto in Common form and Constitute Mr David Rae Advocate Their prors for that purpose In witness whereof these presents Consisting of this and the two preceeding pages written on Stamped paper by Archibald Graham writer in Glasgow are subscribed with the Marginal Note on the second page written by said Archibald Graham at Glasgow the third day of June in the year seventeen and seventy three before these witnesses Thomas Graham writer in Glasgow and the said Archibald Graham signed John Pagan John Ross Thomas Graham witness Archibald Graham witness

APPENDIX B

No official passenger list from the Hector *has survived the voyage, if indeed there was such a thing since, at that time, the British government did not require them, but two lists were compiled in the 1830s from memory by two of the passengers.*

One list was drawn up by William Mackenzie of Loch Broom in 1837 and was included in Dr. George Patterson's A History of the County of Pictou, *published 40 years later. It is the less complete of the two, listing only the heads of families, but unlike the second list it does include observations about these families. It also includes some names not mentioned in the more complete list.*

Appendix B contains the list, now held by the Public Archives of Nova Scotia, drawn up by Squire William Mackay of East River, and includes wives and children, the wives listed by their maiden names, as was then the custom, and generally noted immediately after their husbands. In the section listing children under the age of two, the father's name is listed first and then the child's. The Mackay listing gives two separate dates, July 8 and 10, for the Hector's *departure from Loch Broom.*

Here follows the names of 179 persons that went out in the Hector John Spier master from Loch Broom to Pictou River in Nova Scotia. 8th July 1773

Full passengers above 8 years old.

Colin Douglas	Isabel MacKenzie	Finlay MacLeod
Cathre^n MacLean	James Murray	Margaret MacLean
Colin MacKay	Lilly Sutherland	John MacKay
Helin Fraser	Margret Murray	Marion MacLeod
Rodrick MacKay	Adam Murray	William MacLeod
Christ^o Grant	Abigal Murray	Mary MacKay
Donald MacKay	James MacDonald	Alex^r MacLeod
Alex^r Falconer	James MacLeod	Elspa MacLeod
Alex^r MacLean	Christ^n Urquhart	Donald Grant
John MacLellan	Walter Murray	David Urquhart
William MacLenan	Christ^n Murray	William MacKay
Hugh Fraser	Hugh MacLeod	John Sutherland
Magdalin MacKenzie	Christ^n MacKay	John Grant
John MacKenzie	David MacLeod	John Sutherland
Donald MacDonald	Mary MacLeod	Alex^r Cameron
Mary MacLean	Alex MacKenzie	Janet Ross
Mary Forbes	Mary Sutherland	Alex^r Ross
Thomas Fraser	Kenneth Fraser	Isabel MacLeod
Robert Innes	Cath^n MacKay	Alex^r Ross
Janet Munro	Donald MacKenzie	Donald Ross
Donald MacKay	Betty Sutherland	John Munro
Robert Lyon	Margret MacKay	Margret Sym
Donald Munro	William Mathewson	William Ross
Colin MacKenzie	Elspa MacKenzie	Archibald Chisholm

Appendix

William MacKenzie
John MacDonald
Kenneth MacKitchi
Alex^r McDonald
Ann Fraser
Charles Mathewson
Donald Cameron
Mary MacDonald
Alex^r Fraser
Alex^r MacKenzie
Hugh Fraser
William Fraser
Ann Smith

Mrs. Fraser
Angus MacKenzie
Margret MacKay
Donald Graham
Alex^r Ross
Mary Mathewson
Marion Ross
Wm. Ross
William MacKay
Janet Fraser
Donald MacKay
William MacDonald
Ann Patterson

James MacDonald
James Grant
Alex^r Grant
Hugh Fraser
Rebecca Patterson
William MacKay piper
William MacKenzie
John MacGregor
Margret MacKitchie
Sara Campbell
Alex^r Fraser

Passengers from 2 to 8 years old

Margaret Douglas
Rodrick MacKay
John MacKay
Mary MacDonald
Katharin MacKenzie
George Murray
Christ^r Murray
Marion MacLeod
Kenneth MacKenzie
Jane MacKenzie
Alex^r Fraser
Adam MacKenzie
Kenneth MacKenzie

Ann Mathewson
William MacKay
George MacKay
Kathrin MacLeod
Angus MacLeod
George MacLeod
Marion MacLeod
Alex^r Cameron
Cathrin Ross
Mary Ross
James MacKritchie
Mary Cameron
Simon Fraser
Cathrin Fraser
Isabel Fraser
Walter Ross

Alex^r Ross
Christian Ross
Donald Ross
James MacKay
Alex^r MacKay
Andrew MacDonald
Elizabeth MacDonald
Janet McDonald
Cathrin MacDonald
Thomas Fraser
Isabel Fraser
Margret Grant
Mary Grant
Jane Fraser
Mary Fraser

Children under 2 years old

Colin Douglas   Child
Colin MacKay
Do
Rodrick MacKay
Robert Innes
Colin MacKenzie
James Murray
Walter Murray
Donald MacKenzie
Do
William Mathewson
Finlay MacLeod
Do
John MacKay

Alex^r
Alex^r
Colin
Ann
Duncan
Colin
Elizabeth
Elizabeth
Elizabeth
William
John
Jannet
William
Ann

Alex^r MacLeod   Child
John Sutherland
Alex^f MacDonald
Do
Donald Cameron
Do
Alex Ross
William MacKay
William MacDonald
James Grant
Hugh Fraser
Andrew Mains
George Morrison

Donald
William
James
Hugh
John
Hugh
Cathrin
Flora
Ann
Jane
Donald
Andrew
Hector

Full passengers from Clyde

George MacConnel
Charles Fraser
James Campbell
John Patterson
Andrew Main
Jane Gibson
George Morrison
Jane Forbes
John Stewart

N.B.

In the preceeding list of passengers on board the Hector for Nova Scotia the number is 189. But there was only 179 shipt by John Ross from Loch Broom the other 10 including a child of George Morrison shipt from the Clyde. The Hector sailed from Loch Broom the 10th July 1773 and arrived at Pictou the 15th September following.

212

APPENDIX C

Official list of the number of families in the District of Pictou as of November 8, 1775.

"Jonas Earl, Robt. Watson, Rob. Watson, jr., Daniel Earl, Daniel Earl, jr., Jas. Watson, Isaiah Horton, Patrick Berry, Wm. Aikin, John Fulton, James Fulton, John Patterson, George McConnell, Mat. Harris, Robt. Harris, John Rogers, Wm. McKenzie, Wm. McCracken, Abram Slater, Moses Blaisdell, Wm. Kennedy, Jas. Davidson, John McCabe, Bar. McGee, John Wall, Colin McKenzie, Alex. Ross, Donald McDonald, Wm. McLeod, Walter Murray, Thos. Fraser, Alex. Fraser, Wm. McKay, Hugh Fraser, Alex. Faulkner, Colin McKay, Colin Douglass, James Campbell, Thomas Troop, James Hawthorn, Joseph Glen, John McLennan, Ken. McClutcheon, Hugh Fraser, John Ross, George Morrison, Robt. Jones, Don. Cameron, Rod. McKay, Robt. Sims, Peter Hawthorn, John McLellan.—November 8, 1775. (Signed) John Harris." A number of these, set down as families, however were unmarried men at this time. Upon this a petition was presented to the Governor to issue a writ for the election of a representative, but the request was not granted.

APPENDIX D

The militia roll of the men of "Pictou or Tinmouth" capable of bearing arms, as of February 12, 1783. (The district was described as beginning at Caribou, encompassing the harbour and its three rivers, and extending to Merigomish.)

"James Grant, William Campbell, Robert Jones, Wm. McCracken, George McConnell, John Patterson, sen., James Patterson, David Patterson, John Patterson, jr., John Rogers, sen., James Rogers, John Rogers jr., David Rogers, James McCabe, John McCabe, Anthony McLellan, James McLennan, Ed. McLean, Joseph Ritchie, William Clark, John McLean, Wm. Smith, David Stuart, John McKenzie, Hugh Fraser, Wm. McLellan, James McDonald, Charles Blaikie, John Blaikie, James Watson, Alex. Cameron, Colin Douglass, Don. McDonald, Robt. Breading (Bryden), John Breading, Alex. Ross, sr., Alex. Ross, jr., James McCulloch, Robt. Marshall, John Marshall, John Crockett, John Crockett, jr., Alex. Fraser, Alex. Fraser, jr., Simon Fraser, Colin McKay, Rod. McKay, jr., James McKay, Donald McKay, Donald McKay, jr., Donald Cameron, Anthony Culton, John Culton, Colin McKenzie, Alex. McLean, John Sutherland, Thos. Turnbull, John McLellan, Wm. McLeod, Hugh Fraser, sr., James Fraser, Esaias Horton, Steatly Horton, Morton (Walter) Murray; George Morrison, Barnabas McGee.

"The above is a true list, given under my hand at Halifax, 12 February, 1783.   Robt. Patterson, Captain."

APPENDIX E

A government document, drawn up in 1809 after the escheatment of the Philadelphia grant for non-compliance with settlement terms, outlining the history of the Grant.

Origin of the Philadelphia Grant

His Majesty's Council, to whom it has been referred to examine the claims of the heirs of John Pagan for a compensation in land for the lands held by him under the Philadelphia Grant reports as follows:

From the statement made by Mr. Robert Pagan and the documents produced by him, it appears—that the year 1772 John Pagan, his nephew, William Pagan and John Witherspoon purchased for the consideration of £225 sterling three undivided shares of 12,857 acres, each, in the Philadelphia Grant from George Bryan, John Bayard and Isaac Wickoff, original grantees under the said Grant.

That in the year 1783 the said William Pagan assigned over all his rights and titles in and to said lands to the said John Pagan—That in the year 1793 the said John Witherspoon conveyed all his rights and title in and to said lands to the said John Pagan in exchange for other lands belonging to John Pagan valued at £211-2-2 Sterling. That between the years 1767 and 1773, 31 families were brought from what are now the United States and settled upon the said Grant by the original grantees all of whom afterwards removed from there, none of those families at present remaining upon it.

That in the year 1773, 72 families consisting of 190 persons were brought into the Province from Scotland through the means of the said John Pagan for the purpose of being settled upon the Philadelphia Grant, (Ship Hector group), the greater part of whom were in the first instance settled by the person acting in behalf of the original propriters within the limits of said Grant, but afterwards removed to other parts of Pictou, a few still remaining within said limits.

That between the years 1773 and 1792 about 25 families were settled by W. Pagan upon the said Grant, but to whom he did not convey any land, who remained a few years upon it and then removed.

That in the year 1793 Robert Pagan, son of the said John Pagan settled 66 families upon the said Grant to whom he conveyed 7306 acres for the consideration of £257.

That the said 66 families still remain upon the said Grant and have cleared and improved according to W. Pagan's estimation, upwards of 1600 acres of land.

Amount expended by John Pagan and his heirs on account of the said lands.

Purchase money of lands from the original grantess.

John Pagan having purchased the whole £225—equal to £250.00

Purchase money of John Witherspoon share £211.2.2 equal to £234.11.3.

Money laid out for provisions for the settlers brought out in 1773 which sum was afterward received from the settlers by Mr. Harris as the Agent of the proprietors and retained by him for his services.

$$£311.2.2$$

Money paid by J. Pagan in Scotland on account of settlers brought in 1773 (on board the Hector) £75.12.8 equal to £ 84.0.8

Legal work   78.7.5

£958.1.6(*sic*)

John Pagan and his heirs received for sale of 7306 acres   257.0.0

Leaving a balance of   £701.1.6

expended by John Pagan and his heirs in the purchase and for the purpose of improving and settling the said land.

Public Archives of Nova Scotia
Vol. 226, doc. 148

APPENDIX F

Ship Hector, the Creation of a Replica

Much of what we know about the *Hector* was passed down through settlers' families. Of the earlier pioneers, all but one Catholic family stayed in the largely Protestant region of Pictou today. That family moved to nearby Antigonish. Hence, there are a great number of people, with stories to tell of their ancestors' voyage on the *Hector*, located in much the same place.

From books written about the voyage, and from a number of sources, researchers determined that the *Hector* was an old Dutch ship, probably 20 years old by the time of the 1773 voyage. It was a 200 tonne, fully-rigged berthing vessel of roughly 90 feet in length, 20 wide and ten to twelve feet deep. Those dimensions form a total of 1800 square feet—roughly the size of a small house—that had to accommodate nearly 200 men, women and children.

Armed with research from this side of the Atlantic about the original *Hector*, two architects were dispatched, one to Holland and the other to the Maritime Museum in London and to Edinburgh. They returned with plans for five possible ships. Two were immediately rejected, one for being too long and the other for being too short. From a process of elimination, the size and shape of the replica was determined. If it hadn't been for a bombing raid during World War II, the researchers would have had no difficulty identifying the right ship. Lloyds of London has kept ship records for hundreds and hundreds of years, but a German bomb destroyed the records for only seven of those years—1768 to 1775.

There have been other ships named *Hector*, of course—five or six up to 1768. There is even an American *Hector*, built later than 1773, but owned by the same person. However, it is unlikely to have been a replica. To find a similar ship, one has to look to other ship-rigged (fully-rigged) sailing ships of the era, such as *The Bounty* (replica built in the 1950s out of Lunenburg, Nova Scotia).

It has been 12 years since the idea of replicating the *Hector* was first floated. Most of the original resources and a lot of the energy were exhausted in those first two years of research. Since 1991, when the keel was laid, construction took place in the summer months only. Progress was slow, but methodical. The workers, according to Vern Shea, chief engineer on the project, tended to be on government grants and were not fully-trained shipwrights. The intention had been to launch the *Ship Hector* in 1998, exactly 225 years after the original had sailed into Pictou Harbour. But that plan was scuttled after a couple of years during which funding was so tight that all Shea and his crew could do during the summer months was routine maintenance to repair the ravages of winter. However, the pace picked up once the fund-raising, supported by community assistance and government funding through the Canadian Millennium Fund, enabled the acquisition of skilled workers on site.

Although modern tools were used, efforts were made to combine traditional materials with current safety guidelines and other specifications. American white oak from the Carolinas and Virginia make up the internal hull as these woods are less likely to rot than native oak. The external planking is Nova Scotia pine and the ceiling is Nova Scotia spruce. The two masts are carved in Douglas fir and await placement. The sails are made from an East Indian cloth that looks and feels like worn canvas, but is resistant to rot. Likewise, the ropes are made of a synthetic material that feels like hemp, but is protected from ultraviolet light.

Ship Hector is painted like a typical merchant marine ship of her time. The topsides are black onto which are painted white stripes that resemble, at a distance, gun portals. making her look like a British naval vessel.

Today the *Ship Hector* awaits the setting of her rigging and the finishing of her interior. Once all is completed, the *Ship Hector* will be moored at the Hector Heritage Quay, a permanent extension of the museum and interpretative centre.

Alexa Thompson. Editor, *Celtic Heritage* magazine
(based on an interview with Vern Shea,
Project Chief Engineer, in the spring of 2000)

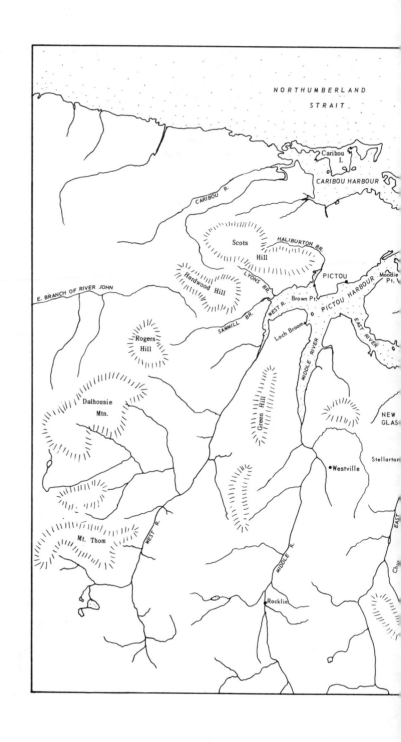

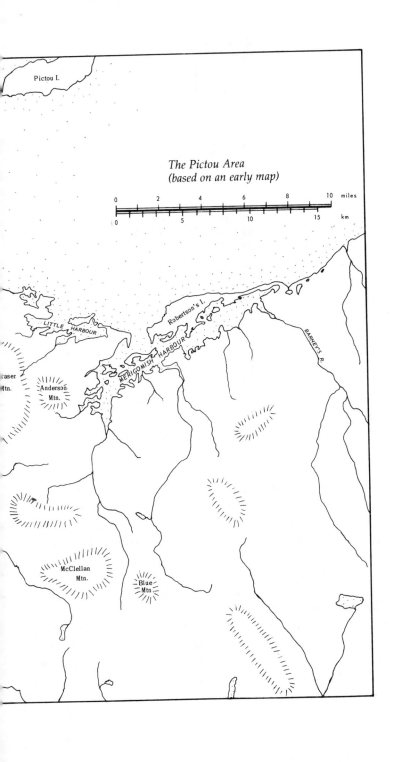

Pictou I.

The Pictou Area
(based on an early map)

0   2   4   6   8   10   miles

0   5   10   15   km

LITTLE HARBOUR

Robertson's I.

BARNEY'S R.

MERIGOMISH HARBOUR

raser Mtn.

Anderson Mtn.

McClellan Mtn.

Blue Mtn.

Postscript

Twenty-three years ago my friend Clyde Sanger, an Ottawa author and journalist, was touring Nova Scotia with his sons Toby and Dan. At Pictou he happened to go into the Bank of Nova Scotia, where he saw an exhibit of children's drawings celebrating the 200th anniversary of the arrival in Pictou Harbour of the brig *Hector* with 189 Scottish men, women and children. After a harrowing voyage the vessel had dropped anchor on September 15, 1773, near a forest clearing that had been settled six years earlier by a handful of Americans.

The passenger list read like a lengthy roll-call of the glens, or several pages of a telephone directory of latter-day Nova Scotia; the names included Chisholm, Munro, Campbell, Stewart, Innes, Graham, Grant, Murray, Cameron, Douglas, Mathewson, MacGregor, Maclean, Urquhart, MacRichie, Falconer, MacConnel and Lyon.

There were Frasers, MacKays and Munros from eastern Inverness; MacLeods, Rosses, MacDonalds, Mac-Lellans and MacKenzies from Loch Broom and Assynt; MacKays, Sutherlands and MacLeods from Sutherland-shire. There were also a few Lowlanders: Patterson, Gibson, Main, Sym, Forbes and Morrison.

By 1803 the population of Pictou had grown to almost five thousand. It had become a thriving lumbering centre and through the port came thousands of Scots on their way to other parts of Nova Scotia, including Cape Breton Island. The people of the *Hector* made history because they created the first focal point for Highland settlement in the province and also because of the influence their descendants were to exert on the 19th-century educational institutions of Nova Scotia and Canada.

The *Hector* story was new to Clyde Sanger, who has a lively interest in Highland history. There are Munros among his ancestors, although he did not know at the time there had been a Munro on the *Hector*. Recalling that my own forbears had come from the Highlands via Pictou, he suggested I write a history of the event that had heralded the flowering of Scots in Nova Scotia.

There had been little published about the people of the *Hector* since Dr. George Patterson's *History of the County of Pictou* in 1877. So after two years of research and writing had taken me to the Scottish Highlands as well as to Pictou, *Scotland Farewell: The People of the Hector* was published in 1980. Since then, like most books, it has taken on a life of its own.

The arrival of the brig *Hector* on September 15, 1773, is re-enacted every summer during the *Hector* Festival on the Pictou waterfront. A longboat representing the one rowed ashore from the *Hector* is greeted by people acting the parts of those who had settled there earlier from the American colonies.

The Hector Heritage Quay includes an Interpretive Centre where visitors can see a depiction of the voyage and an ongoing reconstruction of the brig *Hector*, using the 18th-century methods by which the original vessel was constructed in Holland. Shown here is the Interpretive Centre on its opening day, July 1, 1995.

Scotland Farewell was one of three semifinalists for the Governor General's nonfiction award and has attracted dozens of letters from people searching for their roots, including one from as far away as Hong Kong.

One correspondent, Thomas R. MacKay, Jr., an amateur genealogist in Glendale, Arizona, particularly brought the saga of the *Hector* back to life for me. He wrote that he believed his ancestor might have been the young Roderick MacKay who escaped from Inverness Jail in order to board the *Hector*. Roderick brought the key with him and it reposes to this day in the Nova Scotia Archives.

I would like to think the book has played a useful role in the imaginative projects in Pictou which, over the past decade, have lifted history off the printed page and transmuted it into virtual reality.

These began in 1987 when an annual Hector Festival

The *Hector* replica under construction. The original ship, which had been old and rotting when she brought the settlers to Pictou, ended her life in the shipbreakers yard not long after her return to Scotland from Nova Scotia.

was conceived and developed by Wayne MacGillivary and John Meir of Pictou's deCoste Entertainment Centre for the performing arts. The Festival, which celebrates its tenth anniversary this year, is held in August to promote Scottish heritage and culture. It draws thousands of visitors from across Canada and the United States to pipe band concerts, highland dancing competitions, genealogical sessions and historical displays. The highlight of the five-day festival is re-enactments, in authentic costume, of the landing of the *Hector* settlers in 1773. At the Hector Heritage Quay, built on reclaimed land, visitors will find an imaginative museum and interpretive centre which includes lifelike figures of the crew and passengers.

Another development in commemoration of the people of the *Hector* came to my attention a few years ago

A carpenter makes blocks for rigging the *Hector*. Known as a brig in the United Kingdom, the *Hector* was described as a "flute-class" vessel in Holland, where it was built in the 18th century.

when I received a query from marine architects seeking more details about the ship. I was pleased to hear that the Pictou Waterfront Development Corporation and the people of Pictou were building an exact wooden replica of the vessel that had ended up in the breaker's yard so long ago. Work began in 1990 and the *Hector* was scheduled to be completed in 1998 in time for the 225th anniversary of the ship's arrival. Funds for the construction, maintenance and operation of the *Hector* are being raised by The Ship Hector Foundation, a nonprofit organization in Pictou staffed by volunteers.

Due to these efforts Pictou has become one of the prime tourist attractions of Nova Scotia.

A sculptor's impression of Capt. John Spiers of the *Hector* in a lifelike pose in the Interpretive Centre, and an announcement that appeared in the *Edinburgh Advertiser*.

For PICTOU HARBOUR in NOVA SCOTIA, BOSTON and FALMOUTH in NEW ENGLAND.

THE SHIP HECTOR, JOHN SPEIR mafter, burthen 200 tons, now lying in the harbour of GREENOCK. For freight or paffage apply to John Pagan merchant in Glafgow, Lee, Tucker, and Co. merchants in Greenock; and in order to accommodate all paffengers that may offer, the fhip will wait until the 10th of May next, but will pofitively fail betwixt and the 15th of that month.

N.B. Pictou harbour lyes directly oppofite to the ifland of St. John's, at the diftance of 15 miles only.

225

Janice Gammon stands near the Ship Hector Quay and
models the Ship Hector Tartan she designed, with the
replica of the ship in the background. The colours Janice
so carefully selected have special meaning: white for the
whitcaps the *Hector* battled at sea, royal blue for the loyalty of the settlers to their homeland, green for the evergreens that lined the Nova Scotia shoreline, black for the
lives lost on the trip and gold for the rising sun. Once
registered with the Scottish Tartan Society of Pitlochry,
the tartan was unveiled at the Hector Festival at the
deCoste Entertainment Centre in Pictou. As Janice says,
"It's a tartan that touches everyone in Nova Scotia."

Work began when the keel was laid in 1990. Funds for construction, maintenance and operation were raised by the Ship Hector Foundation, a non-profit organization of volunteers. Through the years since then, visitors have witnessed the gradual progress of the brig taking shape. Some enthusiasts have actually taken part in construction work, returning frequently to check on progress, some scheduled their vacations as working holidays in order to lend a hand. Altogether over the past years there were twelve different categories of tradesmen at work: these included naval architects, marine draughtsmen, master shipwrights, shipwrights, caulkers and beatlers, planking gang, labourers, painters, blacksmiths and carvers. If a ship like the *Hector* were being built in a regular shipyard today, the cost would be six to seven million dollars Canadian. Construction techniques were essentially the same as they would have been in the 1700s when the original brig was built in Europe, with the exception of modern fastenings and the use of power tools.

Some 15,000 people congregated at Pictou Harbour in Nova Scotia to witness the launch of the *Ship Hector*.

Shipwrights and workmen pre-pare to set the ship free for its sideways launch.

Finally, on September 17, 2000, some 15,000 people gathered to see the long awaited launch-ing. It was, said one of those present, "a day unrivalled in anticipa-tion, excitement and exhilaration." At precisely 2:18:11 p.m. the *Ship Hec-tor*, an exact replica of her long-lost namesake, left her stocks and be-came seaborne, an inspiring vision of an 18th-century sailing ship in Pictou Harbour, more than two centuries after the arrival of "The People of the Hector" off Brown's Point.

In the events of Sep-tember 15 to 17 celebrat-ing the achievement, the Clans were well represented, over thirty different groups. Traditional musical entertainment and highland dancing fed off the post-launch energy on the waterfront. The grand finale was the "Big Sing," an incredible compilation of cho-risters from throughout the county, performing music, hymns and Scottish airs that reflect the themes of the *Ship Hector* launch. The grand Clan March on the Sunday was an act of remembrance for those who lost their lives on that brutal voyage of 1773. In years to come there is to be an annual September celebration—a New Scotland Day—to mark the anniversary, recalling the arrival which so funda-mentally shaped the community and indeed the province.

Cannons are fired to herald the start of the launch.

The two "triggers" are hammered away and the ship is ready to be moved down a series of steps towards the water.

The *Ship Hector* slides silently towards a new life at sea.

Crowds came from across Canada and the United States—some by boat—all in anticipation of this exceptional achievement of the completion of the full-scale replica of the *Hector*.

In recognition of the historic nature of the occasion, a number of people came in costume.

At the Pictou Heritage Quay, which won the Provincial Attractions Award for 2000, guides are on hand to walk visitors through a heritage experience which recreates the life and times of the *Hector* immigrants. Visitors can drop into the working carpenter and blacksmith shops and discuss ancestral craftsmanship and tools with the tradesmen or buy *Hector* keepsakes in a gift shop. A resident artist, David MacIntosh, creates images of the *Hector*, her passengers, and Pictou, past and present.

A visitor to the Pictou Heritage Quay cannot but be struck by the pride of the

Regimental re-enactment players stand to attention.

The *Ship Hector* hits the water, to bob back, making the culmination of ten years work come to a successful conclusion. There is more finishing work to come, but the critical stages are complete. The *Ship Hector* is seaborne.

Flags flying proudly, the *Ship Hector* is towed to a waiting wharf, allowing for the building of a proper wharf.

people of the town in turning a dream into reality, a notable feat of determination and perseverance for a community of 4,000 people.

Donald MacKay
May 2001

REFERENCES

BOOKS

Bain, Robert. *History of the Ancient Province of Ross.* Dingwall, 1899.

Boswell, James. *The Journal of a Tour to the Hebrides with Samuel Johnson.* London, 1786.

Brebner, J. B. *Neutral Yankees in Nova Scotia.* New York: Columbia University Press, 1937.

Burt, Edward. *Letters from a Gentleman in the North of Scotland.* London, 1815.

Cameron, James. *Pictou Country's History.* Kentville, N.S., 1972.

Campbell, D., and MacLean, R. A. *Beyond the Atlantic Roar.* Toronto: McClelland and Stewart Ltd. 1974.

Collins, Varnum Lansing. *President Witherspoon.* Princeton University Press, 1925.

Cowan, Helen I., *British Emigration to British North America, 1783-1837.* Toronto: University of Toronto Press, 1928.

Dunn, C. W. *The Highland Settler.* Toronto: University of Toronto Press, 1953.

Forbes, Robert. *The Lyon in Mourning.* 2 Vols. Scottish Historical Society, 1895.

Graham, H. G. *Social Life of Scotland in the Eighteenth Century.* A. & C. Black Ltd., 1928.

Graham, Ian Charles. *Colonists from Scotland: Emigration to North America, 1707-1783.* Cornell University Press, 1950.

Gullet, Edwin C. *The Great Migration: The Atlantic Crossing by Sailing Ship Since 1770.* Thomas Nelson & Sons, 1937.

Haliburton, Thomas C. *An Historical and Statistical Account of Nova Scotia.* 2 Vols. Halifax, N.S., 1829.

Halifax, N.S. Public Archives of Nova Scotia. "The Pictou Plantation: 1767" [by Henry R. Beer].

_____. Reminiscences of a Long Life, 1792-1884 [by John MacKay].

Harvey, D. C., ed. *Journeys to the Island of St. John.* Toronto: MacMillan, 1955.

Home, John. *A Survey of Assynt.* Edinburgh: Scottish History Association, 1960.

Irvine, Alexander. *An Inquiry into the Causes and Effects of Emigration from the Highlands.* Edinburgh, 1802.

Johnson, Samuel. *A Journey to the Western Islands of Scotland.* London, 1775.

Knox, John. *A Tour through the Highlands of Scotland in 1786.* London.

Macgill, W. *Old Ross-shire.* Inverness, 1909.

MacKenzie, Alexander. *The History of the Highland Clearances.* Glasgow, 1914.

MacKinnon, Ian F. *Settlements and Churches in Nova Scotia, 1749-1776.* Montreal, 1930.

MacLaren, George. *The Pictou Book.* New Glasgow, N.S.: Hector Publishing Co., 1954.

233

MacPhie, J. P. *Pictonians at Home and Abroad.* Boston, 1914.

McRobert, Patrick. *A Tour through part of the North Provinces,* 1776. CO 217/76 PANS.

Martin, Martin. *A Description of the Western Isles.* Glasgow, 1884.

Miller, Thomas. *Historical and Genealogical Record of the First Settlers of Colchester County.* Reprint. Belleville, Ont.: Mika Studio, 1972.

Moorsum, W. Capt. *Letters from Nova Scotia Comprising Sketches of a Young Country.* London, 1830.

Murdoch, Beamish. *A History of Nova Scotia,* Halifax, 1866.

Murray, John. *The Scotsburn Congregation.* Truro, N.S., 1925.

Patterson, Frank H. *John Patterson: The Founder of Pictou Town.* Truro Printing and Publishing Co., 1955.

Patterson, Rev. George. *A History of the Country of Pictou.* Montreal, 1877. Reprint. Belleville, Ont.: Mika Studio, 1972.

_____. *Memoir of the Rev. James MacGregor, D.D.* Philadelphia, 1859.

Pennant, Thomas. *A Tour in Scotland, and Voyage to the Hebrides.* 2 Vols. Chester, England, 1774-76.

Prebble, John. *Culloden.* London: Secker and Warburg, 1961.

_____. *The Highland Clearances.* London, 1963.

Punch, Terrence M. *Genealogical Research in Nova Scotia.* Halifax, N.S.: Petheric Press Ltd., 1978.

Raymond, W. O. *Colonel Alexander McNutt and the Pre-Loyalist Settlements of Nova Scotia."* Royal Society of Canada, 1912.

Robinson, John, and Respin, Thomas. *A Journey through Nova Scotia.* York, England, 1774.

Ross, D. K. *Pioneers and Churches.* New Glasgow: Hector Publishing Co., n.d.

Selkirk, 5th Earl. *Observations of the Present State of the Highlands of Scotland, with a view of the Causes and Probable Consequences of Emigration.* London, 1805.

Seton, Sir Bruce Gordon, and Arnot, Jean Gordon. *The Prisoners of the 'Forty-Five.* 3 Vols., Scottish Historical Society, Edinburgh, 1928.

Sherwood, Roland H. *Pictou Pioneers.* Windsor, N.S.: Lancelot Press, 1973.

Smout, T. C. *A History of the Scottish People.* William Collins Sons & Co., 1969.

Stewart, David. *Sketches of the Character, Manners, and Present State of the Highlanders of Scotland.* 2 Vols. Edinburgh, 1822.

Woods, David Walker, Jr. *John Witherspoon.* New York, 1906.

ARTICLES

Adam, Margaret I. "The Causes of the Highland Immigration of 1783-1803." *Scottish Historical Review* XVII, 1920.

_____. "Eighteenth Century Highland Landlords and the Poverty Problem." *Scottish Historical Review* XIX, 1922.

_____. "The Highland Emigration of 1770." *Scottish Historical Review* XVI, 1919.

Harvey, D. C. "The Intellectual Awakening." *Dalhousie Review* XIII, April 1933.

MacKenzie, Alexander. "First Highland Emigration to Nova Scotia: Arrival of the ship Hector." *Celtic Magazine* VIII, 1883.

MacLeod, Ada. "The Glenaladale Pioneers." *Dalhousie Review* XI, 1931.

MacLeod, R. C. *"The Western Highlands in the Eighteenth Century."* *Scottish Historical Review* XIX, 1922.

Mason, John "Conditions in the Highlands after the 'Forty-five." *Scottish Historical Review* XXVI, 1947.

Patterson, Judge George. "The Coming of The Hector." *Dalhousie Review* 111, 1923.

Sawtelle, William Otis. "Acadia: The Pre-Loyalist Migration and the Philadelphia Plantation." *Pennysylvania Magazine of History and Biography,* 1927.

NEWSPAPERS

Boston Gazette (Massachusetts), 1758.
Caledonian Mercury (Edinburgh), 1772-3, 1791.
Colonial Patriot (Pictou), 1827-28.
Edinburgh Advertiser, 1772-3
Edinburgh Evening Courant, 1772.
Gentlemen's Magazine (London), 1750, 1766.
Glasgow Journal, 1772.
Glasgow Weekly Chronicle, 1773.
Greenock Advertiser, 1805.
London Magazine, 1746, 1766.
Pennsylvania Chronicle, 1766-7.
Scots Magazine, 1746.

PRIMARY SOURCES

Edinburgh, Scotland. Scottish Records Office. Forfeited Estates Papers; Annexed Estates of Lovat and Cromarty; Customs Records for Greenock, Oct. 1772-July 1773 (E504/15/22).

Halifax, N.S. Public Archives of Nova Scotia. These are a major source of information about the people of the *Hector* once they arrived in Nova Scotia. There is a wealth of scattered material in the MG 1 Papers of Families, MG 4 Community Records, RG 1 census reports, Land Grant Petitions, Scrapbook Collections, Vertical MS File, and in the unpublished manuscript "The Pictou Plantation," by Henry R. Beer, 1767.

Ottawa, Ont. Public Archives of Canada. Rev. William Drummond Papers (MG 23 3 1).

Pictou, N.S. Hector Centre. Genealogical Records. Public Archives of Canada. Rev. William Drummond Papers (MG 23 3 1).

CREDITS: NEW EDITION

Cover illustration by David MacIntosh, artist-in-residence at the Ship Hector Foundation.

Postscript
Photographs on pages 221 to 225 courtesy of the Ship Hector Foundation.

Photographs on pages 226 to 232 courtesy of David Thompson.

Appendix F
Courtesy of Alexa Thompson, Editor of *Celtic Heritage* and author of *Destination Nova Scotia*, published by Nimbus Publishing Limited, 1999.

Caption regarding the Ship Hector Tartan extracted from "Ship Hector Tartan Sets Sail: Janice Gammon Designs New Tartan," *Celtic Heritage* Vol. 14, No. 4, Sept/Oct. 2000, pp. 22–23. Used with permission.

INDEX

ABOUT THE AUTHOR

Donald MacKay has had a forty-year career as journalist, broadcaster and author. Descended from Pictou County settlers, and born and educated in Nova Scotia, he was a wartime merchant seaman, has been a reporter for Canadian Press, and covered major stories in a dozen countries for United Press International. He spent a decade as chief European correspondent for  UPI Broadcast Services, based in London, and was general manager of UPI in Canada for five years before turning to writing books. He lives in Montreal.